Delinquency
Prevention

Theory and Practice

Contributors

WILLIAM E. AMOS, *The George Washington University*
CARRIE STREET BASH, *Urban League of Philadelphia*
GARY BELLOW, *United Planning Organization*
IVAR BERG, *Columbia University*
A. F. BRANDSTETTER, *Michigan State University*
JAMES J. BRENNAN (Deceased), *Michigan State University*
CLARENCE RAY JEFFERY, *New York University Law School*
INA A. JEFFERY, *American University*
PETER P. LEJINS, *University of Maryland*
SIDNEY G. LUTZIN, *New York State Division for Youth*
MELVIN B. MOGULOF, *Office of Economic Opportunity*
R. C. OREM, *Children's Center* (District of Columbia)
GEORGE EDWARD POWERS, *Georgetown University*
CLYDE E. SULLIVAN, *Social Restoration Center*
      (Rikers Island, New York)
CHARLES F. WELLFORD, *University of Pennsylvania*
JOHN M. WILSON, *University of Maryland*

Delinquency Prevention

Theory and Practice

Edited by
William E. Amos
Charles F. Wellford

PRENTICE-HALL, INC.
Englewood Cliffs, New Jersey

Prentice-Hall Sociology Series
HERBERT BLUMER, *Editor*

LIBRARY OF CONGRESS CATALOG CARD NO.: 67–12188

Printed in the United States of America   C-19790

Current Printing (last digit):

10 9 8 7 6 5 4 3

PRENTICE-HALL INTERNATIONAL, INC., *London*
PRENTICE-HALL OF AUSTRALIA, PTY. LTD., *Sydney*
PRENTICE-HALL OF CANADA, LTD., *Toronto*
PRENTICE-HALL OF INDIA (PRIVATE) LTD., *New Delhi*
PRENTICE-HALL OF JAPAN, INC., *Tokyo*

To our wives, KIT *and* PAT,
without whose support and assistance
this book would never have been written.

Preface

Early in 1964 we became concerned about the fact that while efforts in delinquency prevention were increasing at a rapid rate, the field was so disorganized that one could not find a basis for directing these efforts or evaluating their theoretical or historical relevance, much less their effectiveness. We decided to attempt to rectify this by bringing together a series of chapters which would summarize developments in prevention and indicate the direction of emerging trends. Our early efforts were given considerable encouragement by Robert Gibbons of Prentice-Hall, Inc. By January of 1965 we had outlined our conception of the organization of the book and selected our authors. In April of 1966 the completed manuscript was given to Prentice-Hall for publication.

This book was written primarily as a text for undergraduate and graduate students in those disciplines dealing with delinquency prevention, but it is also directed toward all those involved or interested in this subject. In keeping with our conception of the nature of the problems under discussion, we have not restricted the book's contents to any one field. We have, however, emphasized the sociological implications in many areas because we believe that the focus of activity has been in this discipline. We have tried, therefore, to build from and upon this base by author selection and editorial direction.

We are, of course, deeply indebted to the contributing authors. In addition, we would like to express our gratitude to many of our colleagues who have read portions of the manuscript and offered many constructive suggestions. Finally, we must especially acknowledge the contribution made by our typist, Miss Shirley Smith. As an earlier author expressed it, "She may not know what it means, but she knows what it meant."

WILLIAM E. AMOS
Washington, D.C.

CHARLES F. WELLFORD
Philadelphia, Pa.

Contents

Foreword

The passing years have produced a steadily growing army of delin-quents and teen-age criminals and there is increasing concern in all quarters over what is regarded as the alienation and estrangement of the young. We cast their dilemma in such concepts and notions as "anomie," "detachment from and lack of identity with society" and "failing personal identity." These notions represent a context in which we see youthful behavior at odds with the conforming patterns of society.

Juvenile delinquency is increasing in sections of our society hitherto relatively untouched and untroubled. No longer can we afford to shrug our shoulders in complacent disregard of the problem as one safely con-fined to the disadvantaged areas of our big cities. Delinquency is not some-thing that happens only "across the tracks," but is increasingly a concern of middle-class neighborhoods, of the more economically advantaged areas of the metropolitan community.

Nor is this the whole story. Not only are children being processed by the police and the courts more often than before, they are also being com-mitted to correctional institutions in increasing numbers.

We can no longer permit these developments to rest unnoticed in official reports. We must face them realistically with full awareness of what they mean. We must take note of what is happening with increasing frequency to young people. More often than before, they are becoming the objects of the official attention of our enforcement and correctional agencies. We must consider what this means in the lives of these young people. Unfortunately, our current enforcement and correctional prac-tices are so organized that no one can be fully processed by them without some scars being left on his personal and social life, his present and future career prospects. The dramatic impact of this experience is such that many young people develop feelings of resentment and conceptions of self that lead toward, rather than away from, criminal careers. For many juvenile offenders these early experiences result in a hardening of delinquent atti-tudes that makes it increasingly difficult for them to change the direction of their development.

The juvenile delinquent is the product of a social process that results from the mal- or covert dysfunctioning of traditional agencies dealing with children. The study of the psychic attributes of single delinquents has been of little value in setting forth the basic outlines and causes of delinquency that lie beyond the individual, in the processes and institutions of community life. Hence the relevant concern for understanding and action in the control of delinquency is not the delinquent act or the individual delinquent as such, but the framework of delinquency, that is, the terms and conditions of delinquent careers. These conditions are not only the perceivable shortcomings of important institutions such as the family, the community, the adolescent peer group, the school, the police and other agencies of correction, but the latent and generally unknown ways in which these institutions alienate and estrange young people.

These institutions and agencies are all too frequently and systematically mishandling the children with minor difficulties who come into their hands. Such failures contribute to the confirmation of delinquency and in themselves offer a focal target for programs of prevention.

We have come to see that the problem must be attacked where the delinquency is produced, and this involves two major considerations. In preventive terms, the major focus is upon those areas and regions which are disproportionately productive of crime and delinquency. And, secondly, we seek to re-examine and increase the capacity of the agencies of criminal justice which now too frequently contribute to an aggravation of the problem by the purely negative measures of arrest and detention.

Considerable time and energy have been expended by American communties with a view to the prevention and treatment of crime and juvenile delinquency. The relatively poor success which has attended these efforts cannot be lightly dismissed. Facts such as have been set forth are not generally accepted, and, when they are, it is too often with the reservation and restraint born out of controversy and opinionated discussion. Delinquency, like the weather, is a subject concerning which nearly everyone has a pet theory or a private opinion. The facts are usually strained in the light of personal cure-all and panaceas. More frequently than not the proposals for doing something about juvenile delinquency have little relation to its etiology or process. Indeed, as is characteristic of social problems in general, the control of juvenile delinquency is confounded by the presence of rather widely entertained popular notions. Like the air one breathes, they are taken for granted notwithstanding the fact that they have been proved wanting and are at odds with the results of objective investigation and study. Doing something about delinquency means that the public and the larger community from which crime springs has decided to do something to itself. To really make a difference may require doing something of quite serious consequence for our traditional affairs and private interests. Most of us have not the slightest idea that the juvenile delinquency or crime we collectively frown upon may involve our own personal and social relations. The general public clings, almost desperately, to views about delinquency which are false and self-defeating. But in so doing, the patterns of treatment and prevention, reflecting as they do these fallacious notions, are also self-defeating.

To deal effectively with delinquency is not alone to find new formulae or methods, or to reveal hitherto unknown facts, but in the main to heed, to make use of what is already known. We must present this knowledge as an antidote to popular fears and fancies.

Delinquency is very often assumed to be evidence of a willful disregard for legitimate authority and/or evidence of personal defect or shortcoming. We have much to learn about the mysteries by which societies generate an abnormal response within their own circle. But this has become increasingly apparent. It is the social structure itself which contributes to such behavior. Indeed, it is the self-same social structure expressing its force and influence in an ambivalent manner which produces on one hand the conforming individual, the person respectful of the social codes, and on the other, the deviant and lawbreaker who are disrespectful of the law. *It may well be that what we observe as delinquency and crime is more often than not recognized as a normal reaction of normal people to an abnormal condition.*

As has been observed, juvenile delinquency is a projection of community life and reflects in time and space the changes which the community is experiencing. On the one hand, delinquency relates to long established local conditions and relationships; on the other hand it relates to the stresses and strains which are accompanying basic transformations in the redistribution and resettlement of the population on a national scale. It is to these facts, conditions, and relationships that any bona fide effort in the control of juvenile delinquency must be addressed. Prevention and effective treatment require that delinquency be recognized in generic terms, that its processes and relationships be grasped, and that it be dealt with as a problem of national proportions. Whatever is proposed must have the effect of sensitizing and enlarging the understanding, and hence competency, of the helping agencies. This means, in a broad sense, increasing the capacity of local communities to recognize the specific problems and difficulties of young people for what they really are. Children in difficulty will be rescued, or their problems will be adequately anticipated, only if the children are regarded in the light of the conditions and processes which are shaping them. The juvenile delinquent is always a person whose spiritual, emotional, educational and/or social needs are not being met. Hence, the target is not the delinquent act, nor the individual person who commits it, but the framework inside of which the delinquent career is initiated, nurtured, and confirmed.

JOSEPH D. LOHMAN
Dean, School of Criminology
University of California at Berkeley

Delinquency
Prevention

Theory and Practice

1 The Field of Prevention

Peter P. Lejins

The idea of preventing crime and delinquency is a popular one, both among scholars and professionals in the field and with the general public. It is hard to deny, from the point of view of theory, that it is preferable to intercept criminal and delinquent behavior before it takes place rather than to act against it after it has occurred. By and large, the general public believes, and justly so, that an ounce of prevention is worth a pound of cure. When addressing a lay audience on the subject of crime, there is no surer way of provoking a round of applause than by shifting from a discussion of what we should do with criminals and delinquents to a suggestion of how we can prevent individuals from becoming offenders. Everyone is in favor of this.

And yet the field of prevention is by far the least developed area of criminology. Current popular views are naïve, vague, mostly erroneous, and for the most part devoid of any awareness of research findings; there is a demand for action on the basis of general moralistic beliefs, discarded criminological theories of bygone days, and other equally invalid opinions and reasons. In scientific and professional circles the subject of prevention has received remarkably little serious attention. Even the basic concepts in the field of prevention lack precision: There has been very little theory-building, and attempted research under such circumstances has failed to produce any significant results. It can safely be stated that before we can expect any significant research findings, the field of prevention has to be "organized": The process of defining basic concepts and some attempt at theory-building must be initiated so that through ensuing criticism and discussion a generally acceptable frame of reference for research and the sound development of the field as a scientific discipline will be accomplished.

The Concept of Prevention

The concept of crime and delinquency prevention is used here in juxtaposition to the concept of control. Prevention is a measure taken *before* a criminal or delinquent act has actually occurred for the purpose of forestalling such an act; control is a measure taken *after* a criminal or delinquent act has been committed. Both prevention and control should be viewed as subcategories of society's negative attitude and action against crime and delinquency. Since, by definition, both crime and delinquency are problems, this implies that society must do something about them. Perhaps the term "crime and delinquency handling" should be used to comprise both concepts: control and prevention.

There are certain areas in which preventive and controlling actions seem to overlap or at least the distinction between them is not obvious and needs sharpening. This is true of both the theory and practice of prevention and control.

Such an overlap and potential confusion in theory occurs because an act of control is an attempt to stop criminality or delinquency and also an attempt to forestall future offenses. The concept of special prevention, developed further by legal theory and discussed later, refers to this future effect. An adequate clarification of this theoretical ambiguity lies in recognizing that any action concerning an offender taken as a result of his having committed an offense should be defined as control, even if it interrupts the continuation of criminal behavior and thereby forestalls future criminal acts. In practice, for instance, a so-called area project in a high-delinquency area attempts both to interrupt criminal careers already in progress and to forestall the involvement of new recruits in criminal activities. Both prevention and control are being practiced in this case. Thus the above distinction applies: If societal action is motivated by an offense that has already taken place, we are dealing with control; if the offense is only anticipated, we are dealing with prevention. This distinction is important also from the standpoint of legal theory: In the area of control, public abrogation of the rights of an individual is more feasible because by committing an offense he has invited the curtailment of his rights; in the area of prevention a compulsory public action is less feasible.

Types of Crime and Delinquency Prevention

The ambiguity of the concept of prevention is one of the main obstacles to discussing prevention meaningfully, to obtaining generally significant research data, and even to describing existing preventive programs. The term prevention refers to several different types of societal action, so different, in fact, that in most cases a clarification of the particular type of prevention in question is indispensable to make communication meaningful. Three types of prevention or three distinct meanings of the concept can be differentiated: punitive prevention, corrective prevention, and mechanical prevention. There may be other types of prevention, but both theoretically and practically these three are the most important.

Punitive Prevention

In punitive prevention the threat of punishment presumably forestalls the criminal act. The conventional punitive crime control system, based on criminal law, used to rely and still basically relies on this kind of prevention. The legal theory of crime prevention further differentiated for some time between special and general punitive prevention. Special prevention means forestalling further criminal acts of an offender by punishing him so that he "learns his lesson." It fits the interpretational model of negative conditioning, where pain, represented by punishment, causes him to avoid repetition of the act that became associated with the pain. Although criminal-law theory uses the term prevention in this case, the so-called special prevention of the legal theorist is not true prevention as it is being defined here, but rather a control measure.

The concept of general punitive prevention is usually connected with the name of Anselm Feuerbach,[1] who saw awareness of the threat of punishment or actual punishment as a motive for not committing an offense. This is prevention in the true sense of the word; at the same time it is, specifically, punitive prevention because it is the prospect of punishment that keeps many potential criminals from committing crimes. Although many jurists have claimed that general prevention is perhaps the main function of criminal law, there have been few social-science studies in this area. The underlying theory is usually relatively simple and consists of the assumption that if the potential offender is aware of the prospective pain of punishment, this knowledge will influence his behavior. The freedom-of-the-will theory usually underlies the entire sys-

[1] Anselm Feuerbach, *Revision der Grundbegriffe des peinlichen Rechts* (1799).

4 Peter P. Lejins

tem, although this is perhaps not indispensable: One could resort to the interpretational model of a motivational setup, with awareness of prospective punishment being one of the determinants of the individual's action.

The judge who tells the accused that he will impose a stiff sentence so that he will think twice before breaking the law again acts in terms of special punitive prevention. The judge who tells a traffic violator, "We have recently had too many accidents. This speeding must be stopped. I will give you the maximum under the law so that people will think twice before they step on the gas," is motivated by general punitive prevention.

The effectiveness of punitive prevention presumably depends on the certainty and severity of punishment. Under the influence of humanitarianism the severity of punishment was greatly reduced, and by the end of the eighteenth century, under the impact of the views of Cesare Beccaria[2] and Jeremy Bentham, the limitation to the indispensable minimum of the suffering imposed as punishment became a basic principle of the classical school of criminal law. However, the importance of the certainty of punishment has been gaining favor.

Corrective Prevention

The concept of corrective prevention is entirely different. Here, prevention is based on the assumption that criminal behavior, just as any other human behavior, has its causes, is influenced by certain factors, and is the result of a certain motivation, whatever the terminology may be. Preventive action means the elimination of those causes, factors, or motivations before the criminal behavior has actually taken place. Such corrective preventive action may be undertaken as a matter of general precaution within the society as a whole, or it may be directed toward specific situations and cases on the basis of symptoms that indicate a threat of criminal behavior. Although prevention in this sense, to a certain extent, seems always to have been used, even in antiquity, it is primarily a product of modern times and is clearly anchored in modern social science. As a matter of fact, when a person with a social-science orientation speaks about the prevention of crime today, he is usually thinking in terms of corrective prevention.

If punitive prevention is associated primarily with punitive crime control and the criminal-law approach to criminality, [corrective prevention is a natural concomitant of the modern criminological approach, applying the principles and methods of modern social science to the problem of crime.]

---

[2] Cesare Beccaria, *Trattato dei delitti e delle pene* (1764).

Mechanical Prevention

The third concept, mechanical prevention, again refers to something entirely different from the first two. Here obstacles are placed in the way of the potential offender that make it difficult or impossible for him to commit an offense. Such preventive action does not involve the personality of the individual. No attempt is made to influence his intentions by threatening punishment or by changing his motivation; hence the suggested term mechanical prevention. An increase in police protection in a neighborhood known for the frequency of certain criminal acts is a typical example. The increased difficulty of committing the offense—for instance, "rolling a drunk"—because of intensified police supervision may well prevent impressionable youths from following the example of their more advanced gang companions. Various security measures, such as dependable locking systems, bars on tellers' windows, signaling systems to be used in case of attack, may serve as further examples of mechanical prevention intended to forestall criminal acts by making their execution more difficult. It should be kept in mind that mechanical prevention, just as punitive and corrective prevention, also has its counterpart in the crime-control area. There it appears as incapacitation of an offender whose criminal career it seeks to interrupt; for instance, by keeping him confined in some kind of preventive detention system.

Current Confusion in the Field of Prevention

The three kinds of prevention defined above are so different in essence that any theory-building and research must clearly differentiate among them in order to have any meaning. Likewise, action programs should include these differences in order to plan rationally and to evaluate what is actually happening. However, we do not find this differentiation and precise definition either in theory or in practice. It is true that some research projects have stated accurately their operational definitions of prevention within the project itself, but no general theory has been abstracted from these studies, primarily because of a lack of effort in conceptualization.

Today the criminal lawyer, the legislator in the area of criminal law, and the citizen who favors punitive crime control often think in terms of passing a punitive statute to prevent a certain kind of undesirable behavior and in terms of increasing the penalty for an offense in order to prevent its too frequent occurrence. Recently, increased public sentiment for reducing the juvenile court age and for waiving jurisdiction by the juvenile courts in favor of the regular criminal courts is a symptom of the vitality of the idea of the punitive threat in both control and prevention. The severe punitive laws recently passed by some jurisdictions in the areas of drug traffic and so-called sexual psychopathy are another example of the eruption of purely punitive control and preventive plans. All these measures involve punitive prevention, and their authors sincerely believe that they are dealing with crime prevention. At the same time they are frequently hostile and derogatory toward the advocates of corrective prevention, either because they do not understand the rationale for this type of prevention or because they consider it ineffective.

On the other hand, theorists and practitioners of corrective prevention frequently do not even recognize punitive prevention as prevention and reject it as they reject its base: punishment. The field of criminology abounds in statements of behavioral scientists that reject punishment as either control or prevention. To them, prevention is only corrective prevention: the removal of the causes, factors, motivations, etc., of offensive acts.

Finally, the law-enforcement administrator will often think about prevention of crime exclusively in terms of mechanical prevention. Doubling the police patrol, using two-way radios, improving alarm techniques—to him these are the real crime-preventive measures. He is usually willing to accept the idea of punitive prevention, but his attitude toward corrective prevention is basically hostile. However, publicly and grudgingly he may give it a certain amount of lip service because he feels he must.

One may expect that clarification of the prevention theory and identification of different types of prevention will have not only theoretical merit but also great practical significance. It may help to end the confusion, defensiveness, and hostility of personnel in systems that differ in their methods of prevention. A new era of research and experimentation could well be the reward of the refinements in theory suggested above.

Corrective Prevention

Although all three kinds of prevention are in operation in modern society, corrective prevention is clearly in the ascendency and dominates interest and practical innovations, especially in the United States. Despite the current preoccupation with corrective prevention, some people consider punitive and mechanical prevention more important. Although the exploration of their role through modern research methods is desirable, they need basic monographic treatment: a kind of reintroduction into modern thought on crime prevention. Because of the limitations of space, this treatment is not included here. Rather, the emphasis is on conceptualiza-tion, theory-building, and structuring in the field of corrective prevention.

Just as the entire field of crime and delinquency prevention needs basic conceptual analysis, so does the field of corrective prevention. Here also is an impressive amount of writing, some true research, much public enthusiasm, and considerable action. But again general theory is lacking, the basic types of corrective prevention are ill defined, and the resulting vagueness and confusion preclude progress. A basic structuring of the field is required, especially in view of recent developments.

At present, three major types or areas of corrective prevention can be distinguished:

1. Manipulation of general societal policies affecting many different aspects of life and also affecting crime and delinquency, so that it can be legitimately claimed that some of these policies constitute preventive measures.

A further distinction can be made between general policies not directly connected with crime and delinquency but nevertheless affecting them (e.g., compulsory public education, child labor laws, social security, and mandatory military service) and those policies that pertain directly to crime and delinquency (e.g., the consumption of alcoholic beverages, gambling, the use of drugs, prostitution).

2. Programs to detect symptoms of crime and delinquency rein-forced by preventive action. These programs are based on the knowledge of characteristics, established through research, of criminals and delin-quents that distinguish them from law-abiding people as well as on the knowledge of typical processes leading to delinquent or criminalistic behavior. Thus instruments have been developed which detect the pres-ence of characteristics or processes indicative of future criminality in persons who are not offenders yet. These instruments are directed at what frequently is referred to as crime or delinquency-proneness. The necessary counterpart of the use of such instruments is the availability of preventive treatment facilities for those who have been identified as offense-prone.

3. Preventive work with crime and delinquency concentrations—spatial or temporal—which are indicated either by exorbitant crime and delinquency rates (such as in slum areas in a modern city) or by crime and delinquency "waves" (an increase in delinquency in time of war). Preventive action in this case is not directed at society as a whole but at the areas of concentration, and it consists in the elimination of the causes of the continued involvement of new recruits in criminal or delinquent activities. In practice, this preventive program is usually combined with a parallel control program for established offenders. The "Chicago area project" is a classic example of this type of preventive program.

The above classification provides a frame of reference into which most current preventive discussions and actions can profitably be placed, profitably in that more or less homogeneous preventive proposals are combined and can be further analyzed and classified so that they become more manageable and flexible for both theory-building and action.

The Manipulation of General Policies

A classification of policies is the initial step in the organization of materials in the first major area of corrective prevention. The distinction between general policies not directly connected with crime and delinquency and those directly connected has already been made. With further distinctions, this classification is as follows:

A. General policies not directly connected with crime and delinquency
   1. Policies dealing with economic security
   2. Policies dealing with socialization of the incoming generation
      a. education
      b. employment
      c. defense
B. General policies pertaining directly to crime and delinquency
   1. Policies for the regulation of undesirable behavior by institutionalized criminal-law enforcement
      a. Types of behavior to be subjected to law enforcement
      b. Volume of behavior to be subjected to law enforcement
   2. Policies for the organization of law enforcement in relation to the general governmental structural and the population.

The above classification should be considered a tentative one. Further systematic work in this area will add other policy categories and could result in a reorganization of the pattern. Thus the following analysis of the components of the classification is exploratory.

GENERAL POLICIES NOT DIRECTLY CONNECTED WITH CRIME AND DELINQUENCY   Of these numerous policies, two types are most frequently discussed concerning their effect on crime and delinquency: policies dealing with the economic security of the population and policies affecting the socialization of the incoming generation. Education and employment are the most frequent subjects of discussion related to juvenile delinquency. There is an overlap between policies on economic security and those on socialization of the young: The economic security of the main socializing agency—the family—plays a signal role in the socialization process. This aspect is discussed here under economic security. Because the defense of a nation involves not only the adult population but also those whose socialization is not yet completed, such matters as compulsory military training affect the process of socialization, and its potential positive or negative effect on youthful crime is an important issue. This is the reason for including this additional category.

Policies Dealing with Economic Security   Our modern industrial society is characterized by a persistent search for the security formerly provided by the family. Two of the major solutions to this problem are private insurance and social security, supplemented by public and private welfare. Debates over legislative policies in these areas refer, as a rule, to the repercussions that these policies have on delinquency and crime. The general premise is that the economic stability of the individual and the family is an insulator against criminal and delinquent behavior. Thus, legislation regulating private insurance; public social security with provisions for unwed mothers; homes broken by divorce, separation, or desertion; loss of income due to illness, accidents, or death; unemployment; private welfare as well as policies of private welfare agencies are unquestionably important factors in the etiology of delinquency and crime. The significance of these policies for crime and delinquency prevention is not stressed in prevention theory, and they have not been subjected to systematic analysis and research. Students of crime and delinquency have not considered these policies the potentially most important tools at their disposal. It may very well be that the enlargement of a police force by 1000 men or the addition of 1000 probation officers may be much less significant in preventing crime and delinquency than a seemingly slight change in the provisions of the Social Security Act. Minimum wage policies and other management and labor legislation also affect the basic economic structure of society and the distribution of income.

Policies Dealing with Socialization of the Incoming Generation Awareness of the importance of these policies for juvenile delinquency is increasing, but again it is not as great as it deserves to be. Delinquent behavior has been conceived as a result of various factors that adversely affect the socialization process. The United Nations' *Comparative Survey on Juvenile Delinquency* states that nothing in the social policies of a nation is without influence on its children, and everything that affects the children can be either a criminogenic factor or a preventive measure.[3]

EDUCATION   For a long time, education of the young has been held in such esteem that the question of public education contributing to juvenile delinquency, youthful offenses, and young adult crime was seldom raised. It was not until the 1940's that requests for an appraisal of the

[3] Translated from the French edition, *Étude comparée sur la délinquance juvénile. Deuxième partie: Europe* (United Nations, 1952), p. 157.

potentially negative effects of the compulsory public education program were voiced. William Kvaraceus' studies on the school and delinquency[4] and Albert K. Cohen's[5] dramatic comments on the conflict between the public school as a middle-class institution and the youth of the lower socioeconomic class in terms of anomie, aspiration, achievement, and opportunity broke wide open the issue of contemporary formal education and delinquency. A number of research projects, supported by private foundations and public funds, were started in the late 1950's and 1960's. The results of some of this research are beginning to have an effect on school curricula. Current interest in the ungraded primary and intensive experimentation with it in delinquency-prevention projects are based on the hypothesis that the elimination of official recognition of a student's failure by nonpromotion might be beneficial in bringing up children who, because of limited opportunities, cannot successfully compete with more fortunate members of the peer group. The currently popular project "Headstart," which consists of summer preparation of culturally deprived children for enrollment in the public school, is another example of an effort with the same objective.[6]

The much older device of channeling a presumably predelinquent youngster who is failing in the conventional academic school program into a vocational curriculum is widely used. It is considered a standard preventive device in all communities that are of sufficient size to afford this differentiation in their school program. The predelinquent nature of such a school population is often toned down to eliminate stigmatization and to facilitate the incorporation of the floundering youths into the general population.

The general issue underlying the compulsory education program is the conflict between the principle of equality of educational opportunity, which leads to uniformity of the curriculum, and the presumably innate differences in individual ability and educational potential. Given the interpretational model of delinquent behavior as a release of frustration resulting from a broad social need, it is understandable that a less able child suffers in recognition or status when he is made to compete with a better-endowed classmate. Biologically inherited and culturally instilled differences among children may lead to delinquency as a result of a program of compulsory education that is not sensitive to this problem.

[4] William C. Kvaraceus, *Juvenile Delinquency and the School* (New York: Harcourt, Brace & World, Inc., 1945).

[5] Albert K. Cohen, *Delinquent Boys* (New York: Free Press of Glencoe, Inc., 1955).

[6] "Headstart" projects are a frequent component of projects financed and developed under the auspices of the President's Committee on Juvenile Delinquency and Youth Crime and subsequently of the Office of Economic Opportunity "Anti-Poverty" programs.

The recent emphasis on appropriately trained pupil personnel workers who deal with problem children in the public schools should be considered a national policy that has prevention of delinquency as at least part of its objective.

EMPLOYMENT   The proper place of employment during the socialization process in modern society has been the subject of concern and legislation for some time. Child labor laws, which had as their purpose the protection of the young from exploitation, the assurance of sufficient time for education, and the development of a well-rounded personality, have been criticized recently for certain negative side effects. It is claimed, for instance, that there are children who are not interested in and do not profit from further education before the child labor laws permit them to be regularly employed. Presumably, a period of idleness and purposeless existence is forced on them just at the time of adolescent storm and stress. Resulting individual and group disorganization may lead to delinquent and criminal responses to the problem situation. Work-study programs have been suggested as a compromise solution. Although concerned with other matters, the policies in this area have important repercussions for delinquent behavior and should be studied by those interested in prevention.

DEFENSE   National defense is such an important matter for every country that policies in this area are usually determined solely by the needs of the nation. Yet these policies and their corresponding programs have great effects on the total life process of the society and thus on crime and delinquency. Because national defense enlists subadult groups, it has a direct effect on socialization. Compulsory military training may come when a youth is in the process of emancipation from the family and perhaps when he has completed his education, but before he has found an adult role and independence through employment.

Compulsory or voluntary involvement in a total institution, to use Erving Goffman's concept, will affect potential criminal responses to problems. Congressional debates on universal military training frequently refer to its advantages of providing young men with something to do, placing them under supervision and discipline, teaching them occupational skills, and in general guiding them through this trying period. The similarity between the functions of military training and the Civilian Conservation Corps and programs of the Economic Opportunity Act is obvious. Whatever the current preferences may be, and whatever research findings may tell us, it is evident that this is another area of national policy that should be watched carefully by criminologists for its effects on youthful crime.

In conclusion, many societal policies pertain to issues that society may consider more important than crime and delinquency, and therefore it makes decisions about these issues regardless of their positive or negative influence on crime. On matters pertaining to national defense or the fair distribution of earnings in industry, a criminologist may not even be consulted about the effects on his field of proposed legislation. Yet it is logical for those on whom our society relies for its perspective on delinquency to study the effects on criminal behavior of *all* policies and programs. Whether these effects will determine the decisions of the people and their legislators is not necessarily the crucial issue. The criminologist should bring his knowledge about the criminogenic side effects of the legislation in question to the attention of the public and the legislators to be weighed with other arguments. Thus, the criminologist will be performing his social and professional function.

POLICIES PERTAINING TO CRIME AND DELINQUENCY   A different type of general societal policy is that related specifically to crime and delinquency. Its importance for control and prevention is more obvious, yet some of its potential preventive implications are often overlooked. This is another area of analysis and action that should be explored further by criminologists.

Policies for the Regulation of Undesirable Behavior by Institutionalized Criminal-Law Enforcement   A survey of the law-enforcement systems of different countries as well as a historical study of law enforcement in any particular country shows that there is great variety in the methods of handling undesirable behavior. Different forms of social control—folkways, mores, and laws—are used differently to accomplish the same basic purpose: to eliminate undesirable behavior. Whereas one society uses institutionalized enforcement and makes objectionable behavior illegal, another society may obtain the same results through its system of mores, which informally prohibits such behavior. One society may shift from one form of social control to another regarding the same offensive behavior. Thus, the issue is raised whether one form of social control is more effective than another for handling the same problem; an evaluation of societal policies using different forms of social control and making potential improvements is called for.

TYPES OF BEHAVIOR TO BE SUBJECTED TO LAW ENFORCEMENT   What kinds of undesirable behavior are best handled under what forms of social control? The classic example in the United States is the question of how consumption of alcoholic beverages, the use of drugs, gambling, prostitution, etc., are to be controlled. Social control systems of different countries handle these types of behavior in various ways: Some relegate them to the area of morality and rely on the mores and informal controls of public opinion, the family, and the church; others place them under law enforcement. The United States generally resorts to law enforcement in this area more readily than do many other countries, perhaps because the strong religious moralism of the founding fathers established the tradition of using public political power against violations of moral norms. Prohibition of alcoholic beverages, limitations on gambling, restrictions of the sale and use of drugs are examples of the use of legal measures—through the police and the courts—where other societies often limit themselves to informal moral control.

Variations in the policies of social control in this area have great preventive significance. It is almost typical for Americans to blame the Volstead Act, which forbade the manufacture and sale of liquor for beverage purposes, for the rise of organized crime and a powerful criminalistic underworld, and it is said that the Act was repealed to stop these developments. Similarly, the large volume of organized interstate gambling is blamed on the statutes that make gambling illegal. In analyzing the relation between mores and laws, the sociologist frequently claims that a conflict between the two leads to the difficulty of enforcing laws and to the expansion of profitable illegal activity that is not sufficiently opposed by the population.

This is not the place for a detailed analysis of the complicated syndrome of developments connected with various prohibitions in this country that deal with borderline immoral-criminal behavior, but it is obvious from the above examples that this is an important area for exploration in relation to crime and delinquency prevention.

VOLUME OF BEHAVIOR TO BE SUBJECTED TO LAW ENFORCEMENT Another question is how much enforcement activity it is advisable to relegate to law-enforcement agencies. How much behavior that must be "controlled" may one take away from folkways and mores and place under the jurisdiction of law-enforcement institutions? As a rule, available law-enforcement manpower is seen as a bottomless barrel. Federal, state, county, municipal, and other legislative agencies produce statutes in a continuous flow, assuming that existing law-enforcement agencies will somehow effect the enforcement. A rational analysis shows that every legislative act should be carefully considered as to the law-enforcement manpower it will require; corresponding additions to the personnel of police departments and the courts should be made when new laws are passed. Instead, the law-enforcement system of this country is hopelessly overworked. Statistics indicate that the police are able to handle only a small portion of offenses committed; prosecuting attorneys are willing to bargain for a plea of guilty on a lesser count in order to avoid time-consuming criminal procedure; and the courts take far too long to process the cases. Feeble suggestions about the necessity for increasing the police force, the number of prosecuting attorneys, and the number of judges are constantly being made. Yet the fundamental question is whether it is possible to have sufficient personnel, given a tendency to place more and more behavior under the supervision of law-enforcement agencies. The truth may be that there is an optimum load for the law-enforcement institutions of any country. Law enforcement deteriorates if it is overtaxed, and it is conceivable that this may lead to an increase in delinquent and criminal activities. Again we are faced with the question of the effect of societal policies—this time pertaining directly to crime and delinquency —on the increase or decrease of criminal behavior. And again, a criminologist concerned with prevention must also be concerned with these policies.

This deterioration under the burden of an excessive work load begins with the enforcement of the law in selected cases rather than as a matter of rule or principle. With the number of violations constantly growing, law enforcement, instead of being actual enforcement, becomes as this writer likes to refer to it, symbolic law enforcement. Given an overpowering barrage of offenses, law-enforcement agencies act on only a few of them as a reminder to the general public that certain behavior is prohibited; this is only a symbolic reminder, because no action is taken in most cases. The degree to which law enforcement becomes symbolic varies. When it reaches substantial proportions, deterioration of the social-control system occurs. The rule of law disappears and yields to administrative discretion or arbitrariness. If a law is enforced in only a few cases, it becomes an administrative decision in which cases it will be enforced. The general public then becomes aware that laws are not being enforced, and disregard for law increases. Infrequent enforcement is exploited by unscrupulous persons who gamble that a violation will be overlooked. Because of symbolic law enforcement, the personnel of law-enforcement agencies face strong corruptive influences: They enforce the laws selectively, professional accountability for their actions disappears, and the opportunity for reward, especially from organized criminals, is a temptation to which they often succumb.

This detailed analysis of the syndrome of excessive control by statute indicates how important the analysis of a prevention expert is for this area. To date, unfortunately, very little has been done to direct and curb criminogenic forces potentially resulting from this situation.

Policies for the Organization of Law Enforcement   Other policies that are influential in stimulating or preventing crime and delinquency concern the location of law enforcement within the total structure of the government and its relation to the general public. Only a brief identification of these policies is attempted here. Law-enforcement agents control the actions of the population; the population of the country presumably has control over its government; and law enforcement is part of this government. The issue is the extent to which the general public influences the law-enforcement branch of the government that is supposed to keep that same general public in line as far as the laws of the country are concerned. In this context one must distinguish between the centralized law-enforcement system and local law-enforcement organization. Examples of centralized systems abound in many continental and South American countries, where the Ministry of Justice, sometimes with some cooperation from the Ministry of the Interior, is responsible for law enforcement in the country and also for the employment, promotion, and retention of all or most of the law-enforcement personnel. If the country is a democracy, its population controls its government, at least in principle. But from the practical point of view, the law-enforcement officer, by being a member of a national agency, is so far removed from the political influence of an offender that unscrupulous coercion is not likely to occur. In the United States, on the other hand, where law enforcement is the concern of local government, the citizen who is controlled by local authorities is very close —in the sense of political control—to law-enforcement agencies. Presumably, in mass urban society this leads to influence by criminalistic elements of a community, and the history of law enforcement in major American cities for the last one hundred years reveals continuous political scandal. The organization of the police and the courts in their relation to the rest of the public is one of the richest grounds for analysis and research concerning the prevention of organized and politically influential criminals.

Programs of Symptom Detection

Quite different from the preventive attempts by manipulation of broad societal policies is the second preventive proposal: a plan to detect the symptoms of incipient delinquent and criminal behavior, followed by the timely removal of its causes. This prevention plan is based on the assumption that if, as the result of research, we learn the distinguishing characteristics and social processes of delinquents and criminals, these characteristics and processes can be observed by a knowledgeable expert or detected by a testing instrument before the offense actually occurs. This plan is perfectly logical from the theoretical standpoint, and it answers a very popular question. How often, while attending juvenile court hearings or reading about a career of juvenile delinquency, does one hear: "Why hasn't something been done about this boy before?

After all, it must have been obvious for a couple of years that something was going radically wrong with him. Didn't somebody see it?" Although symptom detection and preventive action are equally possible for both adults and juveniles, major efforts have been made primarily with juveniles, following the general tendency to apply corrective and preventive measures first to the young.

An important aspect of the symptom-detection plan is the desirability of applying the detective device to the entire population. Actually, the main point of the plan is to discover crime-and delinquency-proneness in those not yet involved in serious trouble. Thus, if the target of the detective device is the entire population, or at least the entire juvenile population, the need arises for instruments that are expedient to apply, adaptable to machine processing, and, in general, suited to mass handling of data. The importance of these characteristics is emphasized by the suggestion that tests for delinquency-proneness be given periodically as the young generation develops, especially if one hypothesizes that delinquency-proneness may be acquired at different points in a person's development. This mass administration of symptom-predictive devices suggests that the cases pointed up by the device will be characterized by the probability rather than by the certainty of delinquent behavior. Therefore, the original mass testing must be followed by intensive case study, and only those individuals that the follow-up study verifies as crime-prone should be given preventive treatment. Because the entire operation takes place before any legally delinquent or criminal behavior has developed, the cooperation of the individuals and their families must remain voluntary. In view of this, the public relations in the program are very important.

The plan outlined above raises the question of whether to select an existing agency to administer the program or to create a special agency for mass testing, developing facilities for case studies, and devising preventive-treatment facilities.

Several kinds of symptom-detection instruments have been suggested and devised. One type utilizes the knowledge of persons who are in contact with the individual in question, for example, the knowledge of teachers and neighbors. Because these persons are asked to name delinquency-prone individuals on the basis of their own opinions, the question arises whether such persons really know the true symptoms of future delinquency or criminality. Therefore, questionnaires or scale-type devices have been developed that request the knowledgeable individual to comment on certain points, which, in accordance with some theory of delinquency, are important indications of future trouble. A rating scale periodically completed by teachers about their students has been used in some schools.

Another instrument is based on the information supplied by qualified raters, who make a special study of the child and may use as sources of information the child himself. At this point, the well-known juvenile delinquency prediction table developed by the Gluecks[7] should be mentioned. This instrument, made public in 1950, has been widely experimented with and tested for its validity and reliability.[8] It utilizes family relationships: the attitudes toward the child and the methods of discipline. This instrument is cumbersome to administer, and the intensive child study it requires makes it unusable for mass operations.

With the third instrument, the youth himself is the source of information, either by means of a schedule filled out as a result of an interview or by means of a paper and pencil questionnaire. Special personality inventories with emphasis on crime-proneness have been developed by some authors. The first step in this type of delinquency prediction was the use of personality inventories devised for more general purposes than delinquency detection. One was the well-known Hathaway and Monachesi study, utilizing the Minnesota Multiphasic Personality Inventory, administered to ninth-graders in Minneapolis with a subsequent study of their involvement in juvenile delinquency and the establishment of reasonably high correlations between this involvement and the ratings on certain scales of the test.[9]

William C. Kvaraceus is well known for his efforts to develop a special instrument for the early detection of delinquency-proneness. His KD Proneness Scale and Check List, to be used with both children and teachers, have been received with considerable attention nationally and have been widely used experimentally.[10] There is no question that the symptom-detection approach to prevention is potentially promising; with the amount of work being done, tangible and practical results are expected.

Concentration of Crime and Delinquency

The third major type of crime and delinquency prevention is the work done in high-delinquency areas and also with crime and delinquency waves. The existence of segments of the population with exorbi-

---

[7] Sheldon and Eleanor Glueck, *Unraveling Juvenile Delinquency* (Cambridge, Mass.: Harvard University Press, 1950).

[8] Charles S. Prigmore.

[9] Starke R. Hathaway and Elio D. Monachesi, *Analyzing and Predicting Juvenile Delinquency with the MMPI* (Minneapolis: The University of Minnesota Press, 1953).

[10] William C. Kvaraceus, *The Community and the Delinquent* (New York: Harcourt, Brace & World, Inc., 1954); also, J. D. Balough and J. C. Rumage, *Juvenile Delinquency Proneness, A study of the Kvaraceus Scale* (Washington, D.C.: Public Affairs Press, 1956).

tant criminality rates is an old and widely known phenomenon. There have always been frequent reports of regions, rural communities, towns, and groups of people that are troublesome and predatory. The range of these phenomena is wide: The criminal tribes of India, the nomadic gypsy camps, the frontier communities pervaded by smuggling, the isolated moonshiner communities in the United States, and some economically deteriorated areas are frequently cited examples.

The outstanding case of delinquency concentration causing special concern in this country is the deteriorated area of the modern city, which, with other social problems, is characterized by excessive crime and delinquency rates. This type of criminal development was also known long before our time, but the application of modern social surveys and social-science methods has given such areas national and world-wide attention. Although interest in modern city slums was on the increase, the dramatic studies of the "Chicago ecological school" ushered in a new era of research and action. The work of Clifford R. Shaw, who started his lifelong attack on this problem by publishing his *Delinquency Areas*[11] in 1929, is well known. By applying the ecological survey techniques developed in the 1920's in Chicago under the leadership of E. R. Park and E. W. Burgess, Shaw identified the areas and characteristics of delinquency concentration in that city, which led to the formulation of the concept of the criminalistic subculture. A tool for combating that social ill was proposed and developed: the famous "Chicago area project." The emphasis of Shaw and his collaborators was on the delinquency involvement of the child living in a high-delinquency area, which process was identified as a usual learning process. E. H. Sutherland's differential association theory of criminality, developed about the same time, served as a further theoretical buttress of this interpretation.[12] Shaw's area projects were aimed at breaking the stranglehold of the criminalistic subculture in high-delinquency areas and at intercepting the recruitment of new candidates. Shaw's emphasis on local leadership and local resources in the project areas and the limitation of the role of outside professional personnel to that of catalyst were the chief characteristics of the program. For a long time, area projects held the leading role in American criminology and social action as delinquency-prevention attempts: The Chicago area project has been copied by innumerable urban communities in this country. It is difficult to evaluate them, primarily because of the multi-

[11] Clifford Shaw *et al.*, *Delinquency Areas* (Chicago: University of Chicago Press, 1929); also Clifford R. Shaw and Henry D. McKay, *Juvenile Delinquency and Urban Areas* (Chicago: University of Chicago Press, 1942).

[12] E. H. Sutherland, *Principles of Criminology* (Philadelphia: J. B. Lippincott Co., 1939).

plicity of the variables involved, but in general they have been evaluated favorably.[13]

A new era in delinquency prevention, related to its concentration in modern cities, began about the mid-1950's. It is characterized by new developments in criminological and general sociological theory and by correspondingly new types of preventive-action programs.

In criminological theory, a return in the mid-1950's to cultural or subcultural interpretations of criminality, pushed from the foreground preoccupation with psychiatric and psychological interpretations of personality problems leading to deviant behavior. In the late 1950's several authors indicated explicitly their return to the interpretational models of the Chicago school of the 1930's. But in the process of this revival the approach was modified: Instead of emphasizing the processes by which new converts are recruited into the criminalistic subculture, the main interest was in exploring the origin of these subcultures.

At this point criminological theory received a new impetus from general sociological theory. Modified by Robert Merton, the old Durkheimian concept of anomie was retransplanted into American sociology. Durkheim stressed the release of modern industrial society's control of the aspirations of its individual members and simply recognized the lack of opportunity to realize these aspirations; Merton stressed this lack of opportunity and addressed himself primarily to it. Merton defined anomie as "dissociation between culturally prescribed aspirations and socially structured avenues for realizing these aspirations."[14] Of crucial importance to the use of the anomie concept in the United States is the recognition of the differential distribution of opportunities for the realization of culturally instilled aspirations. This creates a new orientation, away from the issue of the potential control of aspirations to a more limited, practical and popular task of increasing opportunities for those who especially lack them. The major groups with limited opportunities were identified as the poor and those groups, especially ethnic groups, that are targets of prejudice and discrimination. The deeper issue of whether even equalized opportunities would be sufficient to satisfy uncontrolled aspirations was pushed aside and presently remains inactive. The program with equalization of opportunities in view, however, became extremely popular and represents the core of current projects, especially those financed by the federal government for prevention of juvenile delinquency and youth crime.

[13] S. Kobrin, "The Chicago Area Project—A 25 Year Assessment," *Annals of the American Academy of Political and Social Science* (March, 1959); also A. Sorrentino, "The Chicago Area Project After Twenty-Five Years," *Federal Probation* (June, 1959).

[14] Robert K. Merton, *Social Theory and Social Structure* (New York: Free Press of Glencoe, Inc., 1957), p. 134.

General sociological theory contributed further to criminological interpretations by providing concepts of motivations that lead individuals from anomic states to delinquency and crime. This also was Robert Merton's contribution, and two motivations suggested by him, those of innovation and rebellion, very frequently form a basis for interpretational models of delinquent behavior in the 1960's.

For further developments in interpretation of delinquent behavior one may turn again to the criminologists. Seminal in this respect was the work of Albert K. Cohen who, in his *Delinquent Boys*, published in 1955, developed the striking proposition that group delinquency in the lower socioeconomic, high-delinquency areas is a result of the conflict between lower socioeconomic class students and the compulsory public school, which, as a middle-class institution with middle-class goals, is partly frustrating and partly meaningless for the slum youngster. Perhaps the next most significant development in this school of thought is James Conant's[15] interpretation of dropouts as disappointed youths who refuse to cooperate with society and who therefore lack technological skills, which dooms them to economic frustration in a society that has ever decreasing use for an unskilled person. Another such interpretation is the analysis by Richard A. Cloward and Lloyd E. Ohlin of the processes by which frustrated youths reach delinquent-group solutions to their problems resulting in criminal, violent, and retreatist gangs.[16] The current demonstration and action projects and programs that began in 1961 are perhaps even more of a breakthrough than are the above theoretical advances. The federal grants stemming from the President's Committee on Juvenile Delinquency and Youth Crime and later from the Office of Economic Opportunity as an integral part of the Anti-Poverty Program were and are responsible for new departures and developments. Lloyd E. Ohlin, who was coauthor of the signal work *Delinquency and Opportunity*, was also the first key administrator of the delinquency programs resulting from the Juvenile Delinquency Act of 1961. Because Ohlin was also instrumental in the earlier preparation of plans for Mobilization for Youth in New York under the auspices and with the financial support of the Ford Foundation and the National Institute of Mental Health, one can see continuity in theory and ensuing action programs.

Although the projects developed with federal funds as a result of juvenile delinquency and economic opportunity legislation are still too new to have received a comprehensive analysis, it is clear that prevention of juvenile delinquency is primarily accomplished by increasing oppor-

[15] James B. Conant, *Slums and Suburbs* (New York: McGraw-Hill Book Company, 1961).
[16] Richard A. Cloward and Lloyd E. Ohlin, *Delinquency and Opportunity, A Theory of Delinquent Gangs* (New York: Free Press of Glencoe, Inc., 1960).

tunities for groups that lack them and cannot provide them for the new generation they are raising. Projects for legal aid to the poor and for developing subprofessional aids in underprivileged areas, "headstart" projects, the ungraded primary, to mention only a few, are devised to provide the poor, the culturally deprived, and those discriminated against with make-up opportunities. These opportunities should increase their stake in the life of society and thus their willingness to cooperate and to accept its goals and values as their own.

The prevention programs of the 1960's, directed toward groups with excessive rates of criminality and delinquency, represent an attempt to attack and intercept the causal processes at an earlier point than heretofore. If one differentiates between more immediate and more basic causes of delinquency, then our current preventive effort has turned to the latter.

2 The Prediction
of Delinquency

Charles F. Wellford

In recent years renewed and increased attention of criminologists has been directed to the area of prediction. After the early work of Burgess[1] and Ohlin[2] there was a period of intense activity followed by a longer period of inactivity by criminologists (with the obvious exception of the Gluecks) in prediction studies. In 1955[3] activity was again resumed on a major scale with the publication of the Mannheim and Wilkins study[4] and the report of the Internal Congress of Criminology's Symposium on Prediction, edited by Lloyd Ohlin.[5] Since then Wilkins has continued to extend our understanding of this area methodologically, and the work in California, in particular, has shown the operational possibilities of one form of prediction. However, historically and currently the

[1] Ernest W. Burgess, "Factors Determining Success or Failure on Parole," in A. A. Bryce, A. J. Harno, E. W. Burgess, and J. Landesco, *The Workings of the Indeterminate Sentence Law and the Parole System in Illinois* (Springfield: Illinois State Board of Parole, 1928).

[2] Lloyd Ohlin, *Selection for Parole* (New York: Russell Sage Foundation, 1951).

[3] If the "sociology of criminology" develops as a branch of the sociology of knowledge, someone will have enormous fun commenting on the significance of 1955 for the field. Not only did we have the research impetus from the prediction studies but also the publication of Cohen's *Delinquent Boys* (Albert K. Cohen, *Delinquent Boys* [New York: Free Press of Glencoe, Inc., 1955]) and the renewal of sociological theories of delinquency.

[4] Hermann Mannheim and Leslie T. Wilkins, *Prediction Methods in Relation to Borstal Training* (London: Her Majesty's Stationery Office, 1955).

[5] Lloyd Ohlin, *Symposium on Prediction Methods* (London: International Congress of Criminology, 1955).

efforts in prediction studies have been concerned primarily with recidivism and not with prevention in the sense discussed by Lejins[6] and adopted as the relevant interpretation for this book.[7] This is verifiable by surveying the content of the excellent bibliography on this general subject recently compiled by Leonard Savitz.[8]

The purpose of this chapter is to develop a sociological perspective on prediction, with special attention to prevention and to the issues stated as follows: first, a discussion of some of the recurrent issues in prediction theory as they apply to prevention (in particular the uniqueness argument, the clinical-statistical controversy, and the relationship between prediction and etiology); second, a discussion of the role of prediction in prevention programs and the implications this has for variable selection; third, a brief analysis of the methodology of prediction with emphasis on the modes of approach to this problem; and finally, an evaluation of the currently utilized instruments based on the analysis of the issues already described.

At the outset let me indicate that like anyone else who today discusses prediction in criminology, I am deeply indebted to the work of Leslie Wilkins. It is Wilkins, more than anyone else, who has influenced our current conceptions of prediction in criminology, and on the basis of his most recent book[9] one can predict that this influence will continue to be significant. In particular, his statements on the methodology of prediction and his attempts to implement these statements through research have influenced this author.

Prediction and the Complexity of Behavior

The complexity of the causes of human behavior has suggested to many fine minds that there can never be an explanation of such behavior

[6] See Chapter 1.

[7] Some others, particularly the Gluecks, Kvaraceus, and Hathaway and Monachesi, have been concerned with predicting prior to the first occurrence of delinquency. The essential works are:

Sheldon and Eleanor T. Glueck, *Unraveling Juvenile Delinquency* (New York: Commonwealth Fund, 1950).

William Kvaraceus, *The Community and the Delinquent* (New York: Harcourt, Brace & World, Inc., 1954).

Starke R. Hathaway and Elio Monachesi (eds.), *Analyzing and Predicting Juvenile Delinquency with the MMPI* (Minneapolis: University of Minnesota Press, 1953).

—— and ——, *Adolescent Personality and Behavior* (Minneapolis: University of Minnesota Press, 1963).

[8] Leonard Savitz (compiler), "Prediction Studies in Criminology," Special Bibliography, International Bibliography on Crime and Delinquency, II, No. 1 (U.S. Department of Health, Education, and Welfare, 1964).

[9] Leslie T. Wilkins, *Social Deviance* (Englewood Cliffs, N.J.: Prentice-Hall, Inc., 1965).

(with the implication, usually stated explicitly when discussing sociology, that the search for causes of behavior of the larger human system is therefore absurd). At various times leading criminologists (e.g., Reckless, in *Criminal Behavior*,[10] proposed the concept of categoric risks as a substitution for etiological factors) and, particularly, critics of criminology (most notably Michael and Adler[11]) have stated such a position with direct reference to deviant behavior. Furthermore, those who have attempted to document and interpret the course of criminological studies in the United States have frequently postulated that the impetus for multifactor explanations of crime and delinquency grew out of a similar despair over the complexity issue. Certainly, one should not contend that this was or is the dominant theme in criminology, but it has been a consistent and forceful position that has plagued the discipline and often driven researchers to "the eclectic (i.e., antitheoretical) approach."

Given this condition one can begin to understand why those most interested in prediction have had to defend themselves against the onslaught by those assuming the applicability of the complexity position, which often reduces to the contention that individuals after all are unique. One can understand such a controversy in psychology in terms of the division between clinical and experimental positions. However, unless we use some variation of the above it is difficult to understand such controversy in a field that can trace its modern methodological ancestry back to Durkheim.[12] The failure of sociological criminologists to address seriously the problems of prediction can be traced to some aspect of the complexity problem.

The variations usually concern elements of one or more of the positions that emerge from the above. These include the emphasis on case study or clinical procedures so that the unique, intangible elements of behavior can be surveyed and/or the contention that prediction cannot take place (or at least should not be a major focus) until cause(s) is (are) located. The analysis of what is at stake in these formulations has already been stated with reference to the individual case.[13] However, the more obvious responses in terms of sociological orientation have not been as clearly formulated. In both instances, however, the cause-prediction issue must be handled separately.

[10] Walter C. Reckless, *Criminal Behavior* (New York: McGraw-Hill Book Company, 1940).

[11] Jerome Michael and Mortimer Adler, *Crime, Law and Social Science* (New York: Harcourt, Brace & World, Inc., 1933).

[12] This does not imply that such a tracing of descent is complete or accurate. I simply wish to emphasize that a major concern of Durkheim and many current sociologists was rates of behavior and not behavior by an individual.

[13] Paul Meehl, *Clinical vs. Statistical Prediction* (Minneapolis: University of Minnesota Press, 1954); Leslie Wilkins, "What Is Prediction and Is It Necesssary in Evaluating Treatment?" (mimeo) (New York School of Social Work, 1961).

Meehl has observed:

> Stouffer has treated the question "What can the clinician do with his facts beyond that which can be done by the mechanical application of an actuarial table or a regression equation?" In his discussion Stouffer chiefly emphasizes the fact that the clinician can in special cases give more weight to a factor than it is given in the actuarial table. On what basis can he validly do this? As has been pointed out, if he does so, he must be using some law or other based upon his previous experience, and this law . . . is actuarial.[14]

This represents the key issue within the antiuniqueness argument: questioning what can one operate with besides membership in variable classes. If we grant this, then the concept of a case study is placed in serious jeopardy, for the source of variation in prediction may not be solely or even predominantly in the subject but rather in the predictor, whose perception and weighting of factors cannot be assumed to be as stable as the characteristics under observation.

In addition, we can, as Meehl does at times,[15] indicate that even if the two approaches to prediction are only equal in power the statistical should be selected, for it is the most efficient and therefore frees the "clinician" to perform more purely "clinical" functions. However neither of these arguments directly confronts the uniqueness issue, for one could respond: "I accept the above statements and conclude that neither approach is sufficient." The question then becomes "sufficient for what?" If we can predict statistically the occurrence of deviant behavior of a certain form, within an acceptable margin of error, what difference does it make if we conceptualize the individual as unique or similar? Such a pragmatic response does not resolve the issue, for it does not answer—it ignores. Furthermore, the purposeful-pragmatic formulation can then be extended to the realm of cause, and one can conclude that the predictor variables do not have to relate directly to causes, though they may, they just have to predict. Despite the excellence of their analyses, those authors interested in predicting deviant behavior have not moved beyond the demonstration that formal actuarial procedures are the most efficient and powerful predictors. They have characteristically, and I think necessarily (given their "individual approach") answered the uniqueness and cause questions on the basis of purpose or practicality.

If we move to another level of determinants, the sociological, we can generate more meaningful (at least for sociologists) responses to the uniqueness question. At this level we begin with the postulation that types of differences exist between causally different groups—the emphasis

14 Meehl, op. cit., p. 24.
15 Ibid., p. 138.

is on the communalities as opposed to the individualities. However, the expense of avoiding the uniqueness argument in this way is that of being unable to predict individual behavior. The focus must be on the rates of X as opposed to its individual incidence. Because this may seem to be a limiting condition, we will attempt to demonstrate in a later section why this is not so. At this point, it has been suggested that at the sociological level of analysis, the concept of uniqueness is not applicable and individual prediction is not possible. Previously it has been noted that statistical prediction is superior to clinical prediction. This can be presumed to hold for sociological prediction also, though this assumes a comparable level of variable measurement, an issue that must also be deferred until a later point in this chapter.

The issue of the relationship between etiology and prediction remains to be discussed vis-à-vis sociological, statistical prediction. First, it is clear to this author that the pragmatic justification as developed by Wilkins, despite its common-sense appeal, is not powerful enough to justify prediction efforts and it certainly is not likely to benefit in the long run those who are interested in research, predictive or etiological. The attack Wilkins has recently made on multifactor theories[16] shows his own inattention to this form of justification. For we could make a very strong case for stating that multifactor research and theory is justified on the basis that "it works": that is, the factors, if combined, account for X amount of variation in delinquency. In addition, we can object to such an approach on the basis that it is not efficient because it creates a barrier between two areas of interest that are similar in problem and subsequently in methodology and could potentially contribute to the central question of causes of deviance. It is easy enough to state these and other oppositions to pragmatic variable selection—it is much more difficult to formulate an alternative position. Such a position must be developed, for it is patently obvious that whether we recognize it or not we all operate with some theoretical formulation—without it, research and action are impossible.

A resolving position is easier to develop because we have already indicated our interest in some form of rate predicton and not in individual prediction (as indicated, this will be more fully developed later). This does not ease the conceptual problems, but it does minimize the clamor about predicting on the basis of causal theories without complete knowledge of cause.[17] The conceptual problem remains the same: how to relate prediction to cause while maintaining the value of the former as a guide to current action programs. The question now becomes: "Can we justify, given our current state of knowledge concerning social correlates

16 Wilkins, *op. cit.,* pp. 36–37.
17 Reference is to the official condemnation of such instruments as the Gluecks' because they label an individual a delinquent prior to his committing the act.

of delinquency, the expenditure in time, talent, and funds on large-scale prediction research?" For if prediction is to be immediately beneficial, the state of explanation must be sound enough to offer some promise of payoff. Only then can we justify to ourselves and to the public such endeavors and only then can the feedback from prediction research begin to supplement etiological research. The proposed resolution, which turns out to be little more than a modification of the position that links, inextricably, causation and prediction, then rests on the current state of causal theory and research.

This is not the place to make such an evaluation, but it is necessary to indicate our contention that current etiological research does have significant implications for prediction. Since 1955 we have been experiencing a resurgence of sociological theories of delinquency, particularly urban, adolescent, lower-class, male, gang delinquency. These theories, largely speculative, have prompted not only more theorizing but, more importantly, a series of concentrated research projects, the results of which are beginning to appear. The most prominent of these was the Youth Studies—Y.M.C.A. Project in Chicago.[18] Whereas other research has dealt with a portion of the general problem,[19] this work is by far the most relevant to the present analysis. The focus of the Chicago Project was primarily on the internal processes of gangs that involved them primarily in questions of status conception and attainment. The more interesting portions of their effort for the present analysis concern (1) their implicit conception of cause, (2) their findings on the relationship between community factors and delinquency, and (3) their development of social-demographic criteria for community description.

In their analysis of serious acts of violence, Short and Strodtbeck state:

> It is our hypothesis that much of what has previously been described as short-run hedonism may, under closer scrutiny, be revealed to be a rational balancing, from the actions perspective, of the near certainty of immediate loss of status in the group against the remote possibility of punishment by the larger society *if* the most serious outcome eventuates.[20]

Obviously their emphasis is on a game-theory model that separates the effect and reactions to an initial act, which, when completed in a status testing situation, leads to the increase of the chances of performing a more serious act. Though they do not develop the point, it is clear that this radically alters the classical notion of cause. Wilkins has approached a

---

[18] James F. Short, Jr., and Fred Strodtbeck, *Group Processes and Gang Delinquency* (Chicago: University of Chicago Press, 1965).

[19] See appendix in Marshall Clinard (ed.), *Anomie and Deviant Behavior* (New York: Free Press of Glencoe, Inc., 1964).

[20] Short and Strodtbeck, *op. cit.*, p. 250.

similar formulation in his discussion of the "decision amplifying system." He quotes the following from Maruyama on the implications these types of formulations have on our conception of cause:

> The law of causality may now be revised to state that *a small initial deviation which is within the range of high probability may develop into a deviation of a very low probability* (or more precisely) into a deviation which is very improbable within the framework of a probabilistic uni-directional causality.[21]

If we assume that social actions (as opposed to individual) are best described in terms of purpose, then such a model seems most powerful. Such a conception is new to criminological theory and indicates, we suggest, an increasing sophistication and relevance in this body of knowledge. It is these types of developments that should encourage those interested in prediction, for it indicates that a source is emerging for variable selection that will be useful to action and contributory to the science of the sociology of crime.[22]

We also see in this research effort important contributions to our knowledge concerning gang delinquency and community structure[23] and to our ability to differentiate socially lower-class areas with official statistics.[24] These areas will be more extensively discussed in the following section of this chapter.

In summary, this section relates the central issues in the analysis of prediction from a sociological perspective. The analysis has been made to develop the outline of a justification for statistical prediction using sociological variables that are initially selected from causal theories. This model and the issues it raises have been only minimally explored; to analyze them fully would require more space than is available. It is hoped that the fundamentals have been made clear and therefore can be extended or modified by others.

The Role of Prediction in Delinquency-Prevention Programs

Prediction must occur before the first offense if delinquency prevention, as defined in Chapter 1, is possible. This is a logical statement, one the Gluecks and others have assumed, but, as was indicated earlier,

---

[21] Quoted in Wilkins, *op. cit.*, p. 91.

[22] This is not meant to imply the preferability of microtheories as opposed to general theory. It is a statement that attempts to consider realistically the scope of action programs, past and present, and also indicate the trend seen as dominant in sociology today concerning the road to general theory.

For a complementary approach to the relationship between prediction and cause see T. C. Gibbens and C. P. Hill, "Symposium on Prediction Methods," *British Journal of Delinquency* VI (September, 1955), 87–93.

[23] Short and Strodtbeck, *op. cit.*, Chapter Five.

[24] *Ibid.*, Chapter One.

impossible if one is using "social variables." One can justly raise the question of pre-act labeling if prediction is oriented to identifying individuals. Thus the American Psychological Association and other professional groups have condemned the Glueck method not only because of its methodological limitations, but also because it may be self-verifying (i.e., "cause" those labeled to become what they are labeled). It is not likely that this type of prediction will be possible for some time, if ever.

If this is true, what functions can prediction play in a prevention program? The function it is best suited for is, we suggest, *evaluation:* determining whether changes of the form desired are occurring. It should be obvious that any such instrument could, in its general form, be utilized to predict, but as we have attempted to stress throughout, the prediction could be only in terms of some measure of total behavior and therefore would be of predictive value primarily as an indicator of areas for action and/or intensification of action and of places to refrain from or stop action. The role of the instrument is thus very different from that usually associated with those developed by Wilkins, Ohlin, the Gluecks, etc.

Such a formulation has significant implications for variable selection. It is important to note that in this book, with thirteen different primary authors, a theme has emerged. The emphasis throughout is on the relationship between the social institutions for both explanation and prevention and the necessity for "community action." This is, of course, not a startling discovery (see particularly Mogulof's chapter for a statement of "newness": variation from the area project theme of the 1920's). We also suggest that a major change is in the theoretical sophistication and subsequent focusing of efforts within a community, but it is a "new idea" if we apply it to prediction instruments. It suggests that we must consider the theoretically relevant and measurable variables derivable from these as the predictor variable. The form and suggested content of these variables will be discussed in this section; the method of relating them will be discussed in the following section.

Before proceeding, however, there is another issue to which we must attend. One could ask: "If you are interested in evaluation, why not simply measure the extent of delinquency before and after the prevention program?" Although we must grant that any prevention program has the reduction of delinquency rates as its ultimate goal, it does not follow that this would be the most efficient or relevant measure of success. With regard to efficiency, we are well aware of the difficulty in determining the *occurrence* of delinquent acts[25] and, from this, the inadequacies of

[25] "Hidden delinquency" studies are now quite extensive in our literature and the findings challenge many of our notions concerning delinquency. This has led many into, finally, the importance of the meaning of the act as opposed to simply the action itself. See, for example, Richard Cloward and Lloyd Ohlin, *Delinquency and Opportunity* (New York: Free Press of Glencoe, Inc., 1960), p. 9.

official statistics, especially for the evaluation of preventive action. Furthermore, it may well be that a measure other than one based on occurrence must be developed before we can evaluate the extent of delinquent behavior, for a change of importance may occur not in rates but in form or content. The work of Sellin and Wolfgang[26] on a "seriousness" measure is indicative of this latter measurement. However, here we are still limited by the statistics source and the fact that behavior is complex and that no program one evaluates can attend to the full range of supposed etiological factors. In terms of relevance, we could comment that measures of extent do not allow for this and other types of partial success, nor does it allow us to identify specific sources of program failure. Thus we conclude that a program is a "failure" when it may have been limitedly successful. Therefore, we can conclude that extant measures, though necessary, cannot at this time be considered solely adequate evaluators of program success. To the extent that they measure something more than occurrence, these measures become more relevant to the evaluation of prevention programs (reduction in community seriousness scores may be indicative of success though delinquency rates may not decline), but this is only an increase in relevancy, not a basis for substituting this type of measure for more direct (in terms of program) evaluative instruments. This discussion reinforces a procedural point made earlier that the use of a prediction instrument of the type we are suggesting is necessary: it would be used to determine those areas where our limited resources could be applied and then used to evaluate change periodically. This also means that a before-after design of some form is built into our knowledge of the purpose of the instrument.

To make this section more concrete we can begin to describe those types of variables that have been referred to as social, institutional, and community descriptive. It would seem that there are two distinguishable sources of information in any research—those one generates and those already available. The former are what we have referred to as the causally relevant predictive variables; the latter would be of a more descriptive (usually economic) nature, although the dichotomy is nowhere near this tight. The descriptive or "existing" variables are usually labeled demographic or social-demographic variables. For example, Short and Strodtbeck used, in their community description, a standardized public assistance rate, a median income, median gross rent, and percentage of male workers in professional or technical occupations.[27] Lander [28] used a

26 Thorsten Sellin and Marvin Wolfgang, *The Measurement of Delinquency* (New York: John Wiley & Sons, Inc., 1964).

27 Short and Stradtbeck, *op. cit.*

28 Bernard Lander, *Towards an Understanding of Juvenile Delinquency* (New York: Columbia University Press, 1954).

variety of community measures and found such factors as percentage of owner-occupied homes, percentage of overcrowding, percentage of non-whites, percentage of substandard housing, median rentals, and median years of education to be significantly correlated with delinquency rate. We could generate a number of such variables and then empirically determine their contribution to community description. As is apparent, we could consider some of these causally relevant.[29] However, this is not the point we wish to make. The point is that we have a vast literature concerning variables, similar in form, that can be ascertained easily, especially in large urban areas, and used as social correlates of delinquency and thus as predictors of areas to be "treated" and as measures of "success." Furthermore, these are for the most part quantitative and thus easy to analyze. Although programs may be interested in some of these directly and not others, yet, because such programs are, or at least should be, guided by some coherent ideas concerning patterns of cause, the category of variables to be generated would probably be more directly relevant for evaluation. However, we must not neglect this other source of data in our rush to what we at some point in our efforts define as relevant. The results of the "war on poverty and crime" may well be first reflected in such measures as indicated above.

What are the community variables that are causally relevant? Although we cannot answer this in the absolute sense, we can begin, on the basis of current theory and emerging research, to identify a complex of such variables that is at least "food for thought."

Since Sellin's[30] seminal paper on culture conflict, we have been interested in the conflict of conduct norms. The modern rendition of this is to be found dominant in Korbin[31] and Cloward and Ohlin,[32] and has been recently tested with reference to gang delinquents by Short and Strodtbeck. Theoretical emphasis has been on the causal influence of community value systems and social structure on gang delinquency. This is explicit in the concepts of legitimate and illegitimate opportunity structures and in the emphasis on the integration of age levels, the integration of the carriers of conventional and illegitimate values (which leads us to a discussion of community power structure—a body of methods and data that could easily be adapted to delinquency studies), and "un-integration." Those who have attended to the viable elements in delinquency theory and research that culminated in opportunity structure

[29] *Ibid.* For example, Lander explained the relationship between a set of the variables he used and delinquency rates by reference to anomie theory.

[30] Thorsten Sellin, *Culture Conflict and Crime*, Bulletin No. 41 (New York: Social Science Research Council, 1938).

[31] Solomon Korbin, "The Conflict of Values in Delinquency Areas," *American Sociological Review*, XVI (October, 1951), 653–661.

[32] Cloward and Ohlin, *op. cit.*

theory will recognize the hypothesized importance of these variables. What we have not done is to attempt to use such criteria as the basis of a predictive-evaluative instrument. This is particularly important because so much current preventive action is based on the theory from which these were taken. The point is simply that we have been, for years, developing ways of describing communities that are now relevant to criminological theories of delinquency. The concept of the lower-class culture that generates delinquency, stressed by Miller,[33] provides us with an even more explicit dimension to measure what would be relevant to certain types of action programs. As has been observed: "Whatever the causes, community-level differences clearly influence patterns of juvenile behavior, and in some measure account for differences in our gangs."[34] To the degree that programs are based on the type of comprehensive programs described in this book and the degree of our commitment to the selection of causally relevant variables, we should be developing prediction instruments to select areas for intervention and for evaluation of effectiveness, based on the types of variables, both descriptive (which may be also causal) and causal.

The Methodology of Prediction

As indicated earlier it is in this portion of the general problem of prediction that Wilkins has made the most significant contribution in criminology. Other developments that have altered some of the methodological problems are computer programs for multidimensional statistical techniques and texts that describe the mathematical models underlying prediction in terms more readily understandable by those of us who are not primarily mathematicians.[35] Therefore the statistical procedures are readily available in simplified form. The basic text remains the Social Science Research Council Report of 1941,[36] although, as has been indicated earlier, the application of this body of knowledge to criminology has been most convincingly done by Wilkins. This type of prediction—regression analysis—is dominant today, and we assume that it is applicable to the types of problems discussed earlier. This method does raise the problem of measurement, but this is not the relevant issue it used to be,

[33] Walter B. Miller, "Lower Class Culture as a Generating Milieu of Gang Delinquency," *Journal of Social Issues*, XIV (1958), 5–19.
[34] Short and Strodtbeck, *op. cit.*, p. 115.
[35] In particular, Paul Horst, *Matrix Algebra for Social Scientists* (New York: Holt, Rinehart and Winston Inc., 1963) and Robert McGinnis, *Mathematical Foundation for Social Analysis* (Indianapolis: The Bobbs-Merrill Company, Inc. 1964).
[36] Paul Horst, *The Prediction of Personal Adjustment*, Bulletin No. 48 (New York: Social Science Research Council, 1941).

for today many work on the assumption that measurement of complex social phenomena is possible at the necessary measurement level. There is little more one can say concerning this approach without simply repeating those works already mentioned. It is a process of correlation and then regression analysis that supplies weights to the variables selected as most predictive (i.e., simple, efficient, repeatable, and valid).

The fact that the measurement problem is no longer a central issue for those interested in prediction does not reduce the relevance of this problem, particularly when we begin to consider the types of variables that were identified earlier as being more than descriptive. Though many continue to scale everything in sight and assume an interval or higher level of measurement, the best methodological minds indicate that they doubt if there are any interval scales of attitudes, values, etc.[37] If this is true then one could seriously question our ability to measure something like "community integration." This leaves us two alternatives: (1) attempt to measure something that "measures" what we are interested in or (2) find some other way to handle the data. It appears to this author that the latter is the preferable procedure.

An alternative procedure for handling variables for prediction is by pattern-analytic methods. Although we cannot develop entirely the bases, techniques, and implications in the space available, we can indicate the general features of this approach. Pattern-analytic analysis is relatively new to sociology, although psychologists have been interested in this for some time, and the mathematical, specific developments that have led to this application are at least thirty years old—this is not a radically new order of application. The uses have primarily been in attitude-pattern prediction,[38] sociometric analysis,[39] gang delinquency,[40] and school achievement.[41]

The essential element in this form of analysis is the patterning of variables that may be measured at different levels, including the ordinal. In prediction one would be interested in identifying the relationship between X and a variety of variable patterns. Thus in delinquency preven-

[37] For example, see Hubert Blalock, *Social Statistics*. However, we are beginning to realize that the transformation of ordinal data to metric scales is possible. See Robert Abelson and John Tukey, "Efficient Conversion of Non-metric Information into Metric Information," *Proceedings of the Social Statistics Section of the American Statistical Association*, 1959, pp. 226–230.

[38] Louis McQuitty, "Isolating Predictor Patterns Associated with Major Criterion Patterns," *Educational and Psychological Measurement*, VII (Spring, 1957), 3–43.

[39] For example, Jack Sawyer and Terrance Nosanchuk, "Analysis of Sociometric Structure," *Proceedings of the Social Statistics Section of the American Sociological Association*, 1960.

[40] Short and Strodtbeck, *op. cit.*, pp. 128–135.

[41] Robert P. Stuckert, "A Configurational Approach to Prediction," *Sociometry*, XXI (1958) 225–237.

tion we would be interested in the relationship between configurations of community variables and a measure (e.g., rates and/or seriousness) of total incidence of first delinquencies and delinquency.[42] The prediction of communities in which limited resources are applied would be on the basis of those most approximating the pattern most closely related to our measure of the delinquency we see as appropriate, and evaluation could take place in terms of the communities' movement away from the configuration and in terms of changes in incidence and/or seriousness.[43] The above does not describe this procedure in a way that enables one to evaluate the suggestion, but hopefully it will lead those interested to the material where more detailed analysis can be found. As in previous sections the attempt has been to identify issues and suggest alternatives to the solution of the issue—this is all *a* chapter can do. This is particularly important to note at this point, for by going further into either of the above procedures the chapter would be violating our statement of purpose as presented in the Preface. Those interested in research will pursue this tack or reject it; those not directly interested will at least be aware of two alternatives in statistical prediction.

Current Status of Prediction Instruments

In analyzing the literature describing current prediction instruments that have been developed for use in the prevention of delinquency (keeping in mind the definition of prevention), we can swiftly conclude that there are none that approximate what has been suggested in this chapter. The only major efforts at community prediction have been in the form of check lists such as one finds in Kvaraceus' now dated and out-of-print text on prevention.[44] These of course are not prediction instruments by any acceptable standards. We can interpret this situation in terms of the issues discussed in the first two sections of this chapter.

This section is then reduced to a history of the types of techniques that have not been discussed here[45] and/or a critique of the important predictive instruments in use in criminology that were identified earlier as being relevant to our conception of prevention: the Gluecks', the Kvaraceus Delinquency Proneness Scale, and the MMPI. A critique of the last two does not seem necessary because the Kvaraceus Scale is no

---

[42] At the initial stage we would not have, as we do now, the weighting of variables that would, perhaps, make the technique more general.

[43] We should also note that pattern analysis based on probabilities may be particularly applicable to the testing of theory based on the change in our concept of cause, indicated earlier. This is what was meant in stating that the change in cause is relatable to the earlier emphasis on multifactor theories.

[44] Kvaraceus, *op. cit.*

[45] For such discussion see Mannheim and Wilkins, *op. cit.*, Chapter One.

longer widely used and the MMPI has been shown to be only mini-mally effective.[46] A very good analysis of the Gluecks' technique is to be found in the chapter on the family and delinquency prevention (Chapter 5). Thus, the avenues open for this section have been traveled many times by others, and we shall not travel them again.

In summary, if one accepts the argument posed in the previous sections, we would then indicate that a sociological prediction instrument has yet to be developed and that those instruments now in operation will continue to fail because their objective has a low probability of occur-rence. The thrust of the position taken in this chapter is toward the development of a causally relevant, sociological, statistical (though not necessarily of the traditional form) instrument for prediction and evalua-tion. Our major concern is that the reader will not see the issues raised as "straw men" we have erected in order to advance a position. It is the author's opinion that the issues are real and have not been addressed from a sociological perspective—this chapter has attempted to focus on these and suggest a model for their clarification.

Conclusion

The movement away from individual prophylaxis to community treatment is now the dominant trend in preventive programs. This is evident through the analysis of current programs by Sullivan and Bash[47] as well as through our knowledge of the types of professionals being called upon to formulate the programs financed by the federal govern-ment. This means that program focus and evaluation must be related to suprapsychological and superindividual factors. In this chapter we have attempted to indicate the implications this has for prediction. We have concluded that the most significant of these relate to the purpose of prediction (identification of areas for intervention and evaluation), the source of variables ("community indices" and, by fiat, those that are causally related), and the method of instrument construction (pattern-analytic methods or the more traditional method, provided data manipula-tions are developed and implemented).

Subsequent chapters will develop more fully this emergent concept of prevention as the authors search for the relevance of various institutions to delinquency causation and prevention. Their attempts should be related to the present effort, for the contextual element of this chapter (e.g., the types and sources of variables) will be found in their analysis, and the adequacy of our conceptualization of prediction depends on its

[46] See Chapter 1.
[47] See Chapter 4.

relevance to their conclusions. It should further be noted what this chapter does *not* say. The criticism of existing prediction instruments does not mean that they are not useful and/or "salvageable." The point was made that they are more applicable to programs having an individualistic orientation. This applies, to a lesser degree, to the currently dominant methodology. Furthermore, no attempt was made to demonstrate that the "case study" approach is invalid. It was indicated that for practical reasons at the least and for empirical reasons at the most, the statistical technique was preferred.

In reading this chapter one must keep the subtitle—a sociological perspective—in mind, as well as the orientation of the book. We have attempted to relate prediction to this perspective and orientation in a more coherent and comprehensive way in order to encourage efforts in this direction and to stimulate recognition of its importance and interest in its development.

SELECTED READINGS

Goodman, Leo A., "The Use and Validity of a Prediction Instrument," *American Journal of Sociology*, LVIII (March, 1953), 503–512.

Horst, Paul, *The Prediction of Personal Adjustment*, Bulletin No. 48, New York: Social Science Research Council, 1941.

McQuitty, Louis, "Isolating Predictor Patterns Associated with Major Criterion Patterns," *Educational and Psychological Measurement*, XVII (Spring, 1957), 3–43.

Mannheim, Hermann, and Leslie T. Wilkins, *Prediction Methods in Relation to Borstal Training*. London: Her Majesty's Stationery Office, 1955.

Meehl, Paul, *Clinical vs. Statistical Prediction*. Minneapolis: University of Minnesota Press, 1954.

Savitz, Leonard, "Prediction Studies in Criminology," Special Bibliography, *International Bibliography on Crime and Delinquency*, II, No. 1 (U.S. Department of Health, Education, and Welfare, 1964).

Wilkins, Leslie T., C. P. Hill, and T. C. N. Gibbens, "Symposium on Predictive Methods in the Treatment of Delinquency," *British Journal of Delinquency*, VI (November, 1955), 82–98.

3 Socialization
and Juvenile Delinquency

John M. Wilson

Section I: Socialization*

Man is a social animal. If he were not, he would perish because he possesses no genetic or "instinctive" behavior patterns for survival. He must learn such behavior patterns through social interaction. Man acquires, however, more than an ability to survive through social interaction: He learns the particular ways that his particular culture judges proper for survival. Fully as important, he also learns the many culturally correct ways of behaving, which may have little or no direct relationship to biological survival but which his culture expects and requires of persons accepted as worthy members. First through his familial experience and then through his more formally structured societal contacts, man is taught the culturally defined ways of eating, playing, dressing, talking, working, loving, hating, worshiping, and, ultimately, of dying. He is taught to observe his culture's customs, traditions, folkways, mores, and laws. In short, man learns how to live within his culture; he is not born with that knowledge.

The Process of Socialization

The process through which an individual acquires cultural knowledge is socialization. The term is appropriate because it recognizes the primary importance of the social factor in learning cultural behavior. The indi-

* Section I of this chapter introduces and gives a brief description of the process of socialization. Section II relates that process to the phenomenon of juvenile delinquency in American society.

vidual understands the functioning of his world through social interaction, although contact with the physical environment does transmit
some important information and knowledge (such as the lesson learned
from touching a hot stove). A vitally important part of this understanding is the individual's concept of himself as a human being, which can be
acquired only through social interaction. The significance of this fact was
recognized during the earliest developmental stages of American sociology and was stated by such noted sociological pioneers as Charles Horton
Cooley and George Herbert Mead.

Cooley, using his analogy of the "looking-glass self," described the
formation of human personality as a process in which the individual
projects a series of images of himself that he imagines others to have of
him and that he accepts as true reflections of his personality. Thus the
individual visualizes himself as he thinks other perceive him. The three
crucial elements that Cooley hypothesized as necessary to the process of
self-conceptualization and personality formation were "the imagination of
our appearance to the other person; the imagination of his judgment of that
appearance; and some sort of self-feeling, such as pride or mortification."[1]
Cooley further elaborated that these elements occur most forcefully
and effectively in primary-group situations rather than in secondary-
group situations. For example, it is the social interaction within the family
(the most basic primary group) that is most important for the adequate
socialization of the societal young.[2]

George Herbert Mead also stressed the necessity of social interaction in
relation to socialization. Mead visualized the individual becoming cog-
nizant of himself as a human being through his assumption of the social
role of others. The child identifies with the behavior patterns (or roles)
of the persons having important relationships with him. Initially this
means the mother and father, but as the identification continues to
expand, it includes other members of the family, close acquaintances, and
ultimately society as a whole. In this manner, Mead postulated, the child
learns to view himself objectively through the eyes of others and to relate
significantly that picture of himself to other members of society. Mead
calls this end result the "generalized other," implying that the individual
has become sensitive to other persons' expectations of his behavior and is
directly influenced to conform with them. In this way socialization has

---

[1] Charles H. Cooley, *Human Nature and the Social Order* (New York: Charles
Scribner's Sons, 1902), p. 152.

[2] The continuing importance of Cooley's seminal ideas, including those briefly
noted above, is indicated by the frequent inclusion of his writings in social-science
texts and readings. For one example, see Charles Horton Cooley, "Primary Groups,"
in *Readings in Sociology*, ed. Edgar A. Schuler, Thomas F. Hoult, Duane L. Gibson,
Maude L. Fiero, and Wilbur B. Brookover (New York: Thomas Y. Crowell Company, 1960), pp. 203–208.

been achieved because the individual understands himself as a personality functioning in an orderly manner within his culture.

Social interaction in Mead's theory of the socialization process is important: It is through interaction that the individual is able to place himself in others' roles and thus to gain insight into his own societal role. It appears that the most important aspect or phase of this process is that occurring within the primary-group situation, particularly in the family. This initial, primary-group interaction is the symbolic base upon which the child builds and extends his understanding of the roles of others increasingly distant from him.

Mead joins Cooley in underscoring the significance of social interaction and the correlative importance of primary-group interaction. Other sociological writers, both past and present, also recognize the essential truth of these early socialization concepts.

Structuring of Socialization

Because the proper socialization of the young is among society's most important tasks, society structures that task in a systematic manner. At a cursory glance it may seem that much of the child's social training is left to random or casual social-interaction processes. In reality, however, his interactional experiences are firmly controlled by society. Folkways and mores are instruments of such control, but institutions are the most influential societal agents in this regard.

Social institutions can be defined as societal mechanisms created to satisfy fundamental human interests. These mechanisms are the societally approved and lawfully recognized behavior patterns that effect such satisfaction. In addition to the procreation and socialization of children, the interests include the economic, political, religious, educational, and recreational requirements of societal members. Different institutions such as the family and the church serve these various requirements, although sometimes the functions of the institutions overlap.

The concomitant of function, the structure of institutions, is revealed in the orderly arrangement of status and role within institutions and in the orderly arrangement of institutions in relation to one another. An example of intra-institutional structure is the differential rights and duties ascribed to the husband-father, the wife-mother, and the child-sibling within the family; an example of interinstitutional structure is the societal dictum that the family bears the primary responsibility for child care and therefore that this sphere of responsibility should not be invaded by other institutions. This would not, however, prohibit other institutions from aiding in child care, but it would reserve to the family certain important rights and duties.

Institutions, then, have structure, and they function in the area of socio-cultural imperatives. They use folkways and mores in their operations but possess moral force, which folkways do not have, and legal force, which mores do not have. Research reveals that institutions are universal—present in all cultures.[3] Careful observation indicates that they are usually the most powerful agents of societal control, thus singularly effective in influencing the quality of the child's social interaction and socialization.

American Institutions and Socialization

An historical perspective must be used to develop further the description of institutional influence on socialization in the United States. The most important facet of this perspective is the rapid social change characterizing American society and its institutions. Over the past century and a half, a relatively short time in comparison to the histories of other nations, the United States has changed from a rural farm economy to an urban industrial economy. For example, at the turn of the nineteenth century, only 6.1 per cent of the American population was classified as urban; in the census conducted in 1960, 69.9 per cent of the population was classified as urban.[4] This rural-urban shift was the result of the large-scale migration to urban areas as rural people sought better economic conditions. The two factors involved were the occupational squeeze caused by increasing farm mechanization and expanding job opportunities created by the demands of the Industrial Revolution for more city workers.

Thus America moved from the farm to the city—radically altering the nature of its institutional action on the socialization processes of society. This alteration is confirmed by comparing the socialization of the former rural community to the socialization of today's urban community.

RURAL AMERICA   In rural America there was little doubt about the identity of the major socializing element: It was the institution of the family. The rural family provided not only the initial social interaction by which the child began to understand himself but also much of the training necessary for him to conform to his culture. The family worked together, played together, and participated in community affairs together. Through these shared activities, the family forcefully transmitted Ameri-

---

[3] A good example of the cultural ubiquity and strength of institutions, with particular reference to familial institutions, is provided by Murdock's study of 250 separate cultures. See George Peter Murdock, *Social Structure* (New York: The Macmillan Company, 1949).

[4] "United States Summary, Number of Inhabitants, Census of Population: 1960," Final Report PC (1)-1A (U.S. Department of Commerce, Bureau of the Census, 1961), Table 20.

can folkways, mores, and laws to the child. A young boy, for example, learned the culture's basic economic values and rules by working with his father on the farm and helping him market the crop. The young girl learned the proper feminine economic role by assisting her mother with household chores and generally sharing responsibility for the smooth functioning of the home. Through such experiences, both boy and girl absorbed many of the peripheral cultural attitudes and values associated with their specific economic roles.

In addition to the economic role, other important aspects of cultural behavior were taught by the family, and such teaching always had the advantage of the strong motivational force inherent in primary-group interaction, thus increasing the effectiveness of the socialization of the child. This motivational force was not limited to familial intra-action but was present to an appreciable degree in the general rural community. Neighbors knew each other on a direct reciprocal-interest basis, frequently participating together in work and recreational activities and counting on mutual assistance in times of crisis. They shared concern for the well-being of the community as a whole and also for particular institutions. Thus the school as an educational institution was not autonomous but integrated closely into community life: Schoolteachers were known to all community members, were respected members of the community, and contributed to the socialization of the children within an extended primary-group or *gemeinschaft* framework.

This interpersonal functioning of the rural community generally preserved the valuable socialization factor of strong motivational force, which was most pronounced within the family but also significant among families and between other local institutions and families. Childhood misconduct directed toward other community members was informally and effectively handled among those members. If a youngster was caught taking a choice selection of ripe apples from a neighbor's apple orchard, the neighbor usually attempted to correct this deviant behavior in one of two ways: He either lectured the youngster directly on a personal basis or if the offense involved a significant number of apples, he contacted the child's parents, frequently with culprit in hand, and informed them of the misconduct. This usually resulted in the parents applying more forceful corrective measures to their errant offspring, who in consequence probably curtailed his apple-picking activities.

Because community members customarily interacted on an intimate, primary-group basis, there was no hesitancy in reinforcing corrective action for deviant cultural behavior. Such corrective action was not official: Only in cases of severe or seriously repetitive juvenile deviance would the community utilize formal law-enforcement agencies. The most effective institutional action was conducted within the informal community framework. In this way, the community exercised a basic social-ization function while further reinforcing the uniquely effective socializa-tion action of the rural family.

URBAN AMERICA   The socialization process of modern urban America presents a dramatic contrast to that of the rural America of the past. The family still remains the major socializing institution of society; however, the scope and effectiveness of familial socialization has significantly lessened as the society has changed from rural to urban, reflecting the changed status and role of the family.

The modern family is a consumer rather than a producer. It is set within an urbanized, industrialized, specialized complex that severely limits familial influence. No longer is it possible for the son to be trained by the father for occupational duties and responsibilities. The father, as the breadwinner, must accommodate himself to an economic system that demands that his work be specialized and that it be performed away from the home. There is no place for the son next to the father on an assembly line: That space is occupied by another workman, likewise a specialist. In this way the industrial requirement of maximum efficiency of production is maintained as is the lengthy period of daily separation of the working father from his family. Millions of American mothers are currently working under similar circumstances of daily separation.

The preceding is just one of many examples of the family's reduced socialization role in contemporary American society. Members of the family are in numerous situations involving significant but autonomous social action. Specialization occurs not only in economic activity but also in education, recreation, and other areas of cultural behavior. One sees this individualization of activity in the following pattern of daily family existence: The father dashes from the house or apartment early in the morning to the business world of the central city. The mother, if employed, does likewise, and if not employed, may spend part of the day shopping or visiting friends after doing her housework; she may have a moment or two more than the father with the children before they go to school for the customary six or seven hours. In the evening the family members, having returned home from their separate activities, probably will dine together. After dinner, however, father may go bowling, mother may attend her ladies' club meeting, and the older children may have dates while the younger visit the recreation park to participate in evening games. The family is functioning only as an *occasionally* inte-grated unit.

Some might object that the preceding picture is overdrawn. It is true that many family situations provide for more sustained interpersonal contact, particularly when preschool-age children are involved. On the other hand, some families may experience more fragmented contact than that described above—families from which the father is frequently away for several days because of business requirements. Regardless of possible specific variations it is a valid generalization that the institution of the modern American family is much less cohesive and less omnipresent in societal affairs than was its rural forerunner.[5] Consequently, its socialization function is restricted in area and reduced in effectiveness.

The reasons for this change are related to the necessity of the family to conform to the structure and requirements of the current industrialized society, which are very different from those of a rural agrarian society. First, today's society encourages high rates of spatial and social mobility, which is essential for the utilization of increased industrial opportunity. Yet this mobility fosters a societal pattern of the settling and resettling of strangers in shifting aggregations of individuals and travel-size family units. The ecological quality of the aggregations is urban—of high population density and clustered around numerous centers of industry and commerce.

Second, economic specialization requires persons to work as coordinated members of large groups apart from the family. In addition to the significant amount of time such separation takes from family intra-action, there is also the frequent development of peripheral interests exclusive of family consideration. Thus a father may find it natural to make bowling his principal recreation rather than to relegate all recreation to the home. In this way, specialized individual interests emerging from economic segregation replace many former family functions.

Third, the permanence and stability of the family has decreased. With the political and economic independence of American women there is also greater tolerance of family dissolution: The increase in divorce rates over the last half-century is symptomatic of that tolerance. Of etiological importance here, however, is not just the lesser dependence of the woman on the family, but the lesser dependence in various ways of all the family members on the family.

Other factors could be traced that are relevant to the activity of the modern American family, but these three are adequate to indicate the reasons for the family's decreasing socialization function.

Increasing Importance of Other Institutions

Society attempts to fill the partial vacuum created by reduced familial socialization by broadening the socialization functions of other institutions and by creating additional institutional structures.

[5] It should be recognized that institutional variation is maximized in a heterogeneous culture such as that of the United States. This does not vitiate, however, the important analysis of major social trends related to gross institutional action.

The school is the best example of a "broadened" institution in this regard. No longer does the formal school curriculum consist of only traditional academic subjects. Classes in social manners, social cooperation, social ethics, and social recreation are direct attempts to teach social behavior. Such classes are conducted by methods stressing maximum interaction among students with the implicit purpose of providing a socialization program that will encourage conformity to society's conduct norms in postschool life.

Institutions employing broader socialization practices could be discussed, such as expanded programs for young people in many church groups, extensive organization of recreational programs at public playgrounds, and so on. The principles involved, however, are similar to those of the school and thus do not require further elaboration in this chapter.

Institutional structures specially created to aid the socialization of the young are juvenile courts, youth divisions of police departments, and other official agencies. Their sphere of socialization activity is usually correction of relatively serious juvenile deviation. The creation of special institutions does not always indicate a deterioration of contemporary juvenile behavior as compared to past juvenile behavior. In many cases it merely reflects the substitution of a formal agency to handle deviant behavior previously managed through informal community action.

The truth of the above statement can be demonstrated by transposing the example of the young farm boy who was caught stealing apples from a neighbor's orchard from a rural setting to an urban setting. The particular act of deviance—technically the act of theft—may have a different form in the modern urban setting. The boy, for instance, may be caught by the owner of a car while attempting to take one of its shiny hubcaps. This change in the form of the act, however, does not mean a change in the quality or content of the act. The theft of a hubcap and the theft of a basket of apples are, after all, of about the same monetary seriousness.

Today's urban society is so structured that it is required to apply correction through more formal means than those employed in the past. The theft is no longer from a neighbor but from a stranger. The owner of the car, not knowing the boy or his family, may summon a police officer and the result may be the referral of the boy's misconduct to the juvenile court. It is then the task of the juvenile court to attempt corrective action so the offense will not be repeated. The court is thus officially engaged in a basic socialization process that formerly would have been effected unofficially within the rural community. In all of this the quality of the juvenile misconduct or deviance has not changed: The method of handling the misconduct has changed.

In concluding this section, a final caution is necessary. The foregoing does not deny an increase in juvenile deviance because of urban living conditions: Such an increase is not only possible but highly probable. The modern institutional system must include in its socialization not only correction of juvenile misconduct previously effected informally but also correction of juvenile misconduct occurring as a product of contemporary America. The implications this has for juvenile delinquency prevention will next be explored.

Section II: The Relation of Socialization to Juvenile Delinquency

The Problem of Definition

The continuing controversy over the definition of juvenile delinquency is well known. A minimum definition, however, includes those cases of juvenile deviation from conduct norms considered sufficiently serious to be handled by the juvenile court or other special agencies. The number of such cases is increasingly large, causing growing societal alarm. The following discussion of the relation of socialization to juvenile delinquency is presented with this definition in mind.

Delinquency and Institutional Socialization

Some of the societal alarm about delinquency is groundless. As already noted, certain types of juvenile misconduct are treated today by special socialization institutions rather than by informal interneighbor communication. Special institutions keep statistics; neighbors do not. Consequently, some juvenile misconduct today is juvenile delinquency because of statistical bookkeeping, not because of a deterioration of juvenile behavior. This is not to imply that the quality of socialization exercised by special institutions is always as high as that formerly exercised by the rural neighborhood. Indeed, the second major point for consideration here is the danger of less effective socialization through these institutions.

The danger is directly related to the differences in motivational force in primary-group action compared to secondary-group action. Earlier in the chapter, it was noted that primary-group action is the most effective motivational force for socialization of the young; it was this action that characterized the rural neighborhood or community. On the other hand, highly specialized institutions—the juvenile court is a good example—usually assume secondary-group characteristics according to their specifically assigned tasks in the modern urban community. Such action usually means a lessening of interpersonal intimacy and hence a reduction of motivational force. It is possible that the juvenile court is attempting to play an important societal role without benefit of the motivational lever so effectively utilized in primary-group institutions.

There is actually a twofold danger in this situation. There is first the danger that specialized institutions will fail to handle competently certain types of juvenile misconduct formerly handled adequately by the non-specialized rural community. Such failure would increase the total incidence of delinquent behavior. There is also the correlative danger that specialized institutions will not be able to control certain other juvenile misconduct that appears to be a natural by-product of modern urban society, further increasing the total amount of delinquency.

The same theoretical principle applies to the institutions that, although not specifically created for handling socialization problems, have expanded their roles because of those problems. The school today provides much socialization training abrogated by the American family. Its success is logically correlated, at least to a certain extent, with the intensity of motivational force imposed on the juvenile. Few people argue that the school does not possess some elements of primary-group activity; therefore, the school could exercise a significant degree of motivational force in its socialization efforts. However, the school does not possess as much primary-group orientation as the American family—particularly the former rural family. The school creates a relatively less intensive motivational force, and therefore the partial substitution of school-socialization for family-socialization incurs a proportional risk of being less effective.

The factor of adequate motivational force is crucial for all modern institutions of socialization: Ineffective institutional action directly increases the incidence of juvenile delinquency and directly decreases the potential for preventing juvenile delinquency. The foregoing discussion is not presented to condemn the expansion or creation of nonfamilial institutions for socialization purposes: It merely points out the risk involved. Awareness of this risk is a prerequisite for more effective institutional socialization, and it is hoped that means will be found to intensify motivational force toward that end.

Delinquency as a Product of Urban Life

Urban life has helped to create a significant amount of delinquent behavior. This is not delinquency resulting from ineffective institutional socialization, but rather that emerging as a natural by-product of socio-economic processes in cities.

Partial evidence of this phenomenon is revealed by comparing delinquency rates of rural areas with urban areas: Almost invariably, higher rates are found in urban areas. More convincing evidence can be obtained by comparing delinquency rates of various sections in certain urban areas, which frequently reveals a uniform pattern of progressively higher rates as one moves from the periphery toward the center of American cities. Thus, the highest ratio of delinquents to nondelinquents is found in the interstitial or transitional zone—commonly referred to as the slums—which encircles the industrial and commercial part of the city. The lowest ratio is found in the suburbs or commuters' zone.[6] This difference in delinquency rates is not accidental: It is directly connected with the different cultural conditions existing between the slums and the suburbs as a consequence of the city's economic requirements.

In describing this relationship it is necessary to note the continual expansion characterizing the centrally located business district in the American urban area. Although this expansion fortunately reflects the growth of the industrial economy, it disrupts the residential zone immediately surrounding the business district. Inevitably, business interests seeking more land space invade and take over the adjacent transitional zone. To a significant degree, it is the common knowledge of this invasion-and-succession process that creates slums. Landlords, anticipating the imminent sale of their property for new business location, do not adequately service their subdivided rental housing. The result is physical deterioration of an area already defined by its proximity to the business district as being the least desirable for residence. Only those who cannot afford to live elsewhere settle in the transitional zone; therefore the transitional zone is populated by the economic failures of society: the alcoholic, the part-time laborer, the family on public welfare, the petty thief, the cheap prostitute, the marginal mental defective.

In such a socially negative situation, it is understandable that the transitional zone has a slum culture and that its value system tolerates—and even encourages—certain behavior considered antisocial by the outside community. In today's slums, for example, the fifteen-year-old boy who steals enough money to buy a pair of expensive shoes is more often approved of than criticized. Approval of his larcenous conduct is frequently given by the boy's street gang and by other personal groups of which he is a close member; not infrequently it is given by the boy's family. Such sanction is extended to many other forms of seriously deviant behavior. What is taking place, therefore, is the socialization of the juvenile under cultural circumstances favorable to antisocial and illegal

[6] Although not all research data and interpretation are compatible in this regard, the weight of the evidence realistically supports the noted pattern of differential delinquency ratios. For elaboration see: Clifford R. Shaw and Henry D. McKay, *Juvenile Delinquency and Urban Areas* (Chicago: University of Chicago Press, 1942); Ruth S. Cavan, *Criminology*, 3rd ed. (New York: Thomas Y. Crowell Company, 1962), pp. 73–76; Sophia M. Robison, *Juvenile Delinquency* (New York: Holt, Rinehart & Winston, Inc., 1960), pp. 90–99.

48   John M. Wilson

activity: In a relatively systematic manner the juvenile is being trained toward such deviance rather than away from it. The effectiveness of this training is substantiated by the high rates of juvenile delinquency in the transitional zone.

The above is logical support for the hypothesis that urban economic conditions create a delinquent syndrome not found in the formal rural community. More specifically, this new delinquency is created by the negative socialization processes of the slum areas, which are also creations of the urban economy.

There are several qualifications to be made at this point. First, the preceding shows differences in delinquency rates between the slums and the suburbs. It is true that there are similar differences between the slums and other areas of the city, but these differences are not as pronounced.

Second, the delinquency pattern in the slums is not unexpected. Many children, however, live in slum conditions and are not classified as delinquent. The etiological problems in relation to this fact are still unresolved.[7] Nevertheless, it is clear that the slum culture does operate to increase significantly total delinquency rates of the slum population.

[7] Although unresolved, the etiological problems of delinquency, particularly of slum delinquency, continue to receive considerable professional attention. Also, certain generic criminological theories are frequently thought to have explanative value for such delinquency phenomena. One example here is Sutherland's theory of differential association. The theory postulates, in part, that criminal behavior is learned principally within personal group situations and that a person becomes delinquent by acquiring an excess of definitions favorable to violation of law over definitions unfavorable to violation of law. This seems directly pertinent to the slum milieu, which contains probably the highest concentration of definitions favorable to law violation, together with a high incidence of personal groups projecting these definitions. The slum child, in association with such definitions, would have a correspondingly greater risk potential for delinquent action than would the nonslum child.

Space restrictions prohibit a more extended discussion of related etiological problems in this chapter. However, two or three of the several theoretical formulations, which have, or seem to have, analytical value for explaining slum delinquency, can be mentioned. The work of Shaw and McKay concerning socialization processes in the transitional zone is well known. Sutherland's differential association has been noted. Glaser's concept of differential identification, which emphasizes identification with criminal teachers, is a valuable addition as is Reckless' formulation of the effect of the delinquent child's self-concept. The work of Cloward and Ohlin relative to anomic structuring of the slum area should also be included.

The reader is referred to the following sources: Clifford R. Shaw and Henry D. McKay, "Social Factors in Juvenile Delinquency," in *Report on the Causes of Crime*, II, No. 13, National Commission on Law Observance and Enforcement (Washington, D. C.: U.S. Government Printing Office, 1931); Edwin H. Sutherland, *Principles of Criminology*, 4th ed. (Philadelphia: J. B. Lippincott Company, 1947), pp. 6–9; Daniel Glaser, "Criminality Theories and Behavioral Images," *American Journal of Sociology*, LXI (1956), 433–444; Walter C. Reckless, Simon Dinitz, and Ellen Murray, "Self Concept as an Insulator Against Delinquency," *American Sociological Review*, XXI, (1956), 744–746; Richard A. Cloward and Lloyd E. Ohlin, *Delinquency and Opportunity* (New York: Free Press of Glencoe, Inc., 1960).

Third, delinquency outside the transitional zone, though less frequent, also poses a problem for society. In this regard, there is increasing concern for the middle-class delinquent. It is important to develop pragmatic analysis of this phenomenon; it is hoped that the discussion in this chapter contributes toward that goal.

Finally, the increased number of objects for delinquent attack in urban America may help raise juvenile delinquency rates. For example, the great number of cars available today offers constant temptation for "joy riding" or even direct theft. Thus, one can add the more mechanistic factor of increased material opportunity to the foregoing interpretations relating delinquency to socialization.

Conclusion

This chapter first described the importance and nature of socialization and then related the socialization process to the phenomenon of juvenile delinquency in American society. This entailed a discussion of the role of social institutions, with particular reference to historical changes in the quality and frequency of their function. In characterizing the rapid change of the United States from a rural economy to an urban economy, it was explained that the family was forced to surrender certain socialization activities to other institutions. The implications for juvenile delinquency concomitant to this shift of socialization emphasis were also explained: the danger of less effective institutional socialization, the creation of specialized institutions for socialization, and the institutional handling of additional delinquency problems created by urban ecological processes.

The roles of certain major social institutions vitally influence the treatment and prevention of juvenile delinquency in the United States. It is to these institutions—the family, the school, the juvenile court, and others—that the following chapters are addressed.

SELECTED READINGS

Berelson, Bernard, and Gary A. Steiner, *Human Behavior, An Inventory of Scientific Findings.* New York: Harcourt, Brace & World, Inc., 1964. Chapters 3 and 4.

Broom, Leonard, and Philip Selznick, *Sociology* (3rd ed.). New York: Harper & Row, Publishers, 1963. Chapters 4 and 5.

Burchinal, Lee G., Glenn R. Hawkes, and Bruce Gardner, "Adjustment Characteristics of Rural and Urban Children," in Bartlett H. Stoodley, ed., *Society and Self, A Reader in Social Psychology.* New York: Free Press of Glencoe, Inc., 1962.

Cavan, Ruth S., *Criminology* (3rd ed.). New York: Thomas Y. Crowell Company, 1962. Chapter 4.

Child, Irving L., "Socialization," in Gardner Lindzey, ed., *Handbook of Social-Psychology*, Vol. II. Reading, Mass.: Addison-Wesley Publishing Co., 1954. Pages 655–692.

Cloward, Richard A., and Lloyd E. Ohlin, *Delinquency and Opportunity, A Theory of Delinquent Gangs*. New York: Free Press of Glencoe, Inc., 1960.

Cooley, Charles H., *Human Nature and the Social Order*. New York: Charles Scribner's Sons, 1902.

Davis, Allison, "Socialization and the Adolescent Personality," in *Readings in Social Psychology*, ed. Guy E. Swanson, Theodore M. Newcomb, Eugene L. Hartley, *et al.* New York: Holt, Rinehart & Winston, Inc., 1952. Pages 520–531.

Glazer, Daniel, "Criminality Theories and Behavioral Images," *American Journal of Sociology*, LXI (1956), 433–444.

Hartley, E. L., and Ruth E. Hartley, *Fundamentals of Social Psychology*. New York: Alfred A. Knopf, Inc., 1952. Chapters 8–12.

Hartley, E. L., and D. C. Krugmon, "Notes on Children's Social Role Perception," *Journal of Psychology*, XXVI (1948), 399–405.

Hsu, Francis L. K., *Psychological Anthropology: An Assessment of Culture and Personality*. Illinois: The Dorsey Press, 1961.

Kvaraceus, William C., *The Community and the Delinquent*. New York: Harcourt, Brace & World, Inc., 1954.

Murdock, George Peter, *Social Structure*. New York: The Macmillan Company, 1949.

Ogburn, William F., and Meyer F. Ninkoff, *Sociology* (4th ed.). Boston: Houghton Mifflin Company, 1964. Chapters 9, 10, and 11.

Reckless, Walter C., Simon Dinitz, and Ellen Murray, "Self Concept as an Insulator Against Delinquency," *American Sociological Review*, XXI (1956), 744–746.

Robison, Sophia M., *Juvenile Delinquency*. New York: Holt, Rinehart & Winston, Inc., 1960. Chapter 7.

Shaw, Clifford R., and Henry D. McKay, "Social Factors in Juvenile Delinquency," in *Report on the Causes of Crime*, II, No. 13, National Commission on Law Observance and Enforcement (Washington, D.C.: U.S. Government Printing Office, 1931).

———, *Juvenile Delinquency and Urban Areas*. Chicago: University of Chicago Press, 1942.

Sherif, Munzafer, and Carolyn W. Sherif, *An Outline of Social Psychology*. New York: Harper & Row, Publishers, 1956. Sections 4 and 5.

4. Current Programs for Delinquency Prevention

Clyde E. Sullivan

Carrie Street Bash

This chapter identifies and clarifies concepts and procedural problems associated with current delinquency-prevention activities in the United States and examines contemporary approaches that have prevention as their goal. Delinquency prevention in the United States is ill defined and unorganized. There are at least three major reasons for this lack of definition and organization:

1. The rise of varieties of ideas, agencies, and practices aimed at delinquency prevention has been characterized by a number of unresolved questions and contradictory issues. Many of these have been retained at the core of what are currently regarded as delinquency-prevention programs.
2. There is no generally accepted or generally useful common frame of reference available to facilitate comparison, classification, and communication between agencies and disciplines.
3. The notion of prevention, per se, involves conceptual and operational ambiguities that raise difficulties for adequate and unequivocal definitions.

The Evolution of Prevention Services

Early programs to prevent delinquency were primarily local efforts, usually initiated by privately supported, family-neighborhood-centered agencies and groups. Gradually, as a result of growing concern about juvenile delinquency and as the requirements of living in an expanding urban society began to be understood, increasingly large segments of society became actively involved. In recent years, a wide variety of community, state, and national agencies and groups have become aware of delinquency problems and have developed prevention programs. However, most of the methods and approaches were little more than continuations and extensions of the traditional practices characteristic of the particular agency involved.

This piecemeal development of services became a fragmented patchwork of vested interest programs: Such isolated responses to the problem of delinquency were not likely to create a network of complementary, integrated services or smoothly interacting agencies. Noting this development, the Children's Bureau, Division of Juvenile Delinquency Service, states:

> By the mid-1950's the delinquency prevention effort in virtually every large city was like a huge jigsaw puzzle of services involving important government departments which had heretofore operated with relative independence. The agencies concerned with delinquency prevention included the schools, recreation departments, public housing authorities, public welfare departments giving family service and administering child welfare, private social agencies and health departments and other medical facilities (including psychiatric hospitals and clinics). The size, shape, strength and position (role in the community) of the various pieces of the delinquency prevention picture varied greatly from one city to another. . . . The format for delinquency prevention services varied from city to city partly because the coordinating agency in each city was the one which happened to be the strongest.[1]

Many agencies had operated previously with only infrequent, formal relations among upper levels of administration and with few working channels of communication at line-worker levels.

> It has been said that winning strategy in the war against delinquency is, in large measure, a matter of having the appropriate community services needed by disadvantaged children and their families available in the right place at the right time in the right amount. Yet day-to-day operations made it evident that something was grossly wrong with agency relationships. A general lack of communication between agencies and between disciplines was increasingly evident, and variations in policies between agencies often made it impossible for them to function effectively together for the benefit of the child.[2]

[1] *Juvenile Delinquency Prevention in the United States* (Washington, D.C.: U.S. Department of Health, Education, and Welfare, Children's Bureau, 1965), p. 12.
[2] *Ibid.*, p. 17.

Finally, because the problem is defined in terms of the prevailing interest of the agency, many essential core issues are ignored or unexamined. There is a tendency to prejudge the etiological basis for delinquency and to prescribe action before the problem has been identified. Moreover, there is no strong motivation to compare notes with other agencies or disciplines because the agency is occupied with its own immediate practical problems. As a result, many of these programs remain provincial and isolated in both theory and practice.

The Lack of a Common Frame of Reference

Much of the confusion about appropriate goals and ways of handling delinquency-prevention problems arises because there are few adequate conceptual frameworks available for making comparisons that suggest relationships and make connections among ideas. It is probably inevitable that this will occur in a developing field. At present, however, the difficulties are compounded by the fact that we are dealing with a rapidly changing world. The growing complexity of American society, the increasing multiplicity of group affiliations among its members, the higher rates of geographic and social mobility, and continuing population growth have severely taxed the patterns of social and institutional organization that sufficed for the smaller and more stable population of the past. Social order is compromised by inadequate social supports and ineffective social controls for the containment of antisocial activity.

Understanding of the nature and meaning of delinquency is also changing: Attention has shifted from a narrow focus on the individual or group exhibiting delinquent behavior to interaction between the individual, his social setting, and society as a whole. The examination of social structure in relation to youth has raised many questions about older conceptions and methods of action.

Problems of Definition

It is difficult to formulate comprehensive, unequivocal definitions for delinquency prevention that clearly identify the population to be considered, specify what is to be prevented, indicate the course of action to be taken, and name the appropriate agent in whose jurisdiction the responsibility falls. The difficulties of defining juvenile delinquency are well known and have been thoroughly discussed in the literature.[3] These difficulties also pertain in establishing a base of action for prevention.

[3] Ruth Shonle Cavan, "What Is Delinquency?" in *Social Problems: Persistent Challenges,* ed. Edward C. McDonagh and Jon E. Simpson (New York: Holt Rinehart & Winston, Inc., 1965), pp. 415–424.

Any critical examination of delinquency-prevention programs is complicated and severely hampered by the fact that the concepts and definitions of prevention are intertwined with the concepts and definitions of correction. Most delinquency-prevention programs have been greatly influenced by the organization of information and the data on clients provided by enforcement, court, and correctional services. This may be unavoidable, but some perspective on differences should be developed and maintained.[4]

Correction of adult or juvenile offenders should be restricted to those legally identified or officially adjudged delinquent. Although statistics vary, there is general agreement that the number of persons processed by official law-enforcement agencies constitutes only a small proportion of the total delinquent population.

In contrast to the precisely circumscribed population that is a target for correctional programs, prevention programs must focus on a vastly larger population. The very nature of prevention goals implies different theoretical and operational problems. In principle, at least, prevention programs are concerned with every individual who experiences social, economic, cultural, psychological, or physical handicaps or needs. In this sense, prevention encompasses a broader, more inclusive radius than does correction.

Further important considerations result from the different character of the target population for correction. Although the prevention population is larger, it is additionally distinguished from the correctional population by being scattered, abstract, and unidentifiable in terms other than those of statistical probability. Consequently, few traditions, institutions, formal occupational statuses, authority hierarchies, or community norms have crystallized to deal with this ambiguous population. Any trend toward the development of prevention as a formal, officially supported, institutionalized activity, therefore, has been meager; in fact, no "field" exists. Prevention programs have not developed a central, organized discipline, body of knowledge, action, or research that can be identified as a theoretical schema.

As a field, correction also cannot claim this kind of theoretical consistency and organization of basic knowledge. Administratively, however, a core population of officially identified offenders does provide the correctional field with a basis for internal organization and development of an extensive system of clients, workers, authority structures, rationales, physical plants, and rehabilitative resources. In contrast, no comparable organizing element and institutional elaboration can be demonstrated at this time in the area of prevention.

There is another factor that distinguishes the development of a

---

[4] For conceptual clarification see Chapter 1.

prevention program from an established correctional program. Although both correction and prevention are confronted with complicated theoretical and procedural problems, prevention programs also face political "hurdles" that are deeply rooted in human psychology in general and in American culture in particular.

Correctional programs are directed toward identifiable, legally adjudicated offenders who are socially perceived as threats to persons or property: They are thought to require custody, punishment, or rehabilitation. In contrast, a prevention program focuses on a *potential* population that is legally nonexistent. The need to deal with this population is not impelled, therefore, by punitive motivations. The question of rehabilitation seems academic, hypothetical, and undefined, and it is of immediate concern only to the most sensitive and responsible observers. In fact, the extent to which the public recognizes a need to deal with prevention at all is open to question.

American society prides itself on its pragmatic approach to disturbing problems, but the tendency with delinquency is to develop efficient ways of handling youthful offenders rather than to tolerate the ambiguity and uncertainty of dealing with the more fundamental sociopsychological conditions that lead certain children to become problems. Society seems to act as if crime and delinquency are being foisted on an innocent and law-abiding community.

A preventive program must necessarily focus on assumed prior conditions in order to forestall probable or hypothesized consequences. This unfortunately raises the nagging and unpopular suspicion that delinquency is endemic to the American social fabric. This suspicion, in combination with the intangible preconditions affecting a population that is only statistically identifiable and leading to the mere probability of delinquent behavior, does not enlist popular support.

Although both correction and prevention appear as unpleasant social obligations, the necessity of prevention has not yet intruded on the public consciousness. Therefore, the legally identified offender has been defined as a public responsibility, whereas the potential offender has not been considered as such. Yet a more thoughtful, but hardly less pragmatic, attitude should recognize the practical need for prevention because of the increasing magnitude and cost of correctional programs.

Notes Toward a Conceptual Framework for Delinquency Prevention

Because delinquent behavior emerges from the problems of children and youth in general, almost any program designed to provide basic services to children or the adults surrounding them can be rationalized as a program for delinquency prevention. In addition, although it is possible to identify legal offenders for correctional service after they have been apprehended, there is no comparable, clearly demarcating basis for distinguishing delinquents and nondelinquents that can be used to select a population for prevention service. At best, such a distinction must be sociopsychological in character, but our enabling tools are inadequate.

We cannot give *the* cause of delinquency or even primary causes: We can only identify certain relationships and factors that increase the possibility of finding delinquency in a certain situation. How then can we take action to prevent delinquency?

From time to time it has been suggested that the only program of delinquency prevention that will have any lasting effect is one that attacks the basic roots of the problem in the social structure. Ferri, for example, believed that crime and delinquency follow the form and nature of the community; that society has the number and kinds of crimes it *deserves* as a result of its structure and values. He recommended a series of broad-scale social changes to replace what he saw as relatively ineffective punitive measures of social control.[5]

Similarly, Saul Alinsky has taken the position that crime and delinquency will be prevented only to the extent that such basic social conditions as poverty, poor housing, unemployment, disease, and racial discrimination are eliminated. The "Back of the Yards Project" in Chicago is a program initiated to bring about such social reorganization. Alinsky advocates the development of a series of neighborhood "peoples organizations," made up of local residents and representatives of local organizations. These groups are essentially political-action groups, which when joined with other similar groups across the nation could exert significant political influence at levels that transcend the community.[6]

According to Taft, none of the methods currently used to control delinquency cut the "deeper roots" of the problem. He points out, however, that

> crimeless society had best be static. To avoid culture conflict
> it should be internally homogeneous. On the economic side, a
> crimeless society must avoid excessive competition and greed for
> material gain and must be planned rather than chaotic. This would
> be essential to avoid such sources of maladjustment as relative
> failure, city slums, struggle for speculative gains, monopolistic
> advantages and various types of exploitation.[7]

[5] Enrico Ferri, *Criminal Sociology*, trans. J. I. Kelly and John Lisle (Boston: Little, Brown and Company, 1917).

[6] Saul Alinsky, "Heads I Win, Tails You Lose," *National Probation Association Yearbook* (1946), pp. 40–50.

[7] Donald Taft, *Criminology: A Cultural Interpretation* (New York: The MacMillan Company, 1950), pp. 666–667.

Social and cultural factors act to define goals and values at all levels of society. Not only are the general conditions that provide a "sufficient" climate for delinquency a consequence of the prevailing social order, but more specifically our emphasis on individuality, aggressiveness, wealth, personal prestige, and personal attractiveness sets a pattern that defines delinquent, as well as nondelinquent, goals. Frequently the suggestion, at least by implication, is that the goals are almost more important than the means used to attain them.

Because of this interlocking of determinants and influences, Taft concludes that caution should prevail in choosing crime-prevention methods:

> The reader may decide for himself, first which of the changes needed to prevent crime he desires, and second whether the criminogenic conditions he would have to sacrifice are or are not more desirable than crime prevention. A program of cultural change solely in the interest of crime prevention would be based upon the, perhaps false, assumption that a crimeless society is the one great good.[8]

Although broad-scale social responsibility and sociocultural development are to be encouraged, it is questionable whether such efforts should be rationalized on the basis that they prevent juvenile delinquency. Particularly at operational levels, such programs of social change as urban renewal, full employment, and the elimination of racial discrimination are a different order of social activity than is delinquency prevention. It must be remembered that of the thousands of children who do not have full access to the American opportunity structure only a minority are labeled as delinquent or problem children. Broad programs of social change should be primarily concerned with these larger problems. It is appropriate that broad programs encompass a concern for the deviant, but delinquency is only one type of deviance. Moreover, it is neither appropriate nor constructive for either the deviant or for the normal population that these efforts be conceptualized in negative and limited terms. They are not efforts to prevent delinquency but efforts to produce a maximally healthy and productive society.

It is shortsighted to talk about delinquency prevention in terms that make prevention services exactly congruent with services for the general welfare and benefit of *all* youth. For example, there is an understandable appeal in the idea that delinquency-prevention programs should be an integral part of such a basic service institution as the school: (1) The school has direct access to almost every child from age six to sixteen; (2) most hard-core delinquents are likely to be school problems; and (3) the

8 *Ibid.*

correlation between school problems and delinquency is sufficiently high to suggest that the school is a setting in which incipient delinquency can be identified.

The strategic position that the school occupies in the life of children and youth does not, however, automatically make the school a strategic context for prevention of delinquency. It is at least open to question whether a basic service institution can serve the special needs of delinquency-prone children without compromising its larger function and whether early detection, identification, and special programing in the general school situation do not create new hazards.

In order to avoid compromising the school system's general responsibilities, special schools for problem students have been established. For the most part these have not been effective because, as critics have pointed out, such schools tend to concentrate antisocial attitudes, thereby creating a setting that reinforces negative values. Being isolated from the general school population generally carries some stigma and reduces the chances for differential association and differential identification. Delinquency reinforcement may thus come from both internal and external sources.

Attempts to develop special programs within the general school situation have invariably run the risk of linking the "potential delinquent" or "person needing special services" with pathology and "badness." Consequently, the process that Merton has called the "self-fulfilling prophecy" is set in motion.[9] Few school systems are realistically equipped to mobilize the qualified personnel and the required sensitivity to counteract this process.

However, the school setting is in an opportune position to reduce the status discontent that many sociologists consider a critical determinant in much urban delinquency. The school provides a protected environment in which the extremes in students' status differential in the community can be minimized or made secondary in importance. Thus students can be provided with an environment that fosters the development of interest in the reward systems of the school.

The advocates of this point of view hypothesize that the student will apply his energies to study and to participation in the school only to the extent that the school becomes a place where he finds gratification and success *meaningful in his terms*. As the child experiences a higher proportion of success, it is expected that self-satisfaction and self-confidence are likely to grow. If legitimate opportunities could be provided for tangible success in school settings, status discontent could be managed more effectively for deprived populations through the critical years of

9 Robert K. Merton, *Social Theory and Social Structure* (New York: Free Press of Glencoe, Inc., 1957), pp. 421ff.

childhood and adolescence, and its crippling effects in these years could be minimized. In addition to academic and intellectual success, outlets would have to be provided to cover other skills, abilities, and needs. However, because the key element in this proposition involves change, it seems unlikely that such programs can be established in the general public school.

Adequate and effective basic service institutions such as schools, recreation departments, and welfare departments provide important social services for both delinquents and nondelinquents. They are the public settings in which incipient delinquency is first likely to be recognized, but their fundamental programs, policies, and methods are not specifically aimed at inhibiting delinquent behavior. It is rare to find a basic service agency that is able to modify its program to create special circumstances for dealing with the special needs of potential legal offenders. Such flexibility is usually impossible because their programs are designed to meet the needs of the majority of their clients.

A socially alert and informed community with effective basic service institutions is desirable. Because of the current general public anxiety about juvenile delinquency, it is tempting for administrators of basic services to rationalize their operations as delinquency-prevention programs, to get public support and additional money. By being opportunistic and imprecise in their claims, widespread support is gained for shallow conceptualization and understanding of delinquency; by casually appropriating concepts and by using "prevention" as a catchword, important distinctions have been lost. In the resulting ambiguity and confusion the formulation of meaningful definitions and the undertaking of important specific tasks are delayed.

Basic service programs and those programs designed to contribute to the general welfare of society should be handled as separate and higher-order concerns. These represent long-range societal values and are matters of general *social growth*. The prevention of delinquency, on the other hand, is largely a matter of *social defense*. As an institutionalized activity, delinquency prevention occupies an intermediate position between broad social activities at one extreme and primary socialization activities at the other.

It is expedient to relate delinquency to the general pattern of deviation associated with general institutional disorganization because then the conditions and circumstances predisposing to delinquency are assumed as part of the general system. On the other hand, if delinquent behavior is regarded as a specialized response, it is necessary to be specific about the predisposing conditions and the kind of intervention that can prevent the emergence of delinquent patterns. We have made this kind of separation implicitly by excluding broad-scale social programs and basic service institutions on the grounds that they are practically ineffective for prevention. We now turn to a consideration of the programs that assume that specific predisposing conditions can be identified and that specific patterns of intervention can prevent individuals and groups from making significant personal commitments to delinquent patterns of behavior.

For the most part these programs are at the local community level. The local community is affected by general sociocultural factors, but important variations in structure and organization do exist among communities. From a practical point of view, the most efficient setting for a delinquency-prevention program is at the local neighborhood-community level. There are three reasons for this point of view:

1. *Delinquency is a social activity.* A great deal of the research data reported in the literature suggests that the beliefs, values, attitudes, and behavior of individuals is determined by primary-group relationships. To the extent that this is true, prevention of delinquency must be local and closely related to primary groups. Sutherland and Cressey note:

> Criminals who are to be reformed and the persons who are to exert influence or change must have a strong sense of belonging to the same groups. The two general processes in reformation are the *alienation* of the criminal from groups which support values conducive to criminality and, concurrently, *assimilation* of the criminal into groups supporting values conducive to law-abiding behavior. The latter process can be accomplished only when the social distance between the criminals and the reformers is small enough to permit a genuine "we" feeling.[10]

2. *Delinquent acts are also individual acts.* A wide variety of individuals and individual acts are identified as "delinquent." Causation in each case is likely to be attributable to a complex of factors; for analytic convenience we distinguish them as "sociocultural factors" and "personality factors." Yet they are not independent of one another: Both delinquent and nondelinquent behavior represent social actions or behavioral choices that reflect the interaction between both sets of factors.

It is unlikely that delinquent acts ever erupt spontaneously without predelinquent antecedents: Uusually it can be demonstrated that the overt act is simply one step in a process that has been going on for some time. Most delinquent acts have a history that is reflected in a characteristic organization of perceptions, expectations, beliefs, attitudes, and values. To the extent that delinquency-prevention activities intend to prevent individual acts, they must be close enough to the individual to be sensitive to these characteristics and to intervene effectively.

3. *The use of available resources will vary from community to com-*

---

10 Edwin H. Sutherland and Donald R. Cressey, *Principles of Criminology* (Philadelphia: J. B. Lippincott Co., 1960), p. 602.

munity. Because rates of delinquency as well as the frequency with which any specific delinquent act occurs vary among neighborhoods and among communities, any effective program of delinquency prevention must fit the needs and circumstances of the local situation. An organization and design that is effective in one locality may be inadequate or inappropriate in another. Helpful ideas and principles may be gathered from studies of similar ventures elsewhere, but ideas and techniques can rarely be transferred without some adaptation. Also, every program to prevent delinquency should involve the community in a ceaseless, systematic study of its resources as well as in a continuous survey of the nature, degree, and location of delinquency.[11]

A Classification Schema for Delinquency-Prevention Programs

It is traditional to classify delinquency-prevention activities as those providing *direct* help and services to individual children and as those helping children *indirectly* by changing their social environment. For most purposes this is a useful division and many programs operate on the basis of one or the other of these goals. However, an examination of the ways in which these objectives are actually implemented in most programs reveals that this dichotomization of the *direct-individual* and the *indirect-environment* emphases is, at best, a logical, analytic model. Neither empirical reality nor programs designed to alter that reality exhibit such neat categorization: In practice, a program objective may begin with one of these goals, but every contemporary program of delinquency prevention seems to extend beyond its expressed aim, thus tending to blur the analytic distinctions.

In the preceding discussion we dismissed broad-scale programs of social change, basic service institutions such as schools, and general welfare programs as too comprehensive for dealing effectively with prevention. Implicit in our discussion was the contention that the concept of delinquency prevention should apply exclusively to any program that has a primary and explicit commitment to activities intended to prevent patterns of delinquent behavior.

Accordingly, we propose the following typology as an organizing principle for the classification of prevention programs:

1. Programs that have explicit primary functions and goals involving deliberate intervention in the lives of specifically identified *individuals* for the express purpose of preventing the occurrence of behavior that

[11] William C. Kvaraceus, *The Community and the Delinquent* (New York: Harcourt, Brace & World, Inc., 1954), p. 15.

would label them as antisocial or as delinquent by the laws and rules of general society.

2. Programs that have explicit primary goals of planned intervention and participation in the development, employment, organization, and inter-relationship of various *social institutions, groups,* and *agencies* in the community with the intention of preventing the formation of patterns of delinquent behavior in specific individuals or groups.

3. Programs that have explicit primary goals of deliberate participation in the *social processes* of reviewing and developing laws, social policies, and public attitudes that have a specific and direct relevance to activities designed to prevent delinquency.

At the most fundamental level, this typology is based on the distinction between *intrinsic* targets and *efficient* targets as focal points for delinquency-prevention strategy. Although all prevention programs have the individual delinquency-prone child as their intrinsic target, some programs do not share identical efficient targets. The separation of intrinsic and efficient targets is clearly related to the historical development of delinquency-prevention efforts.

Earlier conceptions of delinquency as individual pathological traits provided a rationale for preventive programs that made the delinquency-prone child both the intrinsic *and* the efficient target. Whether the causes of delinquency were attributed to biological, physical, temperamental, or psychological factors, it was the "pathological" individual toward whom punitive or rehabilitative efforts were directed. More recently, as sociological conceptions have been increasingly applied to delinquent conduct, programs incorporating such ideas perceive their efficient targets in the social environment while still viewing the individual as the intrinsic target. Contemporary approaches to prevention programs, therefore, cover the entire range from the individual to the society as efficient targets. Consequently, our typology must reflect the initial *identity* as well as the increasing *separation* of the intrinsic and efficient targets.

We might describe what is involved here as the selection of three arbitrarily established points on a continuum of social situations, ranging from that which is primarily individual to that which is primarily societal. In the first program, the individual is the dependent variable, and environment is the independent variable. In the second and third programs, the situation is reversed. In each of the program types, an inevitable intrinsic target is the behaving individual, and ultimately specific kinds of behavior are also intrinsic targets. In first-level types of programing, in which the efficient target is a specific person, the individual is both the efficient target and an intrinsic target. The service strategy at this level characteristically involves deliberate intervention in a person's life. The service strategy of the second prevention program is planned interaction and participation with groups and social institutions in the community. In this case, efficient targets are one step removed from the individual and could be family groups, street groups, neighborhood groups, or social agencies in the community.

In practical applications, the preventive measures used in these groups reflect a general cognizance of the critical quality of individuality as an element in understanding and changing group dynamics, but in terms of strategy the focus is on the group and its influence as a unit. This is demonstrated by examining the direction of choices made by prevention agents who are committed to Type 2 patterns when there is a crisis confrontation that involves the separation of an individual member from the group as a whole. Specific individuals and acts of delinquency tend to be submerged in an overriding concern for the group.

At the societal level of prevention, intervention strategy is mostly one of review and evaluation and of initiating change in pertinent laws and public policies by the judicious introduction of information. To a degree, lobbying techniques are also part of the usual pattern of activity at this level. Efficient targets are legislative bodies and state and national organizations with specific influence in activities relevant to delinquency-identification and prevention programs. Although these political efforts are removed from the level of deliberate, direct inhibition, suppression, or rechanneling of individual behavior, it is nevertheless appropriate to regard such programs as a legitimate aspect of delinquency prevention.

If these three levels of activity are acceptable as covering the range of services identified as delinquency-preventive, we can illustrate our schema by viewing several selected, recent programs.

Beginning with Type 1, involving programs of direct individual intervention in which the intrinsic and efficient targets are identical, we find relatively few contemporary programs that unambiguously fit the criteria, which is to be expected. This approach must logically rest on biological conceptions of deviance (such as atavistic assumptions proposed by Lombroso), physical assumptions (such as those advanced by Kretschmer and Hooten), theories of temperament (for example, Sheldon's typology), and the purely psychological explanations (extreme psychoanalytic and psychiatric approaches). Few of these conceptualizations are accepted today without giving some recognition to intervening social variables. However, it is possible to point out prevention programs that conform in essence and in expressed aims to Type 1 criteria.

The establishment of the first juvenile court in Chicago in 1899,[12] with its correlated psychiatric clinic for children, was aimed at the early detection of delinquency-prone juveniles and sought to prevent them

[12] Sutherland and Cressey, op. cit., p. 398.

from developing into hardened "irremediable" criminals.[13] The juvenile court was based largely on the laws of equity, tempered by the findings of the medical and behavioral sciences. Many quasi-judicial procedures were developed, and the juvenile court, in many instances, operated more as a powerful social agency than as a court. At the same time, however, the juvenile court also retained many elements of the criminal court, and on occasion the procedures initially designed to "protect" the child were used in such arbitrary ways that justice was ignored. Because of these developments and other advances in prevention, the juvenile court today is rarely regarded as performing a preventive function. For the most part, its function has become the adjudication of recidivists. Paradoxically, this has had the effect of confirming the delinquency both in terms of self-perception and of social identification. Nevertheless, as initially conceived, the juvenile court was intended to intervene directly to prevent the individual's developent of patterned delinquency. Thus, the individual was both the intrinsic and efficient target for direct intervention.

Another approach, also primarily in this prevention category, is the child guidance clinic. Here also the individual is identified as the efficient target for intensive prevention service, which takes the form of psychotherapy of varying degrees of intensity. Similarly, family service agencies are placed in this category because as far as their delinquency-prevention aims are concerned their intervention target is the individual problem child. The case of family service agencies illustrates the dilemma of attempting to fit a practical intervention program into a logically ordered conceptual schema. As their name implies, family service agencies recognize that problem children tend to appear within a problem family context. Intervention strategy is designed, therefore, to attack largely through psychotherapy the immediate human environment of the incipiently delinquent child. We find, therefore, the beginning of a separation between the efficient target (the family) and the intrinsic target (the problem child).

The "aggressive" casework approach of the Passaic Children's Bureau (New Jersey)[14] the St. Paul Community Service Project (Minnesota),[15] as well as the New York Youth Board, with its emphasis on multiproblem families, are also efforts that primarily fit our first type of prevention program but overlap into Type 2.

Other approaches that straddle the demarcation line between programs of Type 1 and Type 2 are the Cambridge-Somerville Youth Study

[13] Paul W. Tappan, *Juvenile Delinquency* (New York: McGraw-Hill Book Company, 1949), pp. 167ff.

[14] William C. Kvaraceus, *Juvenile Delinquency and the School* (New York: Harcourt, Brace & World, Inc., 1945).

[15] S. A. Stone, E. Castendyck, and H. Hanson, *Children in the Community*, Publication No. 317 (Washington, D.C.: Children's Bureau, 1946).

program, Big Brother and Big Sister programs, and the Stiles Hall University Y.M.C.A. Project (Berkeley, California). Each of these projects attempts to provide positive role models for its "clients," thus extending their efficient targets slightly beyond an immediate focus on the individual.

Among the prevention programs classified under Type 2 is the Henry Street Settlement House, particularly its Pre-delinquent Gang Project.[16] The strategy of this program made neighborhood gangs the efficient target; the individual remained the intrinsic target through which the ultimate aim of preventing delinquency was to be achieved.

Similarly, the Girls Service League Project of the New York Youth Board sought to influence individual conduct through group therapy. Other programs that fit into this type are those using "aggressive" group-work tactics, generally employing "detached workers" or "street club workers" assigned to neighborhood gangs. Programs using these techniques are the Los Angeles Youth Project, the Hyde Park Youth Project (Chicago), the Unreached Youth Project (Cleveland), the Crime Prevention Association (Philadelphia), and, with qualifications, the Boston Youth Project.[17]

Programs classified under Type 3 are necessarily broad efforts to influence the societal conditions that are variables in the development and maintenance of delinquent patterns. Such programs may take shape as a result of the coordination of various previously independent community projects or they may be created at the highest state or federal levels. In the former case, their activities are frequently directed toward precipitating state or federal action; in the latter, they initiate action or provide enabling measures for community action.

Coordinated planning at the community level and action initiated at the state or federal level are relatively recent developments. Federal programs especially raise political questions that have not yet been fully incorporated into American traditions or resolved in public opinion. For these reasons, prevention strategies that fit the criteria of the third type are only now beginning to achieve some measure of acceptance and stability.

Formal programs for this category at best can only be expected to result from various state-sponsored study commissions, state commissions for children and youth, or the President's Committee on Juvenile Delinquency and Youth Crime.[18] At this point, then, we are not prepared to

[16] R. Tefferteller, "Delinquency Prevention in the Neighborhood," *Crime and Delinquency*, X, No. 3 (July, 1964), 217–230.

[17] "Preventive Work with Street-Corner Groups: Boston Delinquency Project," *The Annals of the American Academy of Political and Social Science*, CCCXXII (1959), 97–106.

[18] *Juvenile Delinquency Prevention in the United States.*

specify concrete, active delinquency-prevention programs that clearly fit this type.

Conclusion

Since the turn of the century, thought about juvenile delinquency and programming for prevention of delinquency have undergone significant changes. Some changes have been rather subtle, so that casual examination and comparison ordinarily would not highlight differences. For example, the theoretical base of child-guidance approaches has been greatly altered by the addition of sociocultural data and insights, although the emphasis on intensive treatement of the individual has remained relatively constant. Other changes have been more obvious: the change from unidimensional attacks on the problem to the current emphasis on multiphasic, comprehensive programs. Most changes, however, may be related to variations in basic ways of understanding and defining the nature and problems of delinquency. Thus, shifts in basic *definitions* regarding the nature of delinquency have resulted in shifts in program *objectives*, with subsequent shifts in strategies for achieving the desired objectives.

For many years the tendency was to define delinquency as a "sickness" of the individual that might be averted if it were diagnosed early enough to permit the introduction of some personal, intensive, physical or psychological treatment or to allow timely manipulation of harmful factors in the child's immediate environment. Later, as research began to demonstrate the importance of sociocultural factors in the socialization of the child, there was a swing in the opposite direction such that *society*, rather than the *individual*, was regarded as the patient.[19] Both of these extreme positions reflect a unitary, diagnostic concern for delinquency etiology. Resulting from either of the causal assumptions during this period was the characteristic research question "What caused this delinquency?"

Gradually, behavioral science has moved to a conceptual position of less preoccupation with identification of unitary causes of delinquency. There is increasing acceptance of the idea that aspects of general, rather than only deviant, life experiences may be significantly related to the development of delinquent behavior. Today the focus of concern is more on social roles and processes occurring in the group setting. The characteristic question for research is now more likely to be some variant of "what is happening?" This is largely a shift from a focus on *pathology* to one on *phenomenology*.

In the first section of this discussion we traced the development of

---

[19] Lawrence K. Frank, *Society as the Patient* (New Brunswick, N.J.: Rutgers University Press, 1949).

delinquency-prevention activity and pointed out some of the problems inherent in its growth. In the second section, a number of programs and projects were reviewed, the theories underlying them were isolated and identified, and the nature of the relations among programs was suggested. In the current section we will move toward a synthesis of some of the ideas mentioned in previous sections and suggest some principles for developing a sound base for programing in delinquency prevention.

Sutherland and Cressey have suggested that the terms "potential delinquent" or "predelinquent" are misleading from an etymological point of view. As they note,

> . . . every child is a potential delinquent, every child in earlier years is a predelinquent, and every able-bodied person who has passed the earlier years of childhood commits delinquencies more or less frequently. The term is used, however, to refer to the children who are believed to be extraordinarily likely to become confirmed delinquents.[20]

As we have seen, a variety of techniques and programs have been proposed to prevent the emergence of *patterned* antisocial behavior. These measures have been used with varying degrees of success. All the approaches that we have reported have been effective with some people under certain specific, but not always specifiable, circumstances. Conversely, there is also evidence indicating that many of the techniques have been ineffective and in some cases even harmful to other people under other circumstances. None of the measures proposed has been universally effective, nor has any one program or combination of techniques demonstrated that it is sufficient in itself to reduce delinquency on a broad scale.

On the whole we are still faced with the same situation that is reflected in the following comment by Witmer and Tufts in 1954:

> . . . we are on our way toward learning what does and what does not prevent delinquency, but we still have far to go. Progress toward that objective will call for close cooperation between practice and research, with both parties looking hopefully to theory and to experience for ideas about the direction in which to move next. Practice cannot and should not wait upon research, nor should research be delayed until practice is well established. We shall be most likely to discover how to prevent delinquency if research is undertaken coordinately with the development of new measures and the refinement of old ones, if research and practice are conceived as inseparable parts of a single process.[21]

[20] Sutherland and Cressey, *op. cit.*, p. 613.
[21] Helen Witmer and Edith Tufts, "The Effectiveness of Delinquency Prevention Programs," Publication No. 350 (U.S. Department of Health, Education, and Welfare, Children's Bureau, 1954), p. 50.

This does not mean that we have not made progress since 1954 or that all current approaches are basically ineffective. It does mean that there are still many ambiguities and contradictions in practice, theory, and research.

Some basic working agreements have been made. There is general agreement that neither delinquent nor nondelinquent behavior patterns are determined by *specific* neurological, physiological, psychological, or sociocultural structures. An almost infinite variety of behavior can develop with any given biopsychological organization of a person. At the same time, different physical-social-cultural contexts create different conditions of stress.

A person having a particular biopsychological personal structure experiences different kinds of stress as he encounters various situations and expectations arising in various sociocultural configurations. In this connection, Bloch comments that

> . . . in a civilization like ours, in which increasingly greater dependence is made upon the individual's intellectual capacities, an individual with deficient intellectual endowment, irrespective of how acquired, may encounter far more serious difficulties in adjusting to the conditions of his environment than an individual who is normally endowed. Among the several possibilities of such maladjustment, delinquency and crime simply represent some of the contingent outcomes. The same can be said for virtually any type of constitutional or neurological defect, whether such defects are matters of physique, temperament, endocrinological imbalance, facial or physical deformities, or a neural instability.[22]

Unfortunately, whenever research and theory have been involved in the development of projects and programs of delinquency prevention, there has been a tendency for the authors of such projects to focus either on psychological or sociological explanations of the phenomena. Too little attention has been given the intervening variables between social and personal factors. There is a serious deficiency of psychosocial explanations of delinquency that take both factors and the interactions between them into consideration.

The development of psychosocial definitions of variables is difficult. The language and organization of the literature do not help. Moreover, as long as one is occupied with small problems taken one at a time, the deficiencies of a conceptual system may not appear unduly large. However, now that some large-scale research has revealed deficiencies, behavioral science should establish a more solid, integrated base for further action. This is not to suggest that small research projects be abandoned or

[22] Herbert A. Bloch, "They Are Not Criminals," *Federal Probation* (September, 1958), p. 18.

that any single program or project be thoroughly detailed and explicit in all aspects of psychosocial interaction but rather that the basic interrelatedness of these variables be recognized.

Noteworthy correlations have been demonstrated for all these variables. As it is highly appropriate to be cautious in the interpretation of such correlations, it is equally unwise to be whimsical in rejecting any of them. If we do not allow ourselves to get trapped in outmoded arguments about unitary causes, we can continue to deal with physiological, neurological, and psychological factors as part of the network of variables that seem to be correlated with delinquency, and we may study the *interaction* between these variables and specific sociocultural variables that also have demonstrable correlations with delinquency.

Bovet has characterized certain children as the "vulnerables" in relation to provocative conditions producing delinquency in various cultures.[23] Personal and social factors that create vulnerability vary from one cultural context to another, but in each society it is possible to describe psychosocial profiles of children who, under stipulated conditions (which are part of the profile), seem to be more prone to delinquency than are other children in that same society.

Commenting on this approach, Bloch and Bovet observe:

. . . there are no children who, for whatever reason, appear to be unqualifiedly predisposed toward delinquency. There are, however, certain children predisposed toward delinquency in *certain* societies and within *certain* social settings. The problems of delinquency, therefore, invariably involve a certain type of peculiarly structured child within a given type of peculiarly predisposing situation which may produce a specific type of delinquent activity. The wholly *relative* and *contingent* nature of this relationship must be continually stressed.

When we examine the situations producing delinquency in this way, and recognize the enormously fluid conditions which produce a variety of different relationships, we may discern, nevertheless, within any given society those recurrent psycho-sociological conditions which may produce specific types of delinquent children. Further, we observe something else; we recognize that children whose personalities have become structured in certain societies in a peculiar way may or may not become vulnerable to delinquency in the particular society or restricted social setting.
. . . There are no inherent delinquent propensities within the structure of the personality itself or in the provocative situation, but rather in the conjoined relationship of both.[24]

23 L. Bovet, cited in Bloch, *ibid.*
24 Bloch, *op. cit.*, pp. 18ff.

Thus, the most useful understanding of delinquency will be achieved by careful study of interpersonal situations and by examination of the interactions among individuals, groups, social institutions, and sociocultural situations. By focusing on the complex of interactions rather than on unit characteristics of individuals, overt acts, or social conditions, the social scientist or the social therapist utilizes a unit of analysis that, like the delinquency itself, is a product of all the forces and factors involved.

From the delinquency-prevention point of view, ameliorative activities must be launched from what is essentially a "normal" base because the problems facing a potential delinquent overlap and are similar to the problems of all children and youth. In view of this and certain factors discussed above, it is reasonable to suggest that the most effective and productive approaches to understanding and preventing delinquency will be made by working with basic dynamics in human relationships and with conditions that are common to all children but that in certain combinations may tilt the scale of adjustment toward delinquent behavior.

Having reached such a conclusion, however, we may further develop classifications and typologies of personal organization, of time, of place, and of circumstance in which the contingency of an act or delinquent rationalization of a human problem will be relatively higher. Such classifications or typologies may be studied in various contexts.[25]

To spell out the range and detail of such classification and typology is beyond the intended scope of this paper. There is a great deal of pertinent literature, but the available data suggest that a relatively small number of psychosocial profiles may be sufficiently helpful to improve vastly our current record of success in preventing delinquency (if we are willing to follow through with sufficient resources and effort). Despite glaring deficiencies in tested, relevant knowledge and despite poor understanding of the ways in which social institutions can be managed, our knowledge is sufficient to introduce programs with significantly improved chances of being effective.[26] This is not to suggest that behavioral science now has all the answers, but only that we do have enough answers and sufficient knowledge to improve our present performance. There is still need to develop focused programs that have a specific, explicit commitment to develop information relevant to problems of delin-

[25] Cf. Michael Argyle, "A New Approach to the Classification of Delinquents with Implications for Treatment," *Inquiries Concerning Kinds of Treatment for Kinds of Delinquents*, Monograph No. 2 (Board of Corrections, State of California, July, 1961), pp. 15–24; Clyde Sullivan, Marguerite Q. Grant, and J. Douglas Grant, "The Development of Interpersonal Maturity: Applications to Delinquency," *Psychiatry* (Spring, 1962), pp. 373–385.

[26] R. Gould, "Are We Being Scientific about Delinquency?" *Federal Probation* (1957), pp. 16–21.

quency prevention. As expressed at the beginning of this chapter, the present cost in dollars and in human values more than justifies such attention.

SELECTED READINGS

Alinsky, Saul D., *Reveille for Radicals*. Chicago: University of Chicago Press, 1937.

Amos, William E., Raymond L. Manella, and Marilyn A. Southwell, *Action Programs for Delinquency Prevention*. Springfield, Ill.: Charles C. Thomas, Publisher, 1965.

Austin, David M., "Objectives of the Service," *Youth Groups in Conflict*, compiled and edited by Mary E. Blake. Washington, D.C.: U.S. Department of Health, Education, and Welfare, 1958.

Bennis, Warren G., Kenneth D. Benne, and Robert Chin, eds., *The Planning of Change: Readings in Applied Behavioral Sciences*. New York: Holt, Rinehart & Winston, Inc., 1961.

"Blueprint for Delinquency Prevention," New York State Youth Commission, 1953.

Bowan, Paul Hoover, "Effects of a Revised School Program on Potential Delinquents," *The Annals*. CCCXXII (March, 1959), 53–61.

California Committee on the Older Girl and the Law, *The Older Girl and the Law*, Governor's Advisory Committee on Children and Youth, State of California (January, 1960).

Children's Bureau Statistical Series, No. 65, "Juvenile Court Statistics—1960." Washington, D.C.: U.S. Department of Health, Education, and Welfare, 1961.

Cook, Donald, and Seymour Rubenfeld, "Settings and Causes of Delinquency," *An Assessment of Current Mental Health and Social Science Knowledge Concerning Juvenile Delinquency*. National Institute of Mental Health, in support of Report to Congress on Juvenile Delinquency, 1960. Appendix II, Chapter 3.

Data Book: *A Program for the Prevention of Delinquency*, Sociology Department, Institute for Juvenile Research, Illinois Department of Public Welfare and the Chicago Area Project. Chicago, Ill., July, 1954.

Douglas, J., and Marguerite Q. Grant, "A Group Dynamics Approach to the Treatment of Non-conformists in the Navy," *The Annals*, CCCXXII (March, 1959), 126–135.

Franklin, Adele, "The All-Day Neighborhood School," *Crime and Delinquency*, VII, No. 3 (July, 1961), 255–262.

Fried, Antoninette, "A Work Camp Program for Potential Delinquents," *The Annals*, CCCXXII (March, 1959), 38–46.

Gandy, John M., "Preventive Work with Street-Corner Groups: Hyde Park Youth Project," *The Annals*, CCCXXII (1959), 107–116.

72   *Clyde E. Sullivan and Carrie Street Bash*

Kvaraceus, William C., "Social Aspects of Delinquent Behavior," *Journal of Social Hygiene*, XXIX (1943), 526–527.

Miller, Walter B., "Preventive Work with Street-Corner Groups: Boston Delinquency Project," *The Annals*, CCCXXII (March, 1959), 97–106.

Moles, Oliver M., Jr., Ronald Lippitt, and Stephen Withey, *A Selective Review of Research and Theories Concerning the Dynamics of Delinquency*, Institute of Social Research. Ann Arbor: The University of Michigan, September, 1959.

Noyes, Arthur B., M.D., and Lawrence C. Kolb, M.D., *Modern Clinical Psychiatry*, rev. ed. Philadelphia: W. B. Saunders Co., 1963. Pages 482–499.

Perlman, I. Richard, "Delinquency Prevention: The Size of the Problem," *Juvenile Delinquency: Facts and Facets*, No. 4. Washington, D.C.: U.S. Department of Health, Education, and Welfare, 1960.

Perspectives on Delinquency Prevention. New York City Youth Board, City of New York, 1955; *Pattern for Prevention*. New York City Youth Board, City of New York, 1952; and *Reaching the Unreached*. New York City Youth Board, City of New York, 1952.

Powers, Edwin, and Helen L. Witmer, *An Experiment in the Prevention of Delinquency*. New York: Columbia University Press, 1951.

Reed, Ellery, "How Effective Are Group Work Agencies in Preventing Delinquency," *Social Service Review*, XXII (1948), 340–348.

Robison, Sophia, "Why Juvenile Delinquency Preventive Programs Are Ineffective," *Federal Probation*, XXV, No. 4 (December, 1961).

Second United Nations Congress on the Prevention of Crime and the Treatment of Offenders, "New Forms of Juvenile Delinquency: Their Origin, Prevention and Treatment" (August, 1960).

Serotkin, Harry, "Youth Services," *Social Work Yearbook*. New York: National Association of Social Workers, Inc., 1960. Pages 607–617.

Shanas, Ethel, and Catherine E. Dunning, *Recreation and Delinquency*. Chicago, Ill.: Chicago Recreation Commission, 1942.

Strahanan, Marion, and Cecil Schwartzman, "An Experiment in Reaching Asocial Adolescents Through Group Therapy," *The Annals*, CCCXXII (March, 1959), 117–125.

Sutherland, Edward H., and Donald R. Cressey, *Principles of Criminology*. Philadelphia: J. B. Lippincott Co., 1955.

Tefferteller, Ruth S., "Delinquency Prevention through Revitalizing Parent-Child Relations," *The Annals*, American Academy of Political and Social Science, CCCXXII (March, 1959), 69–78.

Thrasher, Frederick, "The Boy's Club and Juvenile Delinquency," *American Journal of Sociology*, XLII (1936), 66–80.

Witmer, Helen L., *Psychiatric Clinics for Children*. New York: The Commonwealth Fund, 1958.

5 Prevention Through the Family

C. Ray Jeffery
Ina A. Jeffery

One must first know the variables that cause or are related to juvenile delinquency before it can be prevented through the family. Although it is often stated in the literature that the family is part of the environment that produces delinquent behavior, the exact nature of this relationship has yet to be explicated.

The concept of prevention implies control over the variables that influence delinquent conduct. In this chapter we will discuss and delineate some of the important family-linked variables assumed to be related to delinquency.

The family, as it influences human behavior, may be viewed in at least three general ways: (1) as a biological unit, (2) as a psychological unit, and (3) as a social unit. First a survey of the literature will be made to indicate the ways in which the family is related to delinquent behavior, and then a general statement will be advanced of the ways in which prevention through the family can be effected.

The Family as a Biological Unit

It has been argued for many generations that the causes of crime and delinquency are to be found in biology and in the principles of heredity. If criminal behavior is inherited, the family is a crucial unit in the prevention of delinquency.

Family trees are often examined to determine the influence of heredity. The most famous study in this respect was that of the Jukes family by Dugdale. This study, which purported to show that crime, vice, and degeneracy run in families, was later proved a myth.[1] Studies of twins by Lange, Rasanoff, and others have also been used to show that criminality is inherited. The behavior of monozygotic (identical) twins is compared to that of dizygotic (fraternal) twins on the assumption that because identical twins are more alike genetically than are fraternal twins, they will consequently be more alike behaviorally. The inference drawn from such data is that identical twins are more alike in criminality than are fraternal twins. Ashley Montagu summarized these studies and concluded that they do not demonstrate the hereditary nature of behavior.[2]

Sheldon, Hooton, and others have attempted to relate criminality to body type. Sheldon and Eleanor Glueck found in their investigation that 60 per cent of their delinquent group was mesomorphic (muscular, active), whereas only 31 per cent of the nondelinquent group was mesomorphic, and that 14 per cent of the delinquents were ectomorphic (thin, skeletal) compared to 40 per cent of the nondelinquent group.[3]

Many criticisms of these studies have been made, the major one being that environmental conditions are ignored or uncontrolled. The fact that a son resembles his father behaviorally or that a twin resembles his twin brother does not establish the fact that crime is hereditary. A family reared as a cohesive unit will transmit to its members many behavioral patterns, including speaking and eating, but such patterns are learned, not inherited.

The Gluecks' findings are based on statistical correlations, and correlation is *not* causation. Mesomorphic build could cause delinquency, delinquency could cause mesomorphy, both mesomorphy and delinquency could be related to social class or ethnic origin, or both could be related by chance. Although the Gluecks found a high percentage of mesomorphic types in their delinquency population, they did not discuss any possible process in which body build could be related to behavior. Eysenck and his associates have demonstrated that differences in conditioning rates exist for different physical types. This problem of learning theory and body type will be discussed in greater detail later in this chapter.

Hooton found that in the United States Nordics were rated high in forgery and fraud, whereas Alpines were found high in armed robbery

[1] Edgar A. Schuler *et al., Readings in Sociology,* 2nd ed. (New York: Thomas Y. Crowell Company, 1960), pp. 40 ff.

[2] Richard Korn and Lloyd McCorkle, *Criminology and Penology* (New York: Holt, Rinehart & Winston, Inc., 1959), pp. 199–200.

[3] Sheldon and Eleanor Glueck, *Unraveling Juvenile Delinquency* (Cambridge: Harvard University Press, 1950) p. 193.

but very low in forgery and fraud.[4] Hooton interpreted his data biologically, but it should be pointed out that the Nordics, who migrated to the United States in the seventeenth century, occupied middle-class positions of trust and responsibility: positions conducive to committing fraud and forgery. The Alpines migrated in the late nineteenth century and lived in Italian ghettoes where the rate of robbery was high.

Another criticism of the biological theory is that it regards behavior as a product of heredity, whereas modern biology teaches that any trait or process is a product of heredity interacting with environment. Heredity supplies the potential that develops in one of several ways depending on environmental influences. Heredity may set limits, but environment determines the extent to which this potential develops.

The theory that criminality is inherited has been disproved. Therefore, most modern sociologists and criminologists perhaps too hastily conclude that biological variables can be ignored. We will return to a consideration of the physiological dimension of behavior. As far as the family is concerned we can safely state that the family contributes to the biological basis of behavior, although we do not know what the role of biology is in behavior.

The Family as a Psychological Unit

The Freudian theory of personality development is one of the popular theories of delinquency. This approach, which states that delinquent behavior is a result of abnormal mental or emotional states, is based on the premise that libidinal instincts are shaped by social experiences. The id, or pleasure principle, seeks gratification in an unfriendly social environment; the ego, or reality principle, and the superego, or conscience, control and direct the instinctual appetites of the individual. If these three components of personality are not in harmony, psychotic and neurotic symptoms appear. The Freudian theory is a system of *subjective* assumptions about behavior, thus not applicable to scientific verification. However, the influence of Freud on social work and criminology has been great.[5]

The Freudians assume that personality processes occur within the family. The father represents power and authority and is the punishing agent of society; the mother represents love and affection. It is within the family that the ego and superego develop and sexual impulses are controlled. Psychosexual development moves through the oral, anal, and

[4] Ruth Cavan, *Criminology*, 3rd ed. (New York, Thomas Y. Crowell Company, 1962), pp. 694–695.
[5] Sophia M. Robison, *Juvenile Delinquency* (New York: Holt, Rinehart, & Winston, Inc. 1960), pp. 68 ff.

genital stages, with the Oedipus complex occurring during the genital phase. Much attention is thus paid to child-rearing practices, to socialization within the family, to early toilet training, to sex instruction, and so forth.[6]

It is true that the family is an important social group in the development of personality. Aichorn found, for example, that aggressive youths in Vienna came from families with too much or too little love and affection. Because of this family problem, these youths developed sociopathic personalities. David Levy stated that some delinquents are a product of environmental conditions, whereas others are a product of unsatisfactory parent-child relations. Healy and Bronner studied delinquents and nondelinquents from the same family and found that in 91 per cent of the delinquent cases the delinquent felt rejected by the family, whereas only 13 per cent of the nondelinquent cases had these feelings. Bowlby, in his study of forty-four thieves, discovered early and prolonged separation from the mothers during the first five years of life.[7] The Gluecks concluded from their studies that delinquents were reared in homes of little understanding, affection, stability, or moral fiber, and the parents were usually unfit to be effective guides, protectors, or desirable symbols for emulation. The Gluecks found that indifferent, hostile, or rejecting parents were more likely to have delinquent sons than were warm or overprotective parents. Family discipline in delinquent families was either lax or consisted of severe physical punishment.[8]

In a reevaluation of the Cambridge-Somerville study, William and Joan McCord found that 72 per cent of the neglecting mothers compared to 27 per cent of the loving normal mothers had delinquent sons.[9] They found that the lower rates of delinquency were associated with consistent discipline, whereas the higher rates were associated with erratic discipline. The McCords also found that overprotective mothers had nondelinquent sons, whereas neglecting, rejecting, or passive mothers had delinquent sons. If the mother loved the son and the father rejected him, the rate of delinquency was 36 per cent; if the mother rejected and the father loved, the rate was 46 per cent. A rejecting mother is more influential than a rejecting father in producing delinquent sons. Maternal neglect is more damaging than maternal cruelty (apparently, beating a youth at least shows some concern for him). The delinquency rate is higher if the mother is deviant than if the father is deviant. A loving

    6 William F. Kenkel, *The Family in Perspective* (New York: Appleton-Century & Appleton-Century-Crofts, 1960), pp. 227–436.
    7 Barbara Wootton, *Social Science and Social Pathology* (New York: The Macmillan Company, 1959), pp. 136 ff; Robison, *op. cit.*, pp. 70 ff.
    8 Glueck and Glueck, *op. cit.*, pp. 127–129.
    9 William and Joan McCord, *Origins of Crime* (New York: Columbia University Press, 1959), pp. 98 ff.

mother and cruel father combination produces a low delinquency rate. The absence of love and the presence of a deviant model produces a high delinquency rate. Only when both parents are deviant does delinquency appear to be a result of role models.[10]

Hewitt and Jenkins classified delinquents in the following way: (a) brain damage, (b) schizoid, (c) unsocialized aggression, (d) socialized delinquency, and (e) internalized conflict. They found that unsocialized delinquents came from homes in which there was parental rejection, whereas delinquents with internalized conflict came from homes with little warmth or emotional security.[11]

Abrahamsen, Friedlander, Redl, and others have found seeds of hostility and aggression in the family.[12] Such studies suggest that "sick" personalities are produced by "sick" families.

The only psychiatric category in which more delinquents are found than are nondelinquents in that of character disorder. Delinquency is antisocial behavior by definition, and character disorders are antisocial behavior; so, by definition, character disorders and delinquency are related. To state that lack of parental affection leads to behavioral difficulties is a truism, which neither spells out the causal process involved in human interaction nor furnishes the control of the variables needed to treat or prevent delinquency.

Healy and Bronner found that only 8 per cent of their cases were neurotic.[13] As for the percentage of the sample group recorded as normal, Reiss found 65.7 per cent; Hewitt and Jenkins, 61 per cent; and the Gluecks, 48 per cent.[14]

Friedlander found psychoanalysis of limited or no value for the treatment of delinquents.[15] The Gluecks studied one thousand youths from the Judge Baker Guidance Clinic in Boston and found that 88 per cent of them continued their delinquent activities after treatment. Healy and Bronner write off this approach as just another chapter in the history of criminology.[16]

Any prevention-through-therapy program must recognize that few delinquents are neurotic or psychotic, the normal population holds many

[10] Ibid., pp. 108 ff.
[11] Herbert A. Bloch and Frank Flynn, Delinquency (New York: Random House, Inc., 1956), pp. 164–165.
[12] Jackson Toby, "The Differential Impact of Family Organization," American Sociological Review, XXII, No. 5 (October, 1957), 505–512; Robison, op. cit., pp. 70 ff.
[13] Harry M. Shulman, Juvenile Delinquency (New York: Harper & Row, Publishers, 1961), p. 646.
[14] Ruth Cavan, Juvenile Delinquency (Philadelphia: J. B. Lippincott Co., 1962), pp. 62–63.
[15] Shulman, op. cit., p. 640.
[16] Helen Witmer and Edith Tufts, "The Effectiveness of Delinquency Prevention Programs," Publication No. 350 (Washington, D.C.: U.S. Department of Health, Education, and Welfare, Children's Bureau, 1954), p. 37.

neurotic and psychotic people, and psychotherapy has never influenced the antisocial behavior of the delinquent.

The Family as a Social Unit

The family must be considered a social institution, which influences behavior in many ways. It determines or influences such social variables as place of residence, size of family, criminality in the family, social-class position, education, and race. It has been shown statistically that delinquency is related to the above factors: The chances of becoming a delinquent are great for the slum-dwelling, lower-class Negro or Puerto Rican youth. One of the major difficulties in analyzing the influence of the family on delinquency is that this influence cannot be separated from such variables.

Broken Homes and Delinquency

The broken home in relation to delinquency has occupied a great deal of the researcher's time and effort. Various studies found the percentage frequency among delinquents and nondelinquents (controls) from broken homes to be, respectively: 28 per cent and 16 per cent (Carr-Saunders); 57 per cent and 12 per cent (Trenaman); 13 per cent and 6 per cent (Gibbs); and 60 per cent and 34 per cent (Gluecks). Twenty-two per cent of the delinquents studied by Mannheim and Wilkins came from broken homes compared to an expected rate of 14 per cent for the population. Bagot found that 55 per cent of the female delinquent population and 37 per cent of the male delinquent population came from broken homes compared to 44 per cent and 36 per cent in the control group.[17]

In an early study, Shaw and McKay found that the rate of broken homes was high for Negroes and older offenders, and that if one held race and age constant, the differences in the incidence of broken homes between the delinquent and nondelinquent groups was slight: 42 per cent compared to 36 per cent. Shaw and McKay concluded that broken homes were not a significant causal factor in delinquency.[18] Monahan found that broken homes were more prevalent among Negroes and females than among whites and males. In his attempt to analyze this data, Toby pointed to the fact that Shaw and McKay emphasized the adolescent male rather than the preadolescent or the female. Toby asked whether this finding was because of the leniency shown by the courts in handling females and preadolescents, and he noted that although Monahan found more females than males with broken-home backgrounds, there were no

17 Wootton, op. cit., pp. 118 ff.
18 Toby, op. cit., p. 505.

differences between the sexes in the way offenders were handled by the courts.[19]

Toby concluded that females and preadolescents are more affected by family disorganization than are adolescent males, because the female and preadolescent are more protected by the family from delinquency than are males and older groups. By using statistics from New Jersey, Toby indicated that Negro urban populations have a higher proportion of female and preadolescent delinquents, which would be expected because Negro urban areas are characterized by family disorganization.[20]

Shulman compared eight studies of broken homes in which he found the median for females was 51 per cent contrasted to 34 per cent for males. In all the studies, female delinquents came from broken homes to a much greater extent than did male delinquents.[21]

It can be concluded that higher rates of broken homes are found in socially disorganized areas where poverty and slum conditions exist. It is difficult to assess the influence of broken homes because one is not certain if it is the broken home or poverty or race that is contributing to the rate of delinquency.

As used in these studies, the term "broken home" is defined legally: according to divorce, separation, or desertion. A home can be broken psychologically and yet be a home legally. The detrimental influence of the psychologically broken home may be much greater than that of the legally broken home. A child could be under less stress living with a divorced parent than with two parents who hate each other.

We have never met a delinquent with a good family background (in the psychological sense); however, many youths from broken homes do not become delinquent. Broken homes are related to delinquency, but this is not a causal relationship.

Family, Poverty, and Delinquency

Most studies have pointed out that delinquents come from lower-class families in which the breadwinner is unemployed or engaged in unskilled or semiskilled menial labor. Ferguson found that delinquents came from families of unskilled workers with a poor employment record. Rose found that 40 per cent of his delinquent group had fathers who were unskilled, 27 per cent semiskilled, and 23 per cent skilled. Bagot, Trenamen, East, Carr-Saunders, and Mannheim reported the same general findings.[22]

The Gluecks' data indicated almost equal proportions of the families of delinquents and of nondelinquents engaged in skilled or semiskilled

---

[19] *Ibid*, pp. 507–509.
[20] *Ibid*., p. 509.
[21] Shulman, *op. cit.*, p. 476.
[22] Wootton, *op. cit.*, pp. 100 ff.

trades, but a higher proportion of the delinquent families were in unskilled trades. It was found that the fathers of delinquents were unwilling or unable to work, unwilling to assume responsibility, and had poor work habits.[23] Shaw and McKay discovered that delinquents lived in certain definite ecological areas of the city: interstitial areas bordering the business district characterized by poverty, poor health, mental disease, suicide, and alcoholism. These areas are generally inhabited by the most recent immigrants to the city.[24]

Some sociologists have interpreted the migration of Negroes and Puerto Ricans to the city as an important factor in the disruption of the family. Social control was family-centered in the rural society, but when the family moved to the city the influence of the family on the behavior of youths lessened. The father was no longer the head of the household. The weakening of the family was accompanied by the weakening of other institutional controls found in the church, government, and economy. This left the family in a neighborhood in which few ties existed with the larger community.[25]

The role of the Negro family should be mentioned in this context. Since Frazier wrote *The Negro Family in the United States*,[26] it has been observed that the lower-class Negro family is matriarchal: mother-dominated and mother-controlled. The male plays a weak role and cannot identify as the head of the household. Serial monogamy, in which a woman lives with one male after another, is common; illegitimacy and desertion also occur. Resently the deterioration of the Negro family has been the subject of a Department of Labor report, and the deterioration of the Negro family was blamed for the 1965 riots in Los Angeles.[27]

Although poverty and unemployment are characteristics of many families that have delinquent children, there are poverty-stricken families that do not have delinquent children, and there are middle-class families with delinquent children. Poverty is associated with delinquency through the family, but poverty does not cause delinquency.

Employment of Mother

In the lower-socioeconomic-class family it is common for the mother to work away from the home. This has led to speculation that the employment of mothers outside the home is a causal factor of delinquency. Ferguson found in his study that 10 per cent of the working mothers

[23] Glueck and Glueck, *op. cit.*

[24] Clifford R. Shaw, Henry D. McKay, *et al, Juvenile Delinquency and Urban Areas* (Chicago: University of Chicago Press, 1942).

[25] Cavan, *Juvenile Delinquency*, p. 69.

[26] E. Franklin Frazier, *The Negro Family in the United States* (New York: Dryden Press, 1951).

[27] *Washington Post*, August 18, 1965.

had delinquent boys compared to 12 per cent of the nonworking mothers. He concluded that whether or not the mother is employed outside the home is immaterial. Carr-Saunders observed that where the mother was the sole support of the household, 67 per cent of the delinquents and 52 per cent of the controls had working mothers. Trenaman found that 32 per cent of the delinquents and 33 per cent of the controls had working mothers.[28]

The Gluecks' data indicate that 47 per cent of the delinquent families compared to 33 per cent of the nondelinquent families had mothers who worked outside the home. However, when the data were analyzed as to regular and irregular employment, it was revealed that 20 per cent of the delinquents' mothers and 18 per cent of the nondelinquents' mothers were regularly employed compared to 27 per cent of the delinquents' and 15 per cent of the nondelinquents' mothers who were irregularly employed. The major difference was whether or not the mother was *regularly* employed. From this fact the Gluecks concluded that

> whether the mother is approached from the psychoanalytic point of view of the deleterious effect upon the development of personality and character, or simply from ordinary observation and common experience, maternal neglect and careless oversight of children are accepted as major sources of maladjustment and delinquency, and clearly the mothers of the delinquent boys as a group were much more remiss in the care of their children than the mothers of the non-delinquents.[29]

Maccoby took issue with the Gluecks' findings: She noted that the supervision of the child by the mother was crucial. On this basis, 19 per cent of the boys whose mothers were regularly employed and whose supervision was rated good were delinquent. On the other hand, 32 per cent of those whose mothers were housewives and 32 per cent of those whose mothers worked irregularly were delinquents. Maccoby concluded:

> If the mother remains at home but does not keep track of her child, he is far more likely to become a delinquent than if he is closely watched. Furthermore, if a mother who works arranges adequate care for the child in her absence, he is no more likely to be delinquent than the adequately supervised child of a mother who does not work.[30]

Size of Family

Studies have consistently revealed that delinquents come from families that are larger than are families of nondelinquents. British studies show that families of delinquents have from 4 to 6 children. Selected

[28] Wootton, *op. cit.*, pp. 113 ff.
[29] Glueck and Glueck, *op. cit.*, pp. 112–113.
[30] Robison, *op. cit.*, p. 114.

studies of the number of children per delinquent family compared to the number per nondelinquent family (controls) report, respectively: 6.3 and 3.6 (Trenaman); 5.7 and 2.9 (Bagot); and 6.8 and 5.9 (Gluecks).[31]

The significance of the larger families probably lies in the fact that lower-class individuals have a higher birth rate than do middle-class individuals, and because many delinquents are from lower-class families they come from large families. Illegitimacy, poverty, and overcrowding are aspects of a large family that are also factors related to delinquency. The size of the family cannot be isolated from poverty, social class, economic standards, residence, employment, and the other variables associated with delinquency.

Criminality in the Family

One of the famous theories of criminality is the theory of differential association formulated by Edwin H. Sutherland. The theory proposes that a person becomes a criminal if he associates with criminals or with people with criminal attitudes.[32] Popularly stated, this means that delinquency is caused by delinquent associates: If the family of a youth is delinquent, he may learn from its members to be delinquent.

Ferguson found that 41 per cent of his delinquent group came from families containing other delinquents, whereas only 15 per cent of the nondelinquents had delinquents in the family. Ferguson comments that the influence of another family member is as great as that of any other adverse factors that have been studied. Bagot observed that 47 per cent of his delinquent subjects came from families containing at least one other delinquent. Carr-Saunders found that 4.7 per cent of the delinquents he studied came from delinquent families compared to 0.8 per cent of the nondelinquents.[33]

The Gluecks' study discovered that 65 per cent of the delinquents and 26 per cent of the controls had delinquent siblings; 45 per cent of the delinquents and 15 per cent of the controls had delinquent mothers; and 66 per cent of the delinquents and 32 per cent of the nondelinquents had delinquent fathers.[34]

In recent years the multiproblem family has been studied by sociologists and social workers. A New York City Youth Board study revealed that 1 per cent of the families contributed more than 75 per cent of the delinquents. These families had histories of alcoholism, drug addiction,

[31] Wootton, *op. cit.*, pp. 85 ff.

[32] Edwin H. Sutherland and Donald R. Cressey, *Principles of Criminology*, 6th ed. (Philadelphia: J. B. Lippincott Co., 1960), pp. 77 ff.

[33] Wootton, *op. cit.*, pp. 87 ff.

[34] Glueck and Glueck, *op. cit.*, pp. 101–102.

mental illness, physical illness, child neglect, desertion, and sexual immorality.[35]

The presence of several delinquents in one family does not prove that delinquency is learned from association with other delinquents, any more than the presence of cancer in two or more family members proves that cancer is induced by association with other family members. Environmental conditions that produce delinquency in one member can likewise produce delinquency in a second or third member of a family. It is assumed that family members interact and thus influence the behavior of one another. It is impossible to isolate the influence of family members from that of other variables. Some delinquents come from homes containing other delinquents; some delinquents come from homes in which no other delinquent members are present; and some nondelinquents come from delinquent families.

Methodological Issues

Causation and Correlation

The foregoing survey of the literature reveals that delinquency and the family are related in a number of ways. However, these are clinical and statistical relationships, not causal relationships. The family is related to delinquency in terms of biological, psychological, and social processes. Body build, frustration, rejection, punishment, lack of affection, broken homes, residence, poverty, working mothers, size of family, and criminality of family are statistically and clinically related to delinquency.

Scientific method involves the observation of variables under carefully controlled conditions. Variables are classified as independent or dependent, according to the variable that the experimenter manipulates and the variable that he observes. Scientific method entails prediction and control.[36] A causal statement is a statement of the conditions under which prediction and control of events can be made.

Thus, because of the absence of the scientific method, delinquency-prevention projects have failed to prevent or control delinquency in the United States. The Cambridge-Somerville project, which used a clinical approach to the problem, had negative results. In the treatment group 29.5 per cent had court appearances compared to 28.3 per cent of the control group.[37] The Midcity Project, which utilized a total community

[35] Shulman, *op. cit.*, pp. 398–399.
[36] *Ibid.*, pp. 87 ff.
[37] Edwin Powers and Helen Witmer, *An Experiment in the Prevention of Delinquency* (New York: Columbia University Press, 1951).

approach, including community organizations, family services, and group work, also proved to be a failure.[38] These are only two of many projects that have failed to curb delinquent behavior.

The reason for this is found in the nature of criminological research: A science of human behavior must be developed before behavior can be controlled. The following are relevant to any scientific study of behavior:

(1) Most programs emphasize past events, conveyed through case histories, interview materials, psychoanalytic dialogues, records, and so forth. This is an ex post facto design: After the event has occurred, the investigator attempts to reconstruct the situation surrounding the event. Before treatment, the psychiatrist talks to his thirty-five-year-old neurotic patient in an attempt to relate the patient's neurotic behavior to something that happened at the age of five. The only thing that can be said for the two series of behavior—behavior at the age of five and present neurotic behavior—is that one occurred before the other. A temporal sequence, however, is not a causal sequence, although many investigators regard it as such. The sociologist looks at delinquent behavior after it has occurred and then attempts to reconstruct the conditions that produced it. Delinquency is the dependent variable; environmental conditions are the independent variable. The investigator who uses an ex post facto design, as do the Gluecks, does not control the independent variable or variables; thus, no causal relationship can be assigned to the variables. A broken home, low intelligence score, or delinquent companions may be found in the history of a delinquent, but there is no way to establish the influence of these variables on delinquent behavior. We can measure the influence of a particular variable on behavior only if we manipulate the variable under controlled conditions.

Experimental analysis requires controlled conditions under which observations of behavioral change are made. This means taking the subject in his present state and observing behavioral changes that occur when certain environmental variables are manipulated. The observations are always of future behavior, not of past behavior. Historical case studies are useful for supplying clues as to which variables are involved, but history cannot substitute for experimental analysis: The history of polio or cancer will never substitute for a laboratory study in searching for a cure.

(2) In much criminological research the investigator does not manipulate the variables. He uses a static rather than a dynamic approach, resorting to descriptive studies and naturalistic observation. When a criminologist notes that many delinquents live in a given ecological area, come from

38 Walter Miller, "The Impact of a Total Community Delinquency Control Project," Social Problems (Fall, 1962), p. 190.

broken homes, or are members of a gang, he is observing, not experimenting.

The statistical study of delinquency, which is so popular in delinquency research, does not reveal causal relations but rather correlations. If delinquency is statistically related to broken homes, it can mean that delinquency causes broken homes, broken homes cause delinquency, both delinquency and broken homes are caused by poverty or unemployment, or that they are related by chance. For this reason, statements about the causes of delinquency are couched in terms of probability. Some delinquents have delinquent companions, some do not; some delinquents live in slum areas, others do not; some delinquents are poor, others are not; some young males become delinquents, others do not.

The Gluecks, for example, found a statistical relation between mesomorphic body build and delinquency. Does delinquency cause mesomorphy, or does mesomorphy cause delinquency? They state that a lack of affection of father for son causes delinquency. Is this true, or on the basis of the same facts, can we say that delinquency causes a man to have less affection for his son? Does severe parental discipline cause delinquency, or does delinquency cause a parent to be severe with his son?

(3) A great deal of research in criminology involves mentalistic concepts. This body-mind dualism of a Cartesian nature assumes that the mind influences and controls behavior. Such inferential concepts and intervening variables as ego, motives, needs, drives, attitudes, and values are used to explain delinquent behavior. However, there is no way to prove the existence of these concepts because they are inferred from behavior. A person behaves in a criminal manner, and the criminologist says this is a result of the ego (self-concept) or criminal attitudes. A concept is inferred from behavior and is then used to explain that behavior. This is saying that delinquency is caused by a delinquent ego and we know the ego exists because we have observed the delinquent behavior.

Scientific method demands that the variables be operationally defined and observable—independent of the phenomena we are attempting to explain. When we discuss delinquent behavior in terms of attitudes or values, we are dealing not with two variables but with one.

(4) Many criminological studies are based on indirect observations of behavior. Interviews, questionnaires, and test scores are used with the assumption that they reveal both the behavior and the conditions under which the behavior occurs. These methods are not substitutes for direct observation: Responses to questionnaries are related to variables independent of those controlling the behavior being studied. The responses of a delinquent to a probation officer or sociologist may be governed by the subject's desire to escape punishment—not by his delinquent behavior.

We must study the environment in which misconduct occurs rather than the environment of tests and questionnaires. The criminologist spends much time analyzing test and interview behavior rather than criminal behavior.

(5) Most criminological studies give the investigator no control over the delinquent behavior he is examining. If an investigator discovers that an offender comes from a broken home, has dropped out of school at the age of sixteen, has delinquent companions, or behaves as a sociopath, he can record this in his folder, but it gives him no measure of control over the delinquent. Such investigations do not tell us how to change delinquent conduct: Observations do not lead to the control of behavior.

How does one change a criminal attitude or criminal association? The Gluecks state that lack of discipline and affection in the home contribute to delinquency. How does one establish good discipline and affection in a home? How do we keep students from dropping out of school? How do we motivate students and delinquents to take advantage of opportunities for training and education? It is possible to predict the weather, an eclipse, or the rate of death from cancer without controlling them. Control implies prediction; prediction does not imply control. We do not change the weather by predicting rain; we do not change the incidence of death by selling life insurance based on actuarial tables. Only by manipulating relevant variables can we control the future occurrence of an event. We can control the rate of polio by using Salk and Sabin vaccines, not by predicting its occurrence in the population.

Glueck and Glueck

The problems associated with research in the area of the family and delinquency can best be illustrated by a review of a specific research effort. Probably the most ambitious and fruitful research attempt in this country has been done by Sheldon and Eleanor Glueck of Harvard University. The Gluecks matched five hundred delinquents and five hundred nondelinquents according to age, intelligence, ethnic background, and residence. They studied these one thousand subjects in terms of biological, psychological, and sociological traits. Physical examinations, case histories, psychiatric examinations, and personality tests were used to obtain data on these subjects. Statistical correlations were made on over 400 traits, and a summary report of the results was published in *Unraveling Juvenile Delinquency*.[39]

In the original report the Gluecks made the following statement about causation:

[39] Glueck and Glueck, *op. cit.*

While recognizing the fundamental significance to the idea of cause-and-effect of *sequence in time,* we can rationally assume, further, that if such sequence occurs consistently in a definite order from the presence of a certain combination of factors to the presence of persistent delinquency, then these successive events not only *follow* but *follow from* one another. In other words, we can legitimately assume the existence of a system of cause-and-effect in the generally accepted sense. We can, moreover, test it by experiments designed to modify or eliminate the conditions that have been found to precede delinquency in one sample of cases so that we may check on whether or not the subsequent result in a new sample turns out to be delinquency or non-delinquency.[40]

The research design used by the Gluecks is an ex post facto design: After the youth has become a delinquent the investigator goes back in time to find causal relationships. As was pointed out above, an ex post facto design will never reveal a causal relation: It will only reveal a relation in time. All that one can deduce from such a design is that after the occurrence of thousands of other earlier factors (childhood, body build, psychiatric history, family relations, school records, etc.) delinquent behavior occurs. One does not know which, if any, of these earlier events is related to the consequence of delinquency.

The Gluecks are guilty of the fallacy of post hoc, ergo propter hoc (after this, therefore on account of it). They assume that because two events occur in sequence they are causally related. A temporal sequence is not necessarily a causal sequence. For example, yesterday Paul drank water and today he was paid $50. The fact that these two events occur in sequence does not prove that they are causally related. Paul may have been paid $50 for drinking the water as part of a medical experiment, or the two events may be entirely unrelated. The way to demonstrate that they are related is to start with the present and observe the future. One begins with the independent variable (drinking water) and then, holding other variables constant, observes whether or not the subject is paid $50. The experimenter discovers the cause and looks for the effect, not the reverse. The Gluecks start with the effect (delinquency) and look for causes in the past; they have no way of establishing the fact that past events are those which produced present conditions.

In *Family Environment and Delinquency*[41] the Gluecks modify their position on causation. They state that traits (characteristics of subjects) and factors (environmental conditions) are related in several ways. They

[40] Sheldon and Eleanor Glueck, *Delinquents in the Making* (New York: Harper & Row, Publishers, 1952), pp. 165–166.
[41] Sheldon and Eleanor Glueck, *Family Environment and Delinquency* (Boston: Houghton Mifflin Company, 1962).

state that "the discovery of statistically significant associations between factors and traits does not throw light on the nature of the relationship."[42] This is a refutation of their earlier statement on causation. They now say that "association is not necessarily causation."[43] They point out that

(1) a factor can influence a trait;
(2) a trait may serve as a stimulus to a response in the environment;
(3) a trait and a factor may be dynamically reciprocal in their influence; or
(4) factors, traits, and delinquency may be interrelated in a system of mutual influence.

The Gluecks next analyze sixty-six traits in relation to factors. They find seven traits related to body type but not related in any respect to social factors. Sensitivity and sensuousness are listed as two such traits.[44] Sensitivity is defined as "the acute awareness of conflicting situations and stimuli, resulting in some inhibition of action." Sensuousness is defined as "the inclination to free indulgence of appetites." To regard sensitivity and sensuousness as physical and as unrelated to prior environmental factors such as experience with color, taste, form, food, and sex appears to be a gross misinterpretation of the data. A person's sensitivity or sensuousness is his responsiveness to a given environment, and such responses depend on his past experience in that environment. A certain environment will produce a sensual person, whereas another environment will produce a nonsensual person. Sensitivity and sensuousness are classes of behavior that are *learned* in response to environmental conditions.

The Gluecks also list stubbornness and lack of self-control as probable constitutional traits. Again it must be argued that stubbornness and lack of self-control are learned behaviors, not genetic traits. Such behaviors are socially conditioned, although the Gluecks place them at the biological end of the continuum.

The Gluecks next show the interaction of delinquency-related factors and delinquency-related traits. For example, Factor B (crowded homes) is related to Trait 11 (low verbal intelligence). The Gluecks remark that this is surprising because verbal performance is often assumed to be genetic.[45]

The *social* factors listed by the Gluecks are all *family* factors: crowded home, disorderly home, delinquency of father and mother, alcoholism of father and mother, emotional disturbance, physical ail-

42 *Ibid.*, pp. 18–19.
43 *Ibid.*, p. 20.
44 *Ibid.*, p. 72.
45 *Ibid.*, p. 98.

ments, financial dependence of family, poor work habits of father, poor management of income, careless household routine, lack of cultural refinement, lack of self-respect, poor conduct standards, incompatibility, erratic employment of mother, parental indifference to boy's companions, lack of family cohesiveness, broken home, hostility of mother, unsuitable discipline by father, unsuitable supervision of boy, lack of group recreation, physical punishment, frequent moving, unacceptability of father to boy, and indifference of boy to mother.[46]

The social factors the Gluecks consider most influential are those associated with the emotional ties between parents and children. The criminogenic influence of the factors can be plotted along three dynamic lines: (a) the direct effect of the factors on delinquency, (b) the influence of the factors on the formation of delinquency-related traits, and (c) the catalytic influence of sociocultural factors on certain traits.[47]

Prediction of Delinquency

The Gluecks used five family factors as a device for predicting delinquency: (1) discipline of boy by father, (2) supervision of boy by mother, (3) affection of father, (4) affection of mother, and (5) cohesiveness of family. The New York City Youth Board used this instrument to identify potential delinquency at the age of five or six.[48] The results are given in the following table:

Probability of Delinquency	Total Sample		BEHAVIOR Delinquent		Non-Delinquent	
	Number	Per Cent	Number	Per Cent	Number	Per Cent
Total	301	100	44	14.6	257	85.4
8.6 (low)	243	100	7	2.9	236	97.1
58.2 (chance)	25	100	9	36.0	16	64.0
89.0 (high)	33	100	28	84.8	5	15.2

This table indicates that 97.1 per cent of the subjects in the low-probability group were not delinquent, whereas 84.8 per cent of those in the high-probability group were delinquent. These are impressive figures until the data are examined more carefully. Only 14.6 per cent of the subjects became delinquent. Of the 44 who became delinquent, the prediction table missed 7 "lows" who became delinquent (false negative) and 5 "highs" who did not become delinquent (false positive). Also, the

[46] *Ibid.*, pp. 99–102.
[47] *Ibid.*, p. 129.
[48] Maude M. Craig and Selma J. Glick, *A Manual of Procedures for Application of the Glueck Prediction Table* (New York City Youth Board, 1964).

device missed 25 in the "chance" category because it did not designate these subjects as either delinquent or nondelinquent. This indicates 37 missed out of 44 or an error of 84 per cent. If we exclude the chance category, we have 35 delinquents of which 12 were missed, or an error of 34 per cent. Thus the prediction table misses 34 per cent of the extreme categories. In the borderline cases labeled in the table as "chance," the authors made no attempt to predict future delinquency or nondelinquency. It is for these very cases that a prediction table is needed, not for those whose symptoms are most obvious. If we have a signal-detection device that is supposed to identify enemy aircraft, and we use green for friendly, red for enemy, and yellow (chance category) for unidentified, we must regard the yellow signal as a miss because we do not know whether to fire or not to fire. Such a detection device would not long be in use by our air command. The Youth Board states that it predicted 16 out of 25 in the chance category. This is definitely false, because it did not indicate whether the 16 were delinquent or nondelinquent. Only *after* the youths became nondelinquent did the Youth Board state that it was correct in predicting that these subjects would become nondelinquents.

It may be argued that this is an unfair way to look at the data, but because the purpose of the prediction device is to predict delinquency, the only significant figure is the 44 who became delinquent, not the 257 who remained nondelinquent. By using this instrument we miss all the chance category plus the 34 per cent of the high and low categories. It seems probable that an experienced criminologist could have predicted from case records that certain individuals are more prone than are others to delinquency. Because the variables related to delinquency are fairly well known—broken homes, poverty, slum areas, lack of education, and so forth—one can predict in general a high incidence of delinquency in groups with such characteristics. Three things can be said about prediction of delinquency:

(1) Prediction does not foretell individual delinquency: It predicts group delinquency. Even the two extreme ends of the continuum failed to reveal delinquents in 34 per cent of the cases.

(2) The factors selected by the Gluecks, such as discipline, affection, and cohesiveness, are not necessarily the factors that produced misbehavior. The Gluecks admit that these are correlations, not causal factors. It may be that *delinquency* caused lack of family cohesiveness, lack of affection, or strict discipline. Although the Gluecks claim to deal with multiple causation, they deal only with family relationships. They completely ignore such crucial factors as poverty, residence, education, and ethnic discrimination. One assumes from their studies that the cure for delinquency is better family relations, apart from the influence of such variables as poverty and lack of education.

(3) The Gluecks establish no control over behavior. Prediction is not control, as we pointed out above. The Gluecks do not tell us how to establish cohesive families, fair discipline, or family affection. One could argue that if we know what variables are related to delinquency we can form a prevention program. However, we cannot prevent delinquency until we can control behavior. We can control behavior only if we have a science of behavior based on experimental methods, not on clinical or statistical methods. The prediction method used by the Gluecks rests on past events, and it predicts future behavior from these past events. The scientific method begins with controls over present conditions and variables and predicts future events on the basis of *future conditions*, not *past conditions*. Whether or not Johnny commits a crime eight or ten years from now depends on the environment he is in at that time. The important variable is the future environment; yet the Gluecks emphasized past events, and their prediction device in no way deals with future conditions.

Modern Learning Theory and Delinquency

Learned Behavior

Delinquent behavior is learned behavior. Sutherland's theory of differential association is a statement of this proposition in its classical form.[49] It has recently been reformulated in terms of modern learning theory as the theory of differential reinforcement, which states that delinquent behavior occurs in those environmental situations in which such behavior is reinforced and does not occur in those situations in which such behavior is punished.[50]

The basic principle of modern learning theory is that behavior is governed by its consequences. If a response rate increases because of environmental consequences, then the relation between the response and stimuli is classified as reinforcing; if a response decreases in rate because of the consequences, it is called punishment. There are two types of reinforcement and two types of punishment: the presentation of an aversive stimulus and the removal of a desirable stimulus. The influence of modern learning theory is seen in modern educational technology with its programed instruction materials, teaching machines, and so forth. Social behavior has been handled in terms of learning theory,[51] and the

---

[49] Sutherland and Cressey, *op. cit.*

[50] C. R. Jeffery, "Criminal Behavior and Learning Theory," *Journal of Criminal Law, Criminology, and Police Science* (September, 1965), reprinted in *The Control of Human Behavior*, ed. Roger Ulrich, Thomas J. Stachnik, and John Mabry (Chicago: Scott, Foresman, & Company,1966).

[51] George C. Homans, *Social Behavior: Its Elementary Forms* (New York: Harcourt, Brace, & World, Inc., 1964); Arthur W. and Carolyn K. Staats, *Complex Human Behavior* (New York: Holt, Rinehart, & Winston, Inc., 1963).

principle of reinforcement has been used to rehabilitate delinquents.[52] A re-education and retraining program for high school dropouts in which such principles are utilized is now in operation in Washington, D.C.[53]

The Family as a Reinforcing Agent

The data presented thus far indicate that the family contributes to delinquency in several ways. A reappraisal of this relationship in the light of modern learning theory is valuable.

We have noted that delinquent behavior is related to body build. The Gluecks found that delinquents tend to be mesomorphic. Eysenck and his associates have discovered that classical conditioning procedures occur more readily with certain body types than with other types.[54] Biological conditions are important in any learning theory. Food and sex are reinforcing to man, and much social behavior can be explained by its relation to these variables. The family as a social unit is involved in both food and sex gratification. The young child's first tactile experience is that of being fondled or fed. The sucking response is a stimulus-response relationship that is so well established it is regarded as a reflex. It is understandable that the mother becomes a love object: She is a source of food and comfort, and as such she becomes a secondary reinforcer. The sight of the mother means food, fondling, exciting noises, or a change of diapers. The relation of the mother to the child is crucial because the mother controls the reinforcement and punishment of the child.

The Freudian theory of personality is based on a pleasure-pain principle, as is modern learning theory. The major difference in the two types of psychology (behavioral and Freudian) is that (1) behavioral psychology uses experimental procedures to establish relations between stimulus and response, whereas the clinical psychologist uses a clinical procedure that does not establish causal relationships and (2) behavioral psychology does not explain behavior in terms of mentalistic intervening variables, such as id, ego, superego, ego strength, Oedipus complex, on which the clinician is so dependent. It is understandable that the Freudian psychologist places great emphasis on the family in personality development. Research indicates that negligent, rejecting, or punishing parents may create delinquent children. The clinical concept of "a lack of security" suggests a person who has experienced the loss of reinforcement in his past: His insecurity is based on past conditioning. An "inadequate per-

[52] Ralph Schwitzgebel, *Streetcorner Research* (Cambridge: Harvard University Press, 1964).

[53] A research project of the Washington School of Psychiatry, under the direction of C. R. Jeffery, supported by the Office of the Surgeon General, U.S. Army, and by the U.S. Office of Education.

[54] H. J. Eysenck, *Crime and Personality* (Boston: Houghton Mifflin Company, 1964).

son" is one who has not learned to respond to the environment to gain pleasure and to avoid pain.

Studies have shown that consistent punishment, if moderate, will reinforce nondelinquent behavior. Inconsistent punishment is the most ineffective: By sometimes rewarding, sometimes punishing the same behavior, the individual will respond in anticipation of the reward, not the punishment. Severe punishment is destructive of behavior other than that punished because it reduces the total response rate: A child who is spanked for stealing cookies will avoid the mother in general, not just while she is standing near the cookie jar. This is known technically as generalization. A wife who is hurt by her husband will avoid him in all situations, for example, she will refuse to talk to him or to have sex relations with him. A person will escape, avoid, or "act out" in the face of punishment.

The physical surroundings of the home are significantly related to the behavior of family members. The colors, sounds, and smells of the home condition a great deal of behavior. A sparse environment that lacks stimulation and rewards creates a sparse variety of behavior. An environment filled with loud unpleasant noises, offensive odors, and punishing parents will create a stark and behaviorally deprived person. One of the characteristics of individuals who live in an environment of poverty is having behavioral deficiencies such as low intelligence, an inability to talk or read, or an inability to perceive colors or sounds. Such individuals learn to "tune out": They do not hear the noises or see the filth. Often children from deprived backgrounds are thought to be deaf because they do not respond when spoken to. They have learned that the safest response is no response. The basic idea behind cultural enrichment programs such as Project "Headstart" and Higher Horizons is to subject culturally deprived children to a stimulating environment in which a variety of sensory experiences occur. Such an environment should lead to an increased behavioral output on the part of the child.

The lack of a male figure in the home, as in the case of the lower-class Negro, will lead to a lack of male behavior on the part of the son. The family acts as a reinforcing agent for many behaviors of its members. The father will reinforce a class of behavior that the mother will not: If the father is absent, certain behaviors are not reinforced or reinforced imperfectly.

Verbal behavior is learned behavior. If a child lives in a home in which people grunt, shout, swear, and use one-syllable words as sentences, he will not develop verbal abilities. If a child is given water when he cries or grunts, he will never learn to say "water." A child learns to talk because specific verbalizations lead to rewarding consequences from the environment.

Reading is also learned behavior. Some children are encouraged to read by their parents and find current and stimulating reading materials readily available in the home. Under such conditions the child learns to read and to recognize words and letters. Children from culturally deprived areas enter school at a distinct disadvantage because they do not know how to read, write, speak, or even differentiate colors and sounds.

Youths who fail in school work, who are deficient in basic academic skills, and who drop out of high school are much more prone to delinquency than are those who graduate from high school. The middle-class family gives support to its children by reinforcing good academic behavior. The lower-class family cannot give such support and aid, and as a consequence lower-class children drop out of school, are unemployed and unemployable, and, in many instances, become delinquent.

The delinquent family can reinforce delinquent behavior through verbal approval, actual example, disinterest, and so forth. A parent may come home drunk or may engage in theft, and the son or daughter learns that such behavior is approved or at least not scorned. We say that the child learns by example: He observes that certain antisocial acts are not punished in the family.

However, the family need not be criminalistic to produce a delinquent son or daughter. The family may be poverty stricken, in which case delinquent responses may result from material deprivation. Likewise, a delinquent family may have nondelinquent sons. Because each individual experiences his environment uniquely, depending on his past conditioning history, different responses may be emitted to the same or similar stimuli. This explains the frequent observation that poverty, slum areas, or delinquent associates do not always produce delinquent youths.

The above remarks refer to the lower-class, urban, slum family. How does one account for the delinquent behavior of the middle-class child who does not suffer from poverty, lack of education, or a broken home? Comparisons of the gross incidence of delinquent behavior by middle-class youths and lower-class youths are extremely misleading. To be meaningful, comparisons must be made in terms of the different nature of delinquent acts committed by these two groups. As England and others have noted,[55] middle-class delinquencies are characterized by cheating in the school setting and by the automobile-alcohol-sex combination of antisocial behavior.

Prevention Through the Family

Most delinquency-prevention programs indirectly involve the family, although the primary emphasis may be in the form of a child guidance clinic, a school program, a vocational rehabilitation program, or a housing

[55] Cavan, *Juvenile Delinquency*, pp. 94–95.

program. This illustrates that the influence of the family cannot be separated from the influence of other factors in the environment. Programs using the family as the unit of prevention are usually of a more comprehensive clinical or community action type.

Studies have indicated that social services usually do not reach the lower-class, culturally deprived family[56] but instead are both supported and used by the middle-class family. This fact was appreciated in St. Paul and New York City and led to aggressive social work efforts on behalf of the hard-to-reach, deprived families in these two cities. These programs involve locating and gaining the cooperation of multiproblem families in social work services. Such efforts are only mildly successful, illustrated by the fact that only 18 per cent of the families who cooperated in the St. Paul effort showed improvement. In this respect, Shulman states:

> Findings such as these would suggest that social work as currently engaged in by isolated case work agencies, lacking for the most part both professional staffs adequate to deal with multi-problem families and a sound diagnostic approach to the planned treatment of the entire family, have little to contribute to delinquency prevention or treatment.[57]

Social services fail to reach the lower-class individual because no attempt is made to alter his behavior in a meaningful direction. Dependency rather than self-reliance ensues. To be successful, a program must effect meaningful changes in the behavior of the family involved. Neither therapy nor social welfare has achieved these goals. Increased and improved education and employment are the most promising avenues to pursue.

It has been pointed out that the Negro male lacks a masculine role. He needs an education to find skilled work by which he can support a wife and children. Educaton is crucial in any prevention or rehabilitation program. The family must be reached in such a way that the children complete high school and receive vocational or professional training. Frequently neither the families nor the educational system are able to motivate such children to remain in school. A vicious cycle is thus created in which poverty-stricken families rear uneducated children who then enter adulthood without jobs, thus creating a new poverty-stricken family.

Presently in Washington, D. C., a research project exists that is designed to re-educate high school dropouts.[58] The students are paid for academic performance as well as for vocational work. At present they are

[56] Witmer and Tufts, op. cit., pp. 23 ff.; Robison, op. cit., pp. 497 ff; Frank Reissman, Jerome Cohen, and Arthur Pearl, eds., Mental Health of the Poor (New York: Free Press of Glencoe, Inc., 1964).

[57] Shulman, op. cit., pp. 733–734.

[58] Directed by C. Ray Jeffery.

involved in remedial education through programed instructional materials and in home beautification and community improvement projects in poverty areas. It is hoped that on completion of this training these Negro youths will be able to enter vocational training programs or find suitable employment. All these individuals have illegitimate children and are unable to marry because they are unemployed. Several of the group members have indicated that they plan to marry as soon as they are employed.

Prevention through the family must involve strengthening the economic and social base of the family. The young Negro male must be able to hold a job and thereby earn the respect of his wife and children. This improvement in the family must involve total community resources—schools, police, housing administration, medical services, churches, and local government. The family must be actively involved in the improvement of his community. Most antipoverty programs do not include the indigenous lower-class residents in their action projects. An absence of leadership in the lower-class community is by no means indicative of an absence of concern on the part of the residents for the physical and social well-being of the community.

Conclusion

The family is related to delinquency by a number of factors. It is impossible to separate the influence of the family from such environmental variables as poverty, slum residence, ethnic discrimination, broken homes, lack of education, and lack of affection. Correlational analysis asserts a positive correlation between the above factors and the incidence of delinquency, thereby assuming that a reduction in any one or a combination of the factors will be accompanied by a reduction in delinquent behavior. However, the practitioner must be aware of the fact that this is a statistical, not a causal, relationship.

One can profitably view the influence of the family on the behavior of its members in terms of modern learning theory. Succinctly, this theory states that *reinforced* behavior is likely to occur in the future under similar circumstances. The family is a primary dispenser of such reinforcement as affection, sexual gratification, food, clothing, housing, social status, education, and ethnic identity. Families that do not reinforce social behavior in a socially desirable direction will produce individuals who exhibit a high rate of deviant behavior, including delinquency and crime.

In order to prevent delinquency through the family, we can (1) strengthen the individual family members through education and other training, and (2) strengthen the community health, education, and welfare facilities, which are to interact with local family units. In either case, the change must be made in the environment in which the individual family exists, because behavior is a product of the environment in which it occurs.

SELECTED READINGS

Axelrad, Sidney, "Negro and White Male Institutionalized Delinquents," *American Journal of Sociology,* LVII (May, 1952), 569–574.

Cavan, Ruth, *Juvenile Delinquency.* Philadelphia: J. B. Lippincott Co., 1962.

Clinard, Marshall B., *Sociology of Deviant Behavior.* New York: Holt, Rinehart, & Winston, Inc., 1963.

Frazier, E. Franklin, *The Negro Family in the United States.* New York: Dryden Press, 1951.

Glueck, Sheldon and Eleanor, *Unraveling Juvenile Delinquency.* Cambridge: Harvard University Press, 1950.

———, *Delinquents in the Making.* New York: Harper & Row, Publishers, 1952.

———, *Family Environment and Delinquency.* Boston: Houghton Mifflin Company, 1962.

McCord, William and Joan, *Origins of Crime.* New York: Columbia University Press, 1959.

Merrill, Maud, *Problems of Child Delinquency.* Boston: Houghton Mifflin Company, 1947.

Monahan, Thomas P., "Family Status and the Delinquent Child: A Reappraisal and Some New Findings," *Social Forces,* XXXV (1957), 250–258.

———, "Broken Homes by Age of Delinquent Children," *Journal of Social Psychology,* LI (May, 1960), 387–397.

Nye, F. Ivan, *Family Relationships and Delinquent Behavior.* New York: John Wiley & Sons, Inc., 1958.

Reissman, Frank, Jerome Cohen, and Arthur Pearl, eds., *Mental Health of the Poor.* New York: Free Press of Glencoe, Inc., 1964.

Robison, Sophia M., *Juvenile Delinquency.* New York: Holt, Rinehart, & Winston, Inc., 1960.

Shaw, Clifford R., and Henry D. McKay, *Social Factors in Juvenile Delinquency,* A study for the National Commission on Law Observance and Enforcement, II. No. 13. Washington, D.C.: U.S. Government Printing Office, 1931.

Shulman, Harry M., "The Family and Juvenile Delinquency," *The Annals,* American Academy of Political and Social Science. CCLXI (January, 1949), 21–31.

Shulman, Harry M., *Juvenile Delinquency.* New York: Harper & Row, Publishers, 1961.

Smith, Philip M., "Broken Homes and Juvenile Delinquency," *Sociology and Social Research*, XXXIX (May–June, 1955), 307–311.

Sterne, Richard, *Delinquent Conduct and Broken Homes*. New Haven, Conn.: College and University Press, 1964.

Toby, Jackson, "The Differential Impact of Family Organization," *American Sociological Review*, XXII (October, 1957), 505–512.

Witmer, Helen, and Edith Tufts, *The Effectiveness of Delinquency Prevention Programs*, Publication No. 350. Washington, D.C.: U.S. Department of Health, Education, and Welfare, Children's Bureau, 1954.

Wootton, Barbara, *Social Science and Social Pathology*. New York: The Macmillan Company, 1959.

6 Prevention Through Religion

George Edward Powers

When Harvey Cox writes in *The Secular City* that the "rise of urban civilization and the collapse of traditional religion are the two main hallmarks of our era and are closely related movements,"[1] he summarizes the problem of the churches on the modern American scene. More dramatically, a Negro boy expressed the same truth during a showing of the movie, "Black Like Me." In a mood of dejection the hero of the film walks into a church and kneels in front of a large crucifix. As the camera focuses on the thorn-crowned head of Christ, the boy in the theater shouted out in anger, "What does that mother ____ have to do with it?"

The church of the Middle Ages developed its hierarchical system in the feudal society of which it was an important part. Its traditions and teachings have remained more or less constant during this millennium. The principal virtues of such a system are loyalty, obedience, and defense of the system. Even the Protestant reformers did not completely reach outside this structure. Thus, at the midpoint of the twentieth century, the Christian churches have begun to awaken to the reality of their irrelevancy. They have found themselves on the one hand defensive against the secularization of the major institutions of society and on the other incapable of unburdening themselves of the bureaucratic structure that hinders the mobilization of their inner forces for self-renewal and for impact on society. Some prophets (usually those outside the ecclesiastical

[1] Harvey Cox, *The Secular City* (New York: The Macmillan Company, 1965), p. 1.

structures) have issued their warnings. Gibson Winter has written, "The institutional crisis of Christianity arises, thus, from the preoccupation of the religious community with private concerns while the forces that are shaping human destiny dominate the public realm. . . . Religious leaders have been unable or unwilling to face the alienation of the churches from the dynamic of the contemporary world; hence, they deny the inadequacy of the inherited structures of the churches."[2]

The Church and the Delinquency Problem

In no area is the church's irrelevancy more critical than in that of human behavior, whether it is the scientific approach to the study of man through the behavioral sciences or through the practical therapies affecting individuals and groups. The church's problem is intensified when the behavior under discussion is termed "deviant" and then therapy is directed toward the rehabilitation of so-called abnormals or toward the prevention of future patterns of abnormality in individuals or in groups.

In 1952 John Edward Coogan published several articles in *Federal Probation* criticizing the authors of criminology textbooks for their lack of concern for religion. In "The Myth Mind in an Engineer's World," he claims that "disregard of or even contempt for religion" predominates among such noted authors as Harry Elmer Barnes, Lowell Juilliard Carr, Ruth Shonle Cavan, Walter C. Reckless, Edwin H. Sutherland, Donald Taft, and Negley K. Teeters.[3] Coogan implies that many of these authors follow a philosophical determinism that is "pure materialistic dogmatism, with no scientific proof even attempted."[4] He further charges in another article that "not a single paper is listed under church or religion in the 1947 and 1948 Yearbooks of the National Probation and Parole Association" and that "the three subsequently published Yearbooks are as silent on religion."[5] In reply to Coogan, two of the authors reiterated their convictions about the churches. Negley K. Teeters wrote that "religion, as we know it, is of little value in deterring people from delinquency and crime."[6] In reference to the reduction of the amount of crime and to the rehabilitation of criminals, Harry Elmer Barnes claimed that "the failure

<hr/>

[2] Gibson Winter, *The New Creation as Metropolis* (New York: The Macmillan Company, 1963), pp. 30, 67.
[3] John Edward Coogan, "The Myth Mind in an Engineer's World," *Federal Probation*, XVI (March, 1952), 26.
[4] *Ibid.*, p. 29.
[5] John Edward Coogan, "Religion a Preventive of Delinquency," *Federal Probation*, XVIII (December, 1954), 29.
[6] Lowell Juilliard Carr, Harry Elmer Barnes, and Negley K. Teeters, "Replies to Father Coogan's Articles," *Federal Probation*, XVI (September, 1952), 6–7.

of orthodox Christianity to produce such results has been amply demonstrated by centuries of experience."[7]

Two other authors of criminology textbooks in 1952 assessed the situation:

> The blame we may attach to the church must be for its failing to offer parishioners (particularly young persons) vital help in meeting and adjusting to life problems. . . . Part of the reason the churches have failed to help the delinquents and criminals is that most of them have not reached beyond their own portals.[8]
> It is exceedingly difficult to ascertain the role of organized religion in the lives of maladjusted youth. There is little information available on the meaning of church attendance and influence of religious instruction.
> It is significant that little space is devoted to the church and religion by writers on delinquency. Those who do devote space to it frequently do so in order to bring indictment against the church for its failure to concern itself with delinquent non-churchgoers.[9]

More recently, authors have followed the trend of disregarding religion in their books. Sheldon Glueck edited a 1,182 page book on delinquency (almost encyclopedic in its content) in 1959, but there was not one "religion" listing in the Index. There were, however, five references to articles concerning the chaplain's role in a correctional institution, and there was also one item entitled "Church Attendance."[10] Don C. Gibbons in a 1965 publication described as containing "relevant and effective kinds of therapy which can be applied to these individuals in order to change them into law-abiding citizens,"[11] makes no mention of religion as one of the helpful therapies. In *Juvenile Delinquency: Research and Theory*, published in 1965, Herbert Quay categorizes socializing agencies as "legal, social welfare, educational, medical, familial, and religious," and he lists the goals of the agencies' operations as "constraint and control," "remediation and reformation," and "construction and formation," but he does not indicate how religion or the churches can affect behavior patterns; in fact, religion is not mentioned again.[12] Generally speaking, the church is on the defensive as far as delinquency studies are concerned.

[7] *Ibid.*

[8] Mabel A. Elliott, *Crime in Modern Society* (New York: Harper & Row, Publishers, 1952), pp. 366–367.

[9] Pauline V. Young, *Social Treatment in Probation and Delinquency* (New York: McGraw-Hill Book Company, 1952), p. 445.

[10] Sheldon Glueck, *The Problem of Delinquency* (Boston: Houghton Mifflin Company, 1959).

[11] Don C. Gibbons, *Changing the Lawbreaker* (Englewood Cliffs, N.J.: Prentice-Hall, Inc., 1965).

[12] Herbert Quay and contribs., *Juvenile Delinquency: Research and Theory* (Princeton, N.J.: D. Van Nostrand Co., Inc., 1965).

Religion and Delinquency: Fifty Years of Studies

It is difficult to evaluate the studies of the influence of religion on the lives of juvenile offenders. If conclusions were validated by numbers alone, the statement of Walter A. Lunden in his recent publication, *Statistics on Delinquents and Delinquency*, would best describe the present agreement of social scientists as well as psychologists: "In spite of the general opinion that religion creates 'good' conduct and irreligion causes delinquency the statistical data available tend to prove the contrary almost to the point of a paradox."[13] Accepting the Bonger hypothesis in a 1916 study, "As irreligion increases, crime tends to decrease,"[14] the advocates of this position can now declare, after almost fifty years of investigation: "Hypothesis proven."

It is impossible to present a chronological list of these studies. They are so numerous and complex that they defy easy grouping. Some have been conducted on a large scale with careful scientific controls; others have been personally initiated by church workers without any attempt at scientific validation. Many of these studies have been concerned with religious preference or membership, others with participation in religious activities, with knowledge about religion, or with attitudes toward religion. Some of the conclusions can be indicated here as a means of comparing their content rather than the variety of methods used or the reliability or validity of the measurements.

W. A. Bonger studied the religious backgrounds of individuals convicted of serious crimes in the Netherlands from 1901 to 1909 and he found that Roman Catholics rated highest with 416.5 per 100,000 population, then Protestants with 308.6, Jews with 212.7, and finally, those of no religion with 84.2. He concluded that the nonreligious persons had lower crime rates than those who were affiliated with a church or synagogue.[15]

In 1930, Pleasant Roscoe Hightower published a study, "Biblical Information in Relation to Character and Conduct." He discovered that there was no relation between knowledge of the Bible and cheating in school or lying to escape disapproval. By comparing junior high public school students with those in an institution for delinquents, he concluded that knowledge of religious doctrine was not sufficient in itself to guarantee socially acceptable behavior.[16]

---

[13] Walter A. Lunden, *Statistics on Delinquents and Delinquency* (Springfield, Ill.: Charles C. Thomas, Publisher, 1964), p. 154.

[14] *Ibid.,* p. 155

[15] *Ibid.*

[16] Pleasant Roscoe Hightower, "Biblical Information in Relation to Character and Conduct," *University of Iowa Studies in Character*, III, 33–34.

In Allegheny County, Pennsylvania, church membership of delinquents was studied from 1924 to 1934. Of 11,765 boys, 60.3 per cent were Roman Catholics; 30.3 per cent, Protestants; 8.5 per cent, others; 0.0 per cent, nonreligious. Of 2,328 girls, 47.5 per cent were Roman Catholics; 46.2 per cent, Protestants; 6.1 per cent, others; 0.2 per cent, nonreligious.[17]

In 1934, William W. Wattenberg found that 69 per cent of the delinquents studied in a Wayne University project attended church regularly or occasionally.[18]

At Yale University, William Healy and Augusta Bronner published the findings of a survey of 105 youths in Boston, New Haven, and Detroit. They found that 46 of the delinquents compared with 64 of the nondelinquents were regular church or Sunday school attenders. Only 12 of the delinquents and 8 of the nondelinquents never attended church or Sunday school. The authors concluded, "These figures are difficult to interpret except as they show that church affiliations very frequently were not potent in combating stresses that make for the production of delinquency."[19]

George Rex Mursall, in a doctoral dissertation published in 1940 at Ohio State University, found no significant relationship between religious training and delinquent or nondelinquent behavior.[20]

In measuring the attitudes of delinquent and nondelinquent females, Warren C. Middleton and Paul J. Fay summarized a data sheet of fifteen items: median scores for favorable attitudes toward Sunday observance were 6.71 (delinquents) and 5.29 (nondelinquents); toward war, 3.74 (delinquents) and 3.81 (nondelinquents). The delinquent group showed more favorable attitudes in specifically religious areas.[21]

In a British study of church attendance in 1944, it was reported that 29 per cent of delinquents against 39 per cent of nondelinquents attended church services regularly.[22]

William C. Kvaraceus summarized his Passaic, New Jersey study of 761 delinquents: "No significant differences were noted between the proportion of delinquents who were active church members and the proportion of the general population reported as having church membership

[17] Lunden, op. cit., p. 155.
[18] William W. Wattenberg, "Church Attendance and Juvenile Misconduct," Sociology and Social Research, XXXIV (January, 1950), 195–202.
[19] William Healy and Augusta F. Bronner, New Light on Delinquency and Its Treatment (New Haven, Conn.: Yale University Press, 1936), p. 70.
[20] George Rex Mursall, A Study of Religious Training as a Psychological Factor in Criminality (Columbus, Ohio: Ohio State University, 1940).
[21] Warren C. Middleton and Paul J. Fay, "Attitudes of Delinquent and Nondelinquent Girls Toward Sunday Observance, the Bible, and War," The Journal of Educational Psychology, XXXII (October, 1941), 555–558.
[22] A. M. Carr-Saunders, Hermann Mannheim, and E. C. Rhodes, Young Offenders (New York: The Macmillan Company, 1944).

in the state."[23] Among the delinquents, 67.59 per cent were Catholics or Orthodox; 22.58 per cent, Protestants; 1.99 per cent, Jews; 7.84 per cent, not church members; 54.21 per cent attended church regularly; 20.37 per cent, irregularly; 25.42 per cent, never.

In 1949, the Detroit Police Department reported 2,137 boys as delinquent. In his investigation of the religious practices of the youths, Wattenburg found that 43.56 per cent attended church regularly; 25.54 per cent, occasionally; 15.86 per cent, seldom; 14.15 per cent, never; .89 per cent, no response. The recidivists of the group attended church slightly less frequently than the first offenders: 64.9 per cent compared to 71.0 per cent. Wattenburg thought that his findings were inconclusive: "This would seem to bolster the previous findings that church attendance is part of a way of living which generally reduces tendencies towards juvenile misconduct."[24]

In 1954, Sister Mary Dominic studied 162 female residents of the Good Shepherd Home in Seattle, Washington, where 47.5 per cent of the delinquent girls were Protestants, 28.4 per cent Roman Catholics, and 24.1 per cent nonchurch members. Although 160 had attended church at some time, only 5 had attended regularly (3 Roman Catholics and 2 Protestants). The attitudes toward religion of 95 per cent of the residents were described as "negative, indifferent or actively hostile."[25]

Since 1934, the outstanding students of juvenile delinquent behavior have been Eleanor and Sheldon Glueck. Religious factors, however, have not predominated in their investigations. In *Unraveling Juvenile Delinquency* they presented the following observation: ". . . the delinquent boys attended church with far less regularity than the non-delinquents; but only a few of either group neglected their religious duties entirely."[26]

In 1955 at Southern Methodist University, a study was conducted by Elaine Parks Holcomb, using as subjects 100 Anglo girls and 100 Anglo boys: Both groups were institutionalized in state reform schools in Texas. Holcomb found that 97 per cent had religious preference and 67 per cent belonged to churches; 52.5 per cent to Protestant churches; and 14.5 per cent to the Catholic Church. Over 75 per cent claimed regular or occasional church or Sunday school attendance; only 6 per cent had never attended church or Sunday school; 43.5 per cent stated that they did not attend after the age of 10. Of the respondents, 72 per cent had at least one parent who attended church and 66 per cent claimed that one parent

23 William C. Kvaraceus, "Delinquent Behavior and Church Attendance," *Sociology and Social Research*, XXVIII (March-April, 1944), 289.
24 Wattenburg, *op. cit.*, p. 202.
25 Sister M. Dominic, "Religion and the Juvenile Delinquent," *American Catholic Sociological Review*, XV (October, 1954), 264.
26 Sheldon and Eleanor Glueck, *Unraveling Juvenile Delinquency* (Cambridge: Harvard University Press, 1950), p. 167.

(usually the mother) attended regularly or occasionally. Finally, there was indication of positive belief in the existence of God as well as of favorable attitudes toward the church, the Bible, and Christ.[27]

In a doctoral dissertation published at Harvard University in 1961, Juan B. Cortes found that the difference in religiosity of 200 Boston youths (100 delinquents, 100 nondelinquents) was very significant; in fact, there was no other variable equally discriminating. In subsequent studies of matched pairs (20 of each group), according to their own reports of self-evaluation, the delinquents compared with the nondelinquents lacked intrinsic religiosity. The opinions of the parents of both groups agreed entirely with those expressed by their sons. Cortes says, "Low religiousness is one of the three discriminating variables of family background."[28] In a subsequent manuscript, Cortes suggests that "religiousness" can be used as an important factor in predicting delinquent behavior.[29]

John F. Travers and Russell G. Davis described a 1961 study of 223 Roman Catholic white males, ages 10–17, living in Northeastern urban settings: 120 were classified as nondelinquent, 103 as delinquent; some were institutionalized, some not. The hypothesis, "Youths with a high degree of religious intensity will be lower on juvenile delinquency than non-delinquency," was substantiated according to the chi square value of 16.59, significant beyond the +1 per cent level. The religious motives of the delinquents were significantly different from those of the non-delinquents, who were more oriented toward religion.[30]

The religious beliefs of 2,792 delinquents in Philadelphia in 1961 were reported as follows:

	BOYS		GIRLS	
	White	*Negro*	*White*	*Negro*
Roman Catholics	1,922 (68.8)	559 (10.2)	302 (65.2)	125 (10.4)
Protestants	724 (26.0)	4,910 (89.4)	131 (28.4)	1,068 (88.0)
Jews	111 (4.0)	4 —	25 (5.4)	2 —
Others or none	35 —	20 —	3 —	10 —

It was concluded that most of the white delinquents were Roman Catholics and most of the Protestant delinquents were Negroes because

[27] Elaine Parks Holcomb, *The Role of Religion in the Prevention of Juvenile Delinquency* (Master's Thesis, Southern Methodist University, 1956).

[28] Juan B. Cortes, *Physique, Need for Achievement, and Delinquency* (Doctoral Dissertation, Harvard University, 1961).

[29] Juan B. Cortes, *Delinquency and Crime: A Biosocial Approach* (unpublished MSS).

[30] John F. Travers and Russell G. Davis, "A Study of Religious Motivation and Delinquency," *The Journal of Educational Sociology*, XXXIV (January, 1961), 205–220.

these two groups came from the poorest families, which are more disrupted than the others.[31]

At a residential training school, Leo J. Trese studied the religious backgrounds of 101 delinquent girls: 60 Roman Catholic, 29 Protestant, and 12 with no church affiliation. Only 14 of the 101 had never attended church or Sunday school; 85 per cent attended regularly for one or more years; the mean number of years of attendance was 5.9. Among 43 per cent of the Roman Catholics and 20 per cent of the Protestants at least one parent attended church regularly.[32]

Evaluation of the Studies

The difficulties in evaluating the above studies are multiple. The terms "religion," "religious," and "religiousness" are not defined in the same way by the investigators. The subjects of the investigations have neither understood nor accepted the interpretations of religious terminology equally among themselves. The subjectivity of such studies has been too elusive for adequate measurement, especially by the typical methods of testing and questioning. The factors of church attendance and sacramental participation, for example, are not equally valid as norms of measurement: For a Catholic to attend Sunday Mass "under pain of mortal sin" there is a different connotation of religious observance than for the Protestant youth who is urged to attend Sunday school but not necessarily church services. Some of the above studies were conducted in institutions, where conformity even in thought patterns is highly desirable: It would be difficult for the institutionalized delinquent to verbalize his feelings if they were contrary to "what is expected." Also, there seems to be a bias in favor of religious influence as an aid to good behavior whenever the investigator is a religious leader. Another factor is the limited size of the groups studied: The findings of small groups do not easily lend themselves to adequate interpretation. A final consideration that affects the validity of these studies in their relationship to religion in the context of a formally organized church. For some individuals, participation in church activities can be a form of antisocial or even personally harmful behavior. For example, leaders of certain evangelical sects have been known to visit youths detained in jails and to arouse such sentiments of self-condemnation for sinfulness that suicide attempts have resulted. Church records indicate that teen-agers take less interest in church participation as they grow older. This lack of interest may be due less to the religious attitude of the youths than to the inability

[31] Lunden, *op. cit.*, p. 157.
[32] Leo J. Trese, *101 Delinquent Girls* (Notre Dame, Ind.: Fides Publishers, Inc., 1962), pp. 34–36.

of the organized churches to meet the needs of their adolescent members.

Judging from the present evidence, it is not wise to evaluate the importance of church membership and participation in relation to delinquency prevention. Further scientific investigation is necessary, especially as a cooperative venture of all professionals concerned with this aspect of deviant behavior. It is not only a matter of studying individual youths but of taking a more comprehensive approach involving personal and social relations within the total complex of society.[33] Leroy Bowman suggests that

> it is in the value-system of the culture that the germ of the problem lies hidden. The first step, then, is to search for understanding delinquency which well may be an inspection of the values held by the majority of the population, to see how generally they are accepted, the depth of devotion to them, and particularly, the measure of conformity to them.[34]

What the Churches Have Done for Delinquency Prevention

In view of the available statistics pertinent to the church's influence over delinquent behavior (directly with individual youths, indirectly with the institutional complexities of modern society), it is necessary to see what the churches have done and are doing in this area. The first diagram indicates the polarity of functions performed by the churches.

Church activities relevant to prevention of delinquency can be divided into four categories: religion-centered, person-based; religion-centered, community-based; secularity-centered, person-based; and secularity-centered, community-based. These determinations have been made according to the nature of the activities (religious or secular) and their direction (person or community). It has not always been possible here to

[33] The practical effectiveness of religious education given in parochial schools was questioned by Dr. Paul Mundy in his address, "Changing Educational Patterns Required by Changes in Society and in the Church," given at the 1965 National Catholic Educational Association Convention. A study of 300 Catholic high school seniors (males) indicated that there was little significant difference in their responses to questions of morality, whether they attended Catholic schools or public schools. To one question, ". . . will you also be willing to share our food with people of Communist countries if their need is great?" 58 per cent of Catholic students gave a negative reply, whereas only 30 per cent of the public school students did so. Mundy concludes, "These findings seem to support the judgment of the authors of the NORC report, *The Social Effects of Catholic Education:* 'All one can say is that if the parochial schools are turning out people who are more diligent in practices of love of their neighbors, the fact is not confirmed by the evidence available to us.'" (*Proceedings of the 1965 National Catholic Education Association Convention,* Washington, D.C., 1965, pp. 154–155.)

[34] Leroy Bowman, *Youth and Delinquency in an Inadequate Society* (New York: League for Industrial Democracy, 1960), p. 21.

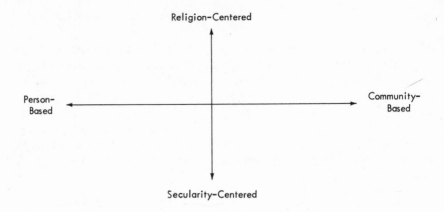

Religion–Centered

Person–
Based

Community–
Based

Secularity–Centered

indicate the degree of determination. There has been, however, an attempt to place the items of the second diagram according to the scales of intensity. Beginning with the religion-centered activities that are person-based and proceeding toward those that are community-based, the functions of the churches in delinquency prevention can be schematically outlined.

Church Activities: Religion-centered, Person-based

The most intimately personal religious involvement on the person-to-person level is "sacramental" or formally determined confession, which has as its purpose not only the objective absolution of sinfulness but the subjective conviction of guilt and resolution of amendment. The value of this religious experience for the delinquent cannot be easily measured except by the individual himself: His future behavior is undoubtedly affected by the extent of his cooperation with the superempirical action involved. The fact is that certain delinquents, especially first offenders, have used "the confessional" as the first step along the road of rehabilitation. In many church groups, pastoral counseling replaces the use of sacramental confession: There is often the same emphasis of expression of guilt, sorrow, and acceptance of forgiveness. Billy Graham has applied this method of direction for youths who are willing "to accept Christ as their personal Savior."

Church youth groups for the most part have not been geared to the needs of the delinquent members of the parish. The Salvation Army and other evangelical churches have been exceptions. In his analysis of the delinquent subculture, Albert Cohen found "that such typically working-class forms of Protestantism as the Holiness sects owe their appeal to the fact that they reverse the respectable status system; it is the humble, the simple, and the dispossessed who sit at the right hand of God. . . ."[35]

[35] Albert K. Cohen, *Delinquent Boys* (New York: Free Press of Glencoe, Inc., 1955), pp. 122–123.

Religion−Centered

Person−Based

"Sacramental" Confession
Pastoral counseling
Church Youth Groups
Religious instructions
Liturgical services
Chaplaincies: agencies, institutions
Church centers, e.g. for Arts
YMCA...YWCA...CYO...youth organizations
Inner City renewal centers, e.g. East Harlem Protestant Parish
Religious Action Groups, e.g. YCW, YCS, and C.F.M.

Community−Based

General counseling
Big Brothers, Big Sisters
Sponsoring: probation, parole
Juvenile institutions
Half-way houses
Community youth centers and clubs
Neighborhood houses
Coffee houses, youth canteens
Education for family planning, etc.
Seminars: crime and delinquency
Study groups: crime and delinquency
Publications and other mass media
Community Action Committees
Social Action Groups, e.g. Back-of-the Yards and Temporary Woodlawn Organization.

Secularity−Centered

Many of the contacts to whom youths in detention facilities are exposed are evangelicals who are concerned enough to make weekly or even daily rounds of jails and receiving homes "to save the sinful." In most churches the religious instruction and liturgical services are directed to the majority of the church membership: The well-behaved are the ones who profit most. It is not unusual for "problem children" to be expelled from church classes or services because they disturb "those who want to learn and to pray." Even the Youth Days and Crusades for Youth have seldom benefited potential or actual delinquents. The promulgation of middle-class standards of conduct by the churches does not often reach into the subculture of delinquency; such standards as "rational cultivation of manners" and "control of aggression and violence," for example, indicate the degree of irrelevancy for "delinquent types."[36]

The chaplaincy of the clergy in public and private institutions and agencies has been popularized in seminaries to such an extent that some ministerial students are trained for specific chaplaincy positions. At the Illinois State Training School for Boys, in-service training of Protestant seminarians has been an important factor in the successful preparation of future chaplains. Because the limits of the personal resources of the individual chaplain will determine his effectiveness with young offenders, the education of the potential chaplain has been extended to include the techniques of counseling and group therapy as well as the basic principles of abnormal psychology and social pathology. One of the important functions of the chaplains of institutions or agencies involved primarily with nondelinquents is to identify the symptoms of antisocial behavior. Experienced chaplains can be very effective in redirecting the dynamic processes of incipient delinquency.

An innovation in religion that has attracted the attention of many New York City youths has been the use of arts and crafts in the churches. At St. Mark's-on-the-Bowerie, a Minister of Arts was recently employed to direct theatrical productions, which are performed in the sanctuary as part of the liturgical services as well as in the church's theater-in-the-round. At Judson Memorial Church in Greenwich Village, the pastor, Howard Moody, has effectively used drama, dance, and music in religious forms. A "Euchararistic Service of Jazz," for example, was presented during a Sunday morning worship service. These attempts to "make religion relevant" have at least achieved the goal of attracting nonchurch-going youths to the churches.

The position on the above diagram of such national organizations as the Young Men's Christian Association, midway between person-centered and community-centered activities, can be justified by the following statement of purpose of the "Y": "Worldwide fellowship of men and boys united by common loyalty for Jesus Christ, for the purpose of developing Christian personality and building a Christian society."[37] Such groups have a dual reason for existence: They work with *individuals* for the betterment of *society* as a whole. In regard to delinquency

---

[36] *Ibid.*, p. 36.
[37] James W. McCandless, *Developing Christian Personality and Building a Christian Society* (New York: Association Press, 1949), p. 7.

prevention they have general as well as specific goals, using individual as well as social methods.

The autonomy of the YMCA and YWCA local organizations prevents an easy analysis of their programs. According to the 1964 Yearbook there are 1,664 associations in the United States with 2,261,634 males and 726,273 females participating; 61 per cent of the members were under the age of 25; the median age was 17.3. The major programs of the "Y's" (besides providing room and board facilities with social clubroom activities) were counseling, camping, physical education and training, and group activity meetings, primarily through the 4-Front Clubs, which numbered 42,045 groups with 14,924,491 members divided into the YIndian Guide, Gra-Y and Tri-Gra-Y, Junior Hi-Y and Junior Tri-Hi-Y, and Senior Hi-Y and Senior Tri-Hi-Y; the senior groups accounted for 5,800,000 teenage members.[38] Although most of the membership is registered as Protestant, about 20 per cent are Roman Catholics and 2 per cent Jews; in 1961, 60 per cent of the "Y's" reported that one or more of the staff employed was Roman Catholic. The first "Y" was organized in 1844 by twelve men in London under the leadership of George Williams. The first "Y" in North America was begun in Montreal in 1851 and in Boston a few months later. (Two other such organizations had already existed in 1848 in Baltimore and Cincinnati but they were not affiliated until later with the international organization. In 1854 a general convention of YMCA locals was held in North America.[39] The original purpose of the "Y's" was centered on the individual needs of youth, but a program of social reform was soon initiated. (The history of social action for the YWCA, which had sent student delegates to the Geneva Meeting of the YMCA in 1886, actually began in 1911 with the promotion of better wages for women in the United States.[40])

When Bishop Sheil founded the Catholic Youth Organization in Chicago in 1930 he did not realize that it would develop into a national federation uniting 3,200 parish groups and 80 diocesan centers and serving 2,000,000 youths. The programs of the CYO usually include spiritual, cultural, social, and physical activities. Because statistics are not accurately recorded, the National Office of CYO gives only estimates of participation in the various activities. In 1964, for example, more than

[38] *YMCA Year Book and Official Rosters* (New York: Association Press, 1964). See also Richard E. Hamlin, *Hi-Y Today* (New York: Association Press, 1955).

[39] C. Howard Hopkins, *History of the YMCA in North America* (New York: Association Press, 1951); Edgar M. Robinson, *The Early Years* (New York: Association Press, 1950); and Paul M. Limbert, *New Perspectives for the YMCA* (New York: Association Press, 1964).

[40] Elsie D. Harper, *The Past Is Prelude* (New York: The National Board of the Young Women's Christian Association, 1963).

122,000 youths took part in "Holy Hour Services," and more than 109,000 participated in CYO basketball games. In the 1964 Annual Report, 45.3 per cent of the diocesan directors reported that their groups sponsored programs that served the total community, and 37.2 per cent engaged in programs to combat social problems of young people.[41] Clyde Vedder claims that the CYO "has as a major objective the prevention of juvenile delinquency and works towards this goal with one of the most extensive and popular youth programs in the United States today."[42]

As delinquency-prevention organizations, the "Y's" and the CYO, as well as the other national church groups (the Juvenile Protection Project of the Northern Baptist Convention and the Youth Service Projects of the Methodist, Presbyterian, Evangelical, and Reformed Churches), cannot justify the value of their programs. Their purpose gives evidence of the valuable contribution that can be made for the protection of individual youths and for the upgrading of the institutions of society. But their purpose has little relevancy in the subculture of delinquency.

Church Activities: Religion-centered, Community-based

One of the most important developments in church work during the past two decades was begun in 1948 in a storefront church on East 102d Street, New York City. Protestant ministers from eight denominations now continue this work of the East Harlem Protestant Parish from a headquarters on Second Avenue. Their mission in the inner city consists of a church center, a credit union office, a health clinic, a narcotics committee office and recreation center, a family camp and retreat center (out of the city), the parish office, which houses a problem clinic, children's library, information center, rummage sale room, youth program office, and drama-art group rooms. More than 25,000 persons, mostly Puerto Rican and Negro, live in the parish boundaries: 96th to 112th Streets, Lexington Avenue to the East River. The multipurpose program is directed toward the immediate needs of the people whom it serves and among whom it exists. George Webber, the "patriarch" of the group, refers to the Parish as affirming "the secular relevance of the Gospel."[43] He believes that new forms of the Christian parish "achieve nothing unless through them is expressed the spirit of being there in the midst of

41 Thomas J. Leonard, General Survey of the CYO (Washington, D.C.: Catholic Youth Organization, 1965).
42 Clyde B. Vedder, Juvenile Offender (Springfield, Ill.: Charles C. Thomas, Publisher, 1963), p. 62.
43 George W. Webber, God's Colony in Man's World (Nashville: Abingdon Press, 1960), p. 88.

God's World."[44] The Parish conducts weekly Bible study sessions in various apartments in the neighborhood and Sunday services in the Parish churches. Plans are now being completed for a central church building and a halfway house for narcotic addicts. The youth programs are directed by a layman, Ramon Diez, whose success with East Harlem youths has been responsible for the rehabilitation of many offenders and the prevention of delinquency among an even greater number of potential offenders.[45] The impact of the Parish on the community is best shown by the involvement of the church workers in the lives of the people. Webber writes:

> We hope that in East Harlem the issues confronting the church, the struggle to discover again the nature of the Christian community and the mission of the church are at least on the right frontiers, and that as we wrestle with these questions, we are dealing with issues which are of significance wherever the church seeks to be faithful to its Lord. If the churches of America do not struggle with these same issues, the gospel stands in danger, not so much from the world as from the church itself.[46]

Another approach to the reform of community life was begun by a Belgian priest, Joseph Cardijn, in 1912, when he met with twelve young factory workers to plan social action projects for the improvement of their working conditions. The group eventually were known as Jocists ("Young Christian Workers"—"Jeunesse Ouvrières Chrétiennes"). In 1957, 32,000 delegates met in Rome for an International Congress[47] and they represented the thousands of other youths who followed the Jocist goal: "to reform all things in Christ," through the Cardijn Inquiry Technique. More recently organized social action groups following the Jocist methods are the Young Christian Students and the Christian Family Movement, which is the largest Roman Catholic organization of laity directly concerned with community projects. The change of environment is the major purpose of all these groups. An action inquiry used by a group of high school boys who belonged to the Young Christian Students deals with the problem "pressure from other guys as an obstacle to study." Their inquiry proceeded in the following way:

1. *Seeing the problems:* (a) How often have fellows made fun of you for getting good grades or having honors?
(b) Ask three honor students if they

44 *Ibid.,* p. 85.
45 For information about Ramon Diez, see Dan Wakefield, "The Gang That Went Good," *Harper's Magazine,* CCXVI (June, 1958), 36–43.
46 Webber, *op. cit.,* p. 21.
47 Joseph Becaud, *Artisans de la Paix* (Paris: Les Éditions Ouvrières, 1963), p. 80.

have ever been made fun of.

(c) How many scholastic monogram winners have ever worn their monograms so far this year?

2. *Making a judgment:* (a) Why do guys use terms such as "brown nose" and "suck ass"? Do they mean what they say?

(b) Are grades and honors a good sign of success in study?

(c) Why are monogram winners afraid to wear their sweaters with the letters?

3. *Getting to action:* (a) Wear your monogram letter. (b) Try to get two other guys to do the same. (c) Help organize a Scholastic Monogram Club.

These members of the Young Christian Students had previously made a study of the "spirit of the school" and summed up their findings as: "The predominating spirit of the school is to have a good time, which means (1) the fun of getting away with stuff, (2) raising hell for the glory of it, (3) going to school without effort, (4) trying to disturb and oppose teachers, and (5) taking it easy whenever possible."[48] The individual members of the Cardijn groups are helped greatly through their membership, but this help is secondary to the main purpose of their activities, which are community-oriented: They want to change the social habits that encourage delinquency; their work is primarily preventive.

Church Activities: Secularity-centered, Person-based

The concern of Christian churches for nonreligious or nonchurch problems can be rationally explained. Following the Judaic tradition of total commitment to religion as a way of living, the founder of Christianity called his doctrine a "new way" of love[49] through which his followers would be judged by their overt acts of service to others, such as feeding the hungry and visiting the imprisoned.[50] Nothing in this code escapes the determination of religion. The role of the clergy is not limited to specifically religious activities, nor is the concept of laity-action excluded from any area of human behavior. The needy or "people in trouble" have been the special concern of the religious-minded through-

---

[48] These excerpts of meeting notes were taken from a pamphlet published by the Young Christian Students, Cathedral High School, Indianapolis, Indiana, 1951.

[49] "This is my commandment that you love one another as I have loved you," John 15:12, *Revised Standard Version of the New Covenant* (New York: Thomas Nelson & Sons, 1946), p. 223.

[50] "I was hungry and you gave me food; I was thirsty and you gave me drink; I was a stranger and you welcomed me; I was naked and you clothed me; I was sick and you visited me; I was in prison and you came to me. . . . As you did it to one of the least of my brethren, you did it to me." Matt. 25:34–40, *Revised Standard Version of The New Covenant*, pp. 58–59.

out the history of Christianity. It seems, however, that the secularity-centered actions of the churches have been traditionally person-based. As the objects of the churches' attention shift from "people in need of conversion" to society in general, there is less ecclesiastical concern. Keeping members in the organization or recruiting new members would demand the greater portion of church resources as well as the time and talents of church leaders. Environmental needs that are not religion-centered have been neglected to a great extent until recently.[51] The movement of the churches into the arena of community-based, secularity-centered activities is a renewed form of the apostolate.

A seminarian once remarked to a fellow student: "Of all our courses in theology the one I like best is psychiatry!" Undoubtedly this young cleric reflected the opinion of many of his confreres, who had begun to envision their ministry as one of "healing through therapy." Many clergymen have accepted the goals as well as the tools of psychiatry; they have confused the generic differences of theology and medicine, of the superempirical and the empirical. Nevertheless, a clergyman can play an important role in the total process of human rehabilitation. It is still true that many people, especially parents of misbehaving children, will turn to a clergyman first, not necessarily for spiritual guidance: He is often the first available. But the wise minister will recognize his limitations as well as his potentials. It seems that the major contribution he can usually make is that of referral. Once he is acquainted with the symptoms of character and personality abnormalities, he will be able to recommend the appropriate therapist or agency. In some cases the clergyman will be capable of dealing with minor, short-term counseling situations, but if he is aware of his primary functions as a religious leader he will not allow himself to be led beyond his depth.

One role that some clergymen are called on to assume is that of sponsoring parolees or, in small communities where juvenile court personnel is lacking, probationers. This direct contact with the process of delinquency will educate him in practical matters that cannot be taught in seminaries. An important factor in the success of clergy-contacts with delinquents is the attitude of the clergyman toward the offender. In a study conducted at Boston University in 1961 the attitudes of ministers toward juvenile delinquency were measured. Two hypotheses were formulated: (1) A minister's attitude toward juvenile delinquency is related to the authoritarian or supportive tendencies in his personality; and (2) what a minister does in his personal contacts with juvenile

[51] It may be an oversimplification of a fact, but this attitude can partially explain why countries that are predominantly Roman Catholic, such as Mexico, can submit to anti-Catholic political pressures or, such as Cuba, can turn to a mitigated form of atheistic Communism.

offenders is related to his attitudes toward causation and treatment. Both hypotheses were validated through the use of the F (Fascist) Scale, the TFI (Traditional Family Ideology) Scale and a Juvenile Delinquency Attitude Scale. There was a high degree of reliability for the tests and a close correlation in their results. The conclusion was reached that "a minister's deep-lying emotional dispositions, more than his absolute theological beliefs, generally determine the nature, extent and effectiveness of his approach to juvenile delinquency."[52] This study corroborates the conviction that a clergyman will succeed as a counselor or sponsor of juvenile offenders if he is nonauthoritarian and supportive in his relationships with youths. (Characteristics not always associated with the ministry.)

Another person-based approach to juvenile delinquents is found in the Big Brother and Big Sister Movements. These organizations trace their origin to a clerk of the Juvenile Court in New York City, who, in 1904, noted that the majority of boys appearing before the Court were fatherless. After meeting with forty members of his church, the clerk petitioned the Court to accept a Big Brother Plan, by which volunteers would assist the Court in working with the boys. From the very beginning the Movement was determined by a religious identity principle: boys were to have Big Brothers of their own faith. The Catholic Protective Society, which had been organized in 1911, joined with the Big Brother Movement in 1916. In the major cities of the United States today there are Protestant, Catholic, and Jewish affiliates with the Movement. Although the organization has proven successful, few potential delinquents and even fewer actual offenders are helped: In 1961 only 5,000 boys were reached through Big Brothers; more than 200 communities were refused assistance in establishing local groups because of lack of personnel and of financial resources.[53]

According to historical records the first institution for juvenile delinquents was established by Pope Clement XI in Rome in 1701. It was called the "Hospice of San Michele" and followed monastic disciplinary rules "for the correction and instruction of profligate youth. . . ."[54] Since that time churches have assumed the responsibility for such institutions; religious organizations such as the Salesians and Good Shepherd Sisters were founded to continue this important work. The best-known institution of this kind is the one begun in 1917 by Father Flanagan.[55]

---

[52] William E. Alberts, *Ministers' Attitudes Towards Juvenile Delinquency* (Boston: Boston University, 1961), p. 72.

[53] "The Door That Never Opened," pamphlet (Philadelphia: Big Brothers of America, Inc., 1962).

[54] Vedder, *op. cit.*, p. 61.

[55] Fulton and Will Oursler, *Father Flanagan of Boy's Town* (New York: Doubleday & Company, Inc., 1949), p. 192.

Boy's Town, Nebraska, now numbers among its alumni thousands of men who were sheltered and educated in this protective environment during their adolescence. Some institutions, unlike Boy's Town, are established for short-term placements, but statistics of recidivism prove their limited value. It seems that the best results are obtained by providing living-in facilities for youths until they are capable of adjusting to society on their own.

Another approach to the problem of institutionalization of young offenders is the half-way house. Many of these foundations have been sponsored by churches. They are semi-institutional, serving as bridges to help youths return from other institutions to normal living in small groups. In New York City and Chicago the YMCA has provided facilities for parolees in a prerelease setting.[56] The late G. Howland Shaw, an expert in the field of delinquency, believed that the use of half-way houses was the greatest hope for the future of rehabilitation programs for delinquents.

The need for neighborhood houses, youth clubs, and youth centers, sponsored by church groups, has been outlined in C. Kilmer Myers' *Light the Dark Streets*. The work of St. Augustines on the Lower East Side of New York City was justified in the growth of the Knights, a gang of "toughs," into a social club of well-behaved and fairly well-adjusted young men. From "bopping" and "boozing" the boys turned to discussion, to social action for community betterment, and to some extent, to religion.[57] William Wendt, who had been a curate with Myers, has now organized a youth program in Washington, D.C., at St. Stephen's Church. During the summer of 1965 his many projects demanded a staff of more than 100 workers, directing every type of program from "Headstart" for preschoolers to the Loser's Club for young alcoholics.

The coffee house and teen canteen approach to delinquency prevention, successfully used by Mobilization for Youth in New York City, has now become a part of church life in many cities. One of the best examples of this apostolate is "Through The Gate," a coffee house opened by Larry Lewis at the Capitol Hill Presbyterian Church in Washington, D.C., in 1964. Every weekend more than 300 youths crowd into the dimly-lit basement room, decorated with paintings and sculpture by young artists. Folk singers perform every half-hour from 9:00 P.M. to 2:00 A.M.; on some occasions the singing is replaced by poetry readings or the presentation of scenes from plays. Lewis' motivation in this coffee house ministry is not to save the souls of these kids, because they are too

---

[56] Kenneth S. Carpenter, "Half-way Houses for Delinquent Youth," *Children*, X (November-December, 1963), 224–229.

[57] C. Kilmer Myers, *Light the Dark Streets* (Greenwich, Conn.: The Seabury Press, 1957), p. 148.

rebellious against the church, against religious hypocrisy, but rather to keep the channels of communication open through non-structured, non-directed dialogue.

The use of education and the discussion method for family planning and living has been adopted by churches nationally and locally for long-range delinquency prevention. One of the most widely developed programs was set up in 1961 by the National Council on Crime and Delinquency for the United Presbyterian Church. A booklet, "Delinquency—Everybody's Problem," was published for church discussion groups. Topics, such as police, detention, juvenile court, probation, and prevention, were treated in such a way that social inquiries and action would result on the local level. Another program devised by the National Council on Crime and Delinquency was called "You and the Law," which was directed to youths as well as to adult leaders in the community; case histories were presented in such a way that youths would be deterred from misbehavior. Another active organization is the American Temperance Society, sponsored by the Seventh Day Adventist Church. This organization distributes films, periodicals, and pamphlets relevant to the use of alcohol, tobacco, and narcotics.

Church Activities: Secularity-centered, Community-based

The full entrance of the churches into the secular world can be best shown through the specifically community-based activities of community action committees and social action groups. The Federal Government has provided the primary incentive for community action through federal grants, such as those of Public Law 87–274, "The Juvenile Delinquency and Youth Offenses Control Act of 1961." The churches have been able to participate in these projects by permitting the use of their facilities, by urging lay members to act as personnel (paid and volunteer), by fusing federal programs into those already existing as church-sponsored, and by using the clergy on committees for decision-making and planning sessions. In the budget report of fiscal years 1962–1964 the Office of Juvenile Delinquency and Youth Development summarized grants for demonstration projects (planning and action) totaling $10,722,140 and for training projects (training centers, curriculum development, workshops, institutes, seminars, etc.) totaling $6,178,903. Many of these projects were directly related to efforts of community leaders, including churchmen, in every section of the nation. Another program, developed by the Office of Economic Opportunities Act, follows a broad scope of community action: remedial education, academic counseling and guidance services, school social work services, after-school services, tutoring, summer and week-end after-school classes, adult illiteracy programs, special education for migrant or transient families, improvement of living conditions of the elderly, health examinations and health education, rehabilitating and retraining the physically or mentally handicapped, health, rehabilitation, employment, and education for young men unqualified for military service, community child-care centers, youth activity centers, improvement of living facilities, home management skills, preparation of rural families for urban living, recreation and physical fitness services and facilities.

In Washington, D.C., a Roman Catholic priest, Geno Baroni, has served on Neighborhood Community Advisory Committees of the United Planning Organization and on the Board of Directors of the Washington Action for Youth Organization; he is also vice-chairman of the University Neighborhoods Council. His concern for civil rights, poverty programs, and public welfare is, for him, an integral part of his religious commitment. He considers this kind of social action "the new role of the Church in the city. It's not concerned just with taking care of its own. For the American Christian, the great challenge is to overcome the racism and impoverishment in our center cities."[58]

The determination to make environmental changes presents the church with a new function and the clergy with a new role. In relating community activities to the problems of crime and delinquency, some clergymen have assumed responsibility for establishing committees as divisions of coordinating councils and other such welfare organizations in their communities. The duties of one such committee have been defined by the chairman, a clergyman, as: (1) to analyze the community's problems concerning the prevention, control, and treatment of crime and delinquency; (2) to educate the community about such problems by serving as a clearing house of information about probation and parole; (3) to assist in developing effective juvenile, family, and criminal courts; (4) to promote the rehabilitation of juvenile and adult offenders; (5) to initiate and encourage community programs for the prevention and control of crime and delinquency.

The success of social action groups can best be exemplified by the many projects of Saul Alinsky, who initiated the renewal of community life in Packingtown, Chicago, the scene of Upton Sinclair's reform novel, *The Jungle*. In 1938, Alinsky, a Jewish social worker, studied the problem of community deterioration in Packingtown, a predominantly Catholic area centered around the packinghouses, which had hired immigrants a generation earlier and now employed the second generation families. A lack of communication among the various lingual and ethnic groups had led to misunderstanding and suspicion. By convincing the leaders of the

[58] *The Washington Post*, July 20, 1965.

various parish groups that they would be helping their own people if they planned and worked together for the welfare of their total community, he was able to organize a council of citizens, which eventually resulted in the formation of a People's Organization, called "Back of the Yards Council." One typical procedure of the Council was to hold the hearings of juvenile offenders with their parents, teachers, employers, and clergymen in attendance as codefendants on trial. All those responsible for the youths' rehabilitation worked together in the probationary planning. Alinsky has said many times that churchmen have always been his best allies. More than forty community-based People's Organizations have been developed by Alinsky and his team of professional organizers. The Temporary Woodlawn Organization, with its thirty-three groups of citizens united in common effort for social reform "against cheating merchants, slum operators, school segregation, and other basic issues, is one of the most widely known community organizations in the life of Chicago."[59] More recently the Northwest Community Organization in Chicago began a renewal program that provided the churches, whose congregations were waning and whose property was in jeopardy, with the impetus necessary to create a new spirit of cooperation that not only upgraded property values but even more essentially "provided the churches with an arena in which they could find their relevance in the twentieth century."[60]

Church Activities Evaluated

From the variety of church activities dealing with delinquent youths and with society with its serious problems of crime and delinquency, it seems that greater results could be expected. The difficulties hindering success in many cases can be traced to interdenominational disagreements and rivalries, lack of funds and personnel, lack of cooperation with public agencies, inadequate training of religious leaders, and poor coordination of efforts on different levels of authority within the same religious organization. Two suggestions that deserve consideration in evaluating the church's past and future relevancy to delinquency prevention have been stated as: (1) "The challenge facing all churches is to find concrete functions for themselves by tying in with the total community effort to

[59] Saul Alinsky, "Citizen Participation and Community Organization in Planning and Urban Renewal," speech published by The Industrial Areas Foundation, Chicago, 1962, p. 9; see also Saul Alinsky, *Reveille for Radicals* (Chicago: University of Chicago Press, 1946); and Charles E. Silberman, *Crisis in Black and White* (New York: Random House, Inc., 1964), pp. 318–350.

[60] Interview with Robert Smith, organizer of the Northwest Community Organization.

deal with the problem of juvenile delinquency."[61] (2) "With but few exceptions, our churches are conspicuously isolated from this problem. They have become so respectable that to bring the church to the delinquent or the delinquent to the church is to perform a miracle in the conjunction of opposites. We must indeed confess that we are a delinquent church."[62]

The successes of the past can only be measured by the challenges of the future. It is in the sense of Dietrich Bonhoeffer's "religionless Christianity"[63] that many contemporary church leaders look to the church's primary task of secularization before it can directly confront the dynamic processes of community life, especially in the urban centers. Gibson Winter writes:

> A democratic society desperately needs a Church which can participate in its public life without acting as a faction in search of private advantage. . . . Our traditional religious structures are simply inappropriate for a democratic society with a pluralistic religious commitment. The Church will find its ministry of public responsibility through an apostolate of the laity and a ministry of servant-hood in the structures of public life. This is her mission and opportunity in the emerging metropolis, but she cannot belong to this future and share in this ministry without the loss of her traditional structures and their false security.[64]

Perhaps, then, delinquency is one problem that the churches can help solve for the preservation of their own life in society as well as for the resultant benefits to individuals and to society in general.

A Theoretical Approach: Religion as a Socializing Agency

Some attempt must be made to theorize about the proper functions of religion, and more specifically of the church, which will enable it to accept the challenges facing it at the present time. A pragmatic definition of religion must be given, but not necessarily one identifiable with the existing forms of ecclesiastical institutions. There also must be some kind of analysis of the relationship of predetermined norms of religion and morality with personality development. Because Juan Cortes is one of the few theorists in the fields of crime and delinquency who takes religion

---

[61] *A Look at Juvenile Delinquency*, Publication No. 380 (Washington, D. C.: U.S. Department of Health, Education, and Welfare, Children's Bureau, 1960), p. 34.
[62] Robert Lee, "Delinquent Youth in a Normless Time," *The Christian Century*, LXXIX (December 5, 1962), 1475–1478.
[63] Dietrich Bonhoeffer, *Letters and Papers from Prison* (New York: The Macmillan Company, 1962), p. 57. (Available in paperback.)
[64] Gibson Winter, *op. cit.*, p. 145.

seriously enough to find an essential connection between irreligion and immorality with delinquent behavior, his position will be presented here with an optimistic conviction of its validity. The "containment theory" of Walter Reckless is basic to an understanding of Cortes, as well as other theorists.[65]

Religion is primarily a communication between an individual human being and a supremely authoritative being apart from the individual. Although the theory of Sigmund Freud views the need for religion as rooted in frustration resulting in searching for a fantasy father-figure, at least it can be held generally that religion must have as its basis a relationship by which the one can establish contact with the other. The continuation of this relationship will depend on two factors: first, the possibility of contact of the one, the inferior being, with authoritative representatives of the other, the superior being; and second, a systematization of conduct norms given by the other, but understood and responsibly accepted by the one. If either of these two factors is not recognized, or having been recognized is rejected, then irreligion and immorality will result. Thus it can be presumed that delinquent behavior is also irreligious and immoral behavior and every social problem is also a religious and moral problem. Cortes goes a step further by claiming that morality and religion are inextricably bound to each other. Religion is a reality; religion teaches moral behavior; and moral behavior is one of the main elements of responsibility. So these three elements of human behavior—religiosity, reality, and responsibility—must be essentially united. One of the major functions of the churches is to assure the concretization and fusion of these elements. Cortes sums up his position:

> Unless delinquents and criminals recognize their irresponsibility and antisocial behavior as morally or socially wrong, they will not improve; the crime problem is also, and principally, a moral problem . . . therefore, an important aim in our efforts is that the teachings of religion be fully and properly internalized by these persons. Self-worth (or self-esteem) is a basic need of human nature as is the need to love and be loved, if we feel or are considered entirely worthless; since self-worth is obtained through responsible behavior by following acceptable standards of conduct, it follows that only responsible behavior will satisfy fully basic human needs.[66]

Delinquents should be considered irresponsible persons, not sick or mentally ill. Their internal problem is the lack of strong superego development; their external problem is the constant emergence of controls that threaten their needs for extraverted activity.

[65] Walter C. Reckless, *The Crime Problem*, 3rd ed. (New York: Appleton-Century & Appleton-Century-Crofts, 1960), pp. 335-360.
[66] Cortes, *Delinquency and Crimes*, Chapter 12.

From studies that have been conducted during the past thirty years, one consistent factor relating to causality is the absence of a strong father-figure in the lives of the delinquent males. These studies correspond to the generalizations of psychologists about the origin of conscience. Hall and Lindzey write: "The superego is modelled upon the earliest parental images, when the parents were thought to be perfect and omnipotent. . . . Superego takes over the role of external authority figures and exacts conformity to society. The person is then said to be socialized."[67] At the present time, however, the position of the father in the American family has been threatened by a matriarchal value system and as a result the authority basis of identification is missing and the superego is blocked in the emerging personality. The resistance of the Chinese-American and Jewish-American families to the lessening of patriarchal influences has undoubtedly been partly responsible for the relatively few number of youthful offenders in these ethnic groups. When there is no male figure or an inadequate male figure with which to identify, emotional insecurities seriously affect the individual's conscious adherence to norms. Eysenck claims that

> it is conscience, which is, in the main, instrumental in making us behave in a moral and socially acceptable manner; that this conscience is the combination and culmination of a long process of conditioning, and that failure on the part of the person to become conditioned is likely to be a prominent cause in his running afoul of the law and of the social mores generally.[68]

Because extraverted people (or as Cortes calls them, "thick-skinned") are more difficult to condition, there is good reason to predict that if these people have also been deprived of normal personality development through faulty parental relationships then their behavior patterns will more likely be delinquent or criminal. The primary function of religion, psychologically speaking, is to reinforce the superego in its struggle with the basic instincts of the person. Without religion or some other moral, authoritarian power, there is danger that standards will not be accepted at all. Abrahamsen believes that a cultural breakdown in religion has affected the delinquent behavior of youths: "In general it can be said that while previously the individual's superego was supported by definite standards of morality, ethics and values, these standards have now become unstable and relative."[69] Therefore, the only release for the potential

[67] Calvin S. Hall and Gardner Lindzey, "Psychoanalytic Theory and Its Applications in the Social Sciences," *Handbook of Social Psychology*, ed. Gardner Lindzey (Reading, Mass.: Addison-Wesley Publishing Co., 1954), pp. 153, 165.
[68] H. J. Eysenck, *Crime and Personality* (Boston: Houghton Mifflin Company, 1964), p. 120.
[69] David Abrahamsen, *The Psychology of Crime* (New York: John Wiley & Sons, Inc., 1964), p. 64.

delinquent is to act out his inner conflicts apart from controls by being aggressive, defiant, hostile, and unwilling to submit to any authority.

One example supporting this approach to delinquency can be found in the increased crime rate among Negro offenders in the United States. According to the 1964 Uniform Crime Reports, published by the Federal Bureau of Investigation, 4,381,419 crimes resulted in arrests; of this number, 3,053,818 were committed by whites and 1,194,377 by Negroes. Of the 905,128 total arrests of youths under 18 years of age in 1964, 671,477 were whites and 217,057 Negroes. In other words, over 20 per cent of the crimes last year were committed by 10 per cent of the population. When the statistics are broken down by locality, it is reported that suburban arrests for youths under 18 include 185,472 for whites and only 17,575 for Negroes; in the rural areas the percentage distribution is similar with 209,476 white youths arrested and 22,705 Negro youths. The city statistics are much different: 588,585 white youths arrested, 209,396 Negro youths.[70] Delinquency in the cities, therefore, is more than a crime problem: It also involves minority group maladjustments caused by economic and social discrimination and eventual family disorganization. In a speech given at Howard University in June, 1965, President Johnson referred to a confidential report of the Federal Government:

> Nearly one-quarter of Negro births are now illegitimate—and the percentage runs even higher in the big-city black ghettoes. . . . Nearly one-quarter of urban Negro women who have ever been married are divorced, separated, or are living apart from their husbands. . . . The result is that almost one-quarter of Negro families are headed by females—more than double the per cent of white families. . . . Less than half of Negro children reach the age of 18 having lived all their lives with both parents. . . . [quote] "Unquestionably, these events worked against the emergence of a strong father-figure. . . . As a result, the Negro society has been largely matriarchal. The growing boy sees his father as a weakling—if he is around.[71]

There is no doubt that existing evidence points to personality malformation in the cases of Negro youths who lack strong authority controls in their "fatherless" families. Delinquent behavior is closely related to lack of family cohesiveness, which in turn depends upon the religiosity and moral stamina of the individual. Without religion and without effective social norms of morality family life will fail, and in many cases delinquency will inevitably result.

The increase of religious and moral training can be a valuable deter-

[70] *Uniform Crime Reports for the United States* (Washington, D.C.: U.S. Department of Justice, 1965) pp. 115–117.
[71] *The Washington Post*, August 23, 1965.

rent to crime, and the churches can be the important agencies of this training. A warning, however, should be given:

> Rules should therefore be limited to the absolute minimum required to guarantee the survival of society, but within those limits, it is probably most humane to conduct the necessary conditioning process with the greatest possible efficiency, rather than haphazardly and ineffectively, as at present. . . . Modern psychology holds out to society an altogether different approach to criminology, an approach geared only to practical ends, such as the elimination of antisocial conduct, and not cluttered with irrelevant, philosophical, retributory and ethico-religious beliefs. It finally holds to the distinction between private sin and public crime, leaving the former to morality and theology and concerning itself only with the latter.[72]

By de-emphasizing the differences between behavioral scientists and churchmen, it is hoped that all those concerned with the problems of delinquent behavior will work together for the rehabilitation of the offenders and for the eventual upbuilding of a society in which delinquency is less possible.

The mistakes of the church in the past should only serve to encourage churchmen to avoid them in the future. Isolationism, denominationalism, and supernaturalism remove the church from the purpose of its existence. The problems of crime and delinquency, like those of civil rights, now present the church with a cause involving basic human values. It can even be said that the problem of delinquency itself imposes "a test of the church's faithfulness."[73] The church's involvement with delinquency will tax its financial resources and demand personal sacrifices on the part of both clergy and laity. But if the church has truly become "a delinquent church," then its "own sins of omission or commission which allow the complex causes of delinquency to continue to exist"[74] can become a strong incentive for commitment to action. Having looked to the past, recognizing the assets, admitting the liabilities, the church should now accept the challenge that will hopefully give its existence relevancy in the twentieth century.

Conclusion

The major studies dealing with religion and juvenile delinquency during the past fifty years give no clear evidence of the specific influence of the churches as delinquency-prevention agencies. More comprehensive

[72] Eysenck, *op. cit.*, p. 180.
[73] Lee, *op. cit.*, p. 1477.
[74] Robert and Muriel Webb, *The Churches and Juvenile Delinquency* (New York: Association Press, 1957), p. 29.

investigations conducted scientifically and cooperatively by all those concerned with the many complex factors of crime and delinquency are needed.

The work of the churches for the rehabilitation of youthful offenders and for the development of environmental structures that protect potential delinquents has been outlined according to division of activities into person-based and community-based and into religion-centered and secularity-centered.

It is necessary to devise an adequate theory of personality development relevant to religiosity. The concept of the function of religion as reinforcing the superego in its struggle with the basic instincts of the person seems best adaptable to an analysis of an individual delinquent's behavior. His internal problem is the lack of superego strength; his external problem is the presence of controls that threaten his need for activity.

The challenge of the churches is to provide the religious and moral "climate" conducive to healthy individual growth to maturity.

SELECTED READINGS

Abrahamsen, David, *The Psychology of Crime*. New York: John Wiley & Sons, Inc., 1964.

Bowman, Leroy, *Youth and Delinquency in an Inadequate Society*. New York: League for Industrial Democracy, 1960.

Carr, Lowell Julliard, Harry Elmer Barnes, and Negley K. Teeters, "Replies to Father Coogan's Articles," *Federal Probation*, XVI (September, 1952), 6–7.

Coogan, John Edward, "Religion a Preventive of Delinquency," *Federal Probation*, XVIII (December, 1954), 29.

Cortes, Juan B., "Juvenile Delinquency: A Biosocial Approach," *Family, Church and Community*. New York: P. J. Kenedy & Sons, 1965.

Cox, Harvey, *The Secular City*. New York: The Macmillan Company, 1965.

Elliot, Mabel A., *Crime in Modern Society*. New York: Harper & Row, Publishers, 1952. Pages 366–367.

Eysenck, H. J., *Crime and Personality*. Boston: Houghton Mifflin Company, 1964.

Gibbons, Don C., *Changing the Lawbreaker*. Englewood Cliffs, N.J.: Prentice-Hall, Inc., 1965.

Glueck, Sheldon, *The Problem of Delinquency*. Boston: Houghton Mifflin Company, 1959.

Healy, William, and Augusta F. Bronner, *New Light on Delinquency and Its Treatment*. New Haven, Conn.: Yale University Press, 1936. Page 70.

Kvaraceus, William C., "Delinquent Behavior and Church Attendance," *Sociology and Social Research*, XXVIII (March–April, 1944), 289.

Lee, Robert, "Delinquent Youth in a Normless Time," *The Christian Century,* LXXIX (December 5, 1962), 1475-1478.

Lunden, Walter A., *Statistics on Delinquents and Delinquency.* Springfield, Ill.: Charles C. Thomas, Publisher, 1964.

Middleton, Warren C., and Paul J. Fay, "Attitudes of Delinquent and Non-delinquent Girls Toward Sunday Observance, the Bible, and War," *The Journal of Educational Psychology,* XXXII (October, 1941), 555-558.

Mursall, George Rex, *A Study of Religious Training as a Psychological Factor in Criminality.* Columbus, Ohio: Ohio State University, 1940.

Quay, Herbert, and contributors, *Juvenile Delinquency: Research and Theory.* Princeton, N.J.: D. Van Nostrand Co., Inc., 1965.

Sister M. Dominic, "Religion and the Juvenile Delinquent," *American Catholic Sociological Review,* XV (October, 1954), 264.

Wattenberg, William E., "Church Attendance and Juvenile Misconduct," *Sociology and Social Research,* XXXIV (January, 1950), 195-202.

Winter, Gibson, *The New Creation as Metropolis.* New York: The Macmillan Company, 1963.

Young, Pauline V., *Social Treatment in Probation and Delinquency.* New York: McGraw-Hill Book Company, 1952. Page 445.

7 Prevention
Through the School

William E. Amos

Education is one of the most potent forces in the development of an individual or of a nation. The acceptance of this thesis has influenced the public schools of our country to adhere to the philosophy that every child is entitled to an education that will allow him to develop to his fullest and give him the opportunity of freedom of choice in making life's decisions. A democracy is based on the assumption that all men are valuable and have dignity and worth. However, the problem, even in a democracy, is whether this assumption concerning human nature will be allowed to become a reality.

What is the nature of human nature? Scores of books by authorities from various fields have attempted to answer this question. For the purpose of our discussion we will define it in a single word. This is not an attempt to oversimplify or to cast reflection on the scholarly studies that have described in detail the very complex nature of the subject. It is an attempt, however, to relate it meaningfully to the problem at hand: the behavior of young people in the educative process. The descriptive term that we would use is *potentiality*. A child at birth possesses no learned behavioral skills: He is only a few pounds of potentiality waiting to be shaped by his life experiences. As a result, we say that the child is a product of his culture. One of the principal purposes of any culture is to pass on its way of life to the young. This includes the attitudes and values of the group as well as its artifacts and institutions. From his many experiences and the meanings that he applies to them, the child develops the concept of himself as a person. In other words, we say that the self-concept is a derivation of meaning from experiences.

The school as one of the principal socializing agencies of our culture has a unique opportunity to influence behavior and to mold the character of the youngsters in its charge. From the expressions of discontent from many sources during the past decade, one could assume that the schools have completely failed in their responsibilities. In some ways this criticism is warranted and in others it is completely unjust. The public school system has greater holding power today than ever before in its history. Over two-thirds of all youngsters who enter the first grade remain to complete high school. The technical, cultural, and humanistic advances of the past decade emerged from the foundation laid by a public school system that has been given responsibilities far beyond that of any other social agency in our culture. The school, through a combination of public apathy, home neglect, and public pressure, has attempted to become all things to all children without the resources, knowledge, or public support to succeed. The school may feed, clothe, teach, treat, transport, and counsel our young. These services have been influenced and molded by the middle-class philosophy of our school as the principal agency to shape our youth.

Because of its universality as well as its actual and potential resources, the school is in a central position to mount an attack on juvenile delinquency. However, the primary causes for delinquent behavior lie outside of the school. Although it is obligated to carry its share of the community's load in detecting and controlling norm-violating behavior, whether of a psychological or cultural etiology, it has neither the obligation nor the resources to carry the primary burden of effecting cures. Its functional role is performing the teaching-learning process within which it will maximally contribute to the prevention of norm-violating behavior.

At this point it is important to note that although some of the norm-violating behavior manifested by youngsters is due to emotional disturbances (25 per cent), the cause of the vast majority of the cases can be traced to cultural deprivation (75 per cent, of which all but five per cent are members of the lower class).[1]

What is required are programs of education that effectively meet the needs of all—"good" schools—including the needs of the potential delinquent as well as those of the slow learner, academically gifted, physically handicapped, and other special categories in addition to the "normal" youngster.

Although the quality of education varies widely from community to community, and much remains to be done, the schools as a whole have

---

[1] William C. Kvaraceus and Walter B. Miller, *Delinquent Behavior: Culture and the Individual* (Washington, D.C., National Education Association, 1959), pp. 54–55.

made substantial progress in recent years in improving programs for those youngsters who have come from homes that fall in the social categories between lower-middle-class and upper-middle-class, those in which delinquency due to cultural deprivation is uncommon. The effect on upper-class youngsters has been less pronounced because many are exposed to the environment of private institutions. However, for those youngsters who are members of lower-class society—the poverty culture—the disadvantaged youth—the schools have not been as successful in meeting the challenge. Various cities concerned with this lack of success have made efforts to develop imaginative programs.

Gary, Indiana, is one of the cities in the United States that has established special classes and schools for truants, delinquents, and pre-delinquents. These schools give special consideration to the size of classes, curriculum adjustment, specially trained teachers, and, above all, the individual needs and interests of the children. Attendance is not compulsory, and the sessions last only half a day. Casework counseling is provided for the parents.[2]

The well-known "600" schools of New York City operate on a similar "special school" system. They provide intensive services to disruptive and delinquent children. In addition to other assets, these schools relieve regular classrooms of severe behavioral problems. New York City has also developed the "700" schools for children with more serious and consistent problems, especially youths convicted by the courts who could not be placed in appropriate institutions because of lack of space.[3]

Criticisms of both programs are the same. They handle only a fraction of the children needing specialized attention and there is some disagreement as to how participating students should be selected. The principals usually pick the children that they feel should be sent to a special school. Some authorities believe that the Bureau of Child Guidance should have this responsibility.

In December, 1956, a unique program to stimulate disadvantaged children to higher scholastic achievement was begun in Junior High School No. 43 in Manhattan. The program, later known as Higher Horizons, included increased guidance and counseling personnel, and a number of special instructional and remedial services were provided. Methods were devised to broaden the children's cultural experiences, and contacts between school personnel and parents were intensified. When necessary, even medical and financial assistance was provided.[4]

[2] Herbert C. Quay, *Juvenile Delinquency* (Princeton, N.J.: D. Van Nostrand Company, Inc., 1956), p. 324.

[3] *Ibid.*, p. 325.

[4] W. E. Amos, Raymond Manella, and Marilyn Southwell, *Action Programs for Delinquency Prevention* (Springfield, Ill.: Charles C. Thomas, Publisher, 1965), pp. 86–94.

Based on the results of this project, an expanded program was launched in 1959. By 1962, 76 public schools serving over 64,000 pupils were involved. The regular staff of the participating schools was augmented by hundreds of additional teachers and counselors. Similar projects have been developed in thirteen major cities. Higher Horizons may not be a panacea for the educational ills of all major urban areas, but the fact remains that thousands of pupils have improved scholastically while participating.

Kingston, New York, hopes to change behavioral patterns of children with poor backgrounds and to instill in them the importance of proper school behavior and achievement to enable them to accomplish their goals. This is attempted in a number of ways: instruction in reading, writing, and language arts; group and individual counseling sessions; development of cultural interests; in-service teacher training; visits to the community and the homes; guest speakers; and an improved student-teacher ratio. All participants in this program are from a low socioeconomic area and are between the fourth and eleventh grades.[5]

Milwaukee's work-study program for predelinquents demonstrates the effects of half-time work in combination with half-time school attendance on adolescents who have shown delinquent behavior. Boys from junior and senior high schools throughout the city are participants. They receive academic and vocational training plus remedial work and guidance.[6]

San Diego has initiated a program that is basically an exploration of the relationship among an individual's school experiences, subsequent dropout, and delinquent behavior. The school is examined as a social system to locate sources of strain and tension. Recognition is given to the fact that the school is an ever increasing conditioning agency for attitudes, values, beliefs, skills, and standards. Lower-class youths are led to want certain things, via the prevailing middle-class orientation of the schools, that are not realistically available to them. This project hopes to find answers concerning the sources of frustration and their ramifications within the school.[7]

The Quincy, Illinois, Youth Development Project proposes to enrich the early educational experiences of culturally handicapped elementary school children through a modified curriculum of out-of-school educational experiences and through greater parental involvement in the education of their children. The program aims to prevent school failures, job

[5] *Inventory of Compensatory Education Projects*, School of Education, University of Chicago, Illinois, 1965 (mimeo.), p. 8.
[6] *Ibid.*
[7] *National Institute of Mental Health Grants Related to Crime and Delinquency*, R11–633 (Washington, D.C.: Advisory Mental Health Council, 1965).

failures, and resultant delinquency by supplying experiences prerequisite to the usual school curriculum but neglected in preschool years.[8] There are indications that the program has had some success in reducing delinquency, but it is believed that it must begin in the primary grades to have the desired effect.

The Urban Service Corps of the District of Columbia public school system is composed of volunteers who offer their services through a variety of programs. Under the direct supervision of an Assistant Superintendent of Schools, the volunteers serve as counseling and remedial reading aides, recreation workers, job development personnel, and they help operate various programs aimed toward preventing dropouts and delinquent behavior. Churches have provided space for study centers as well as staff to supervise them. Parents of the children are also given assistance by volunteers in such areas as budgeting, home repairs, and food preparation. The Corps operates its programs for the entire school system as well as for nonschool youth agencies.[9]

Kansas City's work-study program to prevent juvenile delinquency was begun in 1960. The program has three stages. The first is an orientation period that is composed of half-day classroom activities and half-day work assignments. After one to two years at this stage, the child moves to the second level, where the half-day work experience is paid employment. After having reached the age of seventeen or eighteen, a youngster may enter the final stage—full-time employment, still under the supervision of school personnel.[10]

However, in too many instances, these programs have been isolated, fragmented efforts that have had a negligible impact on the social problems of the lower class. A positive ray of hope, however, has emerged in the past few years in the form of public awareness and social consciousness. Efforts are under way to design meaningful, long-term, comprehensive programs that will strike at the heart of the various problems that allow the lower class to contribute such a disproportionate number of juvenile delinquents. In order for these programs to succeed they must be directed at the following:

1. *The development of a new value system.* Young people who are products of deprivation, discrimination, rejection, and frustration have a value system that is not compatible with the expectations of society. They have limited hope for any personal success in their futures. As they go through school they carry with them attitudes, drawn from their home

[8] *Programs for the Educationally Disadvantaged* (Washington, D.C.: U.S. Department of Health, Education, and Welfare, 1963), p. 58.
[9] Amos, *op. cit.*, pp. 64–73.
[10] George W. Burchill, *Work-Study Programs for Alienated Youth* (Chicago: Science Research Associates, Inc., 1962), pp. 133–141.

surroundings, that do not agree with those of teachers, educational organizations, or textbook publishers. Therefore, when these youngsters grow into their teens and stand on the threshold of jobs, the effects of deprivation are sharply etched on their personalities. They bear the marks of poverty and fear, and they are frequently barricaded behind a wall of silence because of a basic inability to relate to a new and alien culture.

The concept of long-term goals is completely unrealistic in the minds of most of these youth. "Live today and be rewarded today" is a philosophy that carries over into antisocial acts on the streets and in the communities. Their value system gives only limited status to academic success, hard work, and dependability. In many cases, a youth from this subculture has never had an opportunity to learn his sex role from a stable adult figure. He has seen the male as a transient who shirks his family responsibility, and he has seen the status figures in his life as the operator, con man, and manipulator. Various studies have shown that the parents of the disadvantaged, in both city and country, may place a high value on education for their children, although they themselves are largely under-educated.[11] Yet in spite of this respect for education per se, a majority of these parents cannot or do not give their children adequate support and encouragement either to attend school regularly or to study at home. This lack of family support places an extraordinary responsibility on the school system. Yet these young people generally go to schools that have the poorest facilities, the most crowded classrooms, and the most over-burdened teaching staffs. When they enter the labor market, the lifetime tradition of disadvantage is continued, and their deprived background is manifested in their unemployability.

2. *Programs to improve employability.* As a result of the problems mentioned above as well as others, the youths from high-delinquency areas may be severely limited in their employability. The programs that creative and responsive school administrators must develop will be concerned with the following manifestations exhibited by the youth in their charge.[12]

(a) They may function below their potential because of a deficiency in educational background or because they do not know of the various employment opportunities to which they could aspire.

(b) They may have such low self-esteem that it is difficult for them to see themselves as able to acquire or hold jobs for which they are otherwise capable. They may even be reluctant to train for better jobs in

[11] Frank Riessman, *The Culturally Deprived Child* (New York: Harper & Row, Publishers, 1962), pp. 10–15.

[12] William E. Amos, "Disadvantaged Youth: Recognizing the Problem," *Employment Security Review* (September, 1964), pp. 42–46.

the belief they will find nothing open to them, which is based on the observed experiences of their friends and families.

(c) They may be socially undeveloped, act impulsively, and have difficulty getting along with co-workers and employers. They may not understand how to accept supervision, to develop and learn under it, or to tolerate any implied criticism. They may be irresponsible, lacking middle-class standards of reliability. They may not show up on time for interviews, be late for work, or not show up at all for several days: Punctuality is often not expected or practiced in their home environments.

(d) Some may be bitter and disillusioned, with hidden or obvious hostility. Others will have a sense of powerlessness in the face of overwhelming obstacles. Some will compensate with an overaggressive manner, but more will be inarticulate and withdrawn from adults.

(e) Many disadvantaged youths are products of inferior segregated schools that have not prepared them to succeed in a competitive society. This is true not only of those young people who have failed to complete high school but also of many of those who have graduated without acquiring the necessary basic skills to enable successful occupational growth.

3. *Improving the self-concept of the delinquency-prone child.* Frederick Elkins defines socialization as the process by which someone learns the ways of a given society or social group so that he can function within it.[13] The child must internalize these experiences and, as a result, develop feelings and attitudes concerning himself in relation to others. The product of these experiences is how the child sees himself. Behavioral scientists have for some years accepted the thesis that how one sees himself is reflected in his behavior. The youth who has been exposed to the socialization process of the lower class develops in many instances a concept of himself as a person who is inadequate, has little chance of success, and must fight for every gain. He may be so insecure and anxious that he reacts physically to any threatening situation. Not only is he inadequate in his own viewpoint, but he sees the world as a place where the strong survive and the weak are overcome. He lacks a strong self-concept that would offer insulation against delinquent behavior and provide internal strength by which he could benefit from whatever resources he has. Too many of these youngsters are pushed out of school and into delinquent behavior because of a negative concept of themselves and the world. This concept may or may not be accurate, depending on the status that the culture places on a particular act, achievement, or thing. For example, it has been shown that delinquents underestimate

[13] Frederick Elkins, *The Child and Society* (New York, Random House, Inc., 1960), p. 4.

their academic and social abilities while overestimating the status-loaded physical capabilities that they may possess.[14]

Students of the problem are in general agreement that in order for the school to take effective steps toward the discharge of its obligation to provide meaningful education to all boys and girls, including special emphasis on the imperatives of delinquency prevention, the following steps must be undertaken:[15]

1. More adequate financial support of education, with emphasis on the equalization of educational opportunity for culturally and financially deprived communities.
2. The professional preparation, recruitment, and rewarding of higher quality teachers who understand the culture, nature, and needs of the children of the community in which they teach.
3. The development and implementation of curricula that will be meaningful and effective in the lives of the children of the community.
4. The integration of special instructional services into the total school program.
5. The provision of pupil personnel and guidance services staffed by guidance counselors and other specialists who understand the culture, nature, and needs of the children of the community.
6. Leadership by the school in the organization and continued operation of coordinated community efforts on behalf of youth, including the prevention and control of delinquency.
7. Where existing administrative structures impede direct and effective services to youth, the recognition and organization of novel administrative structures that can attack the problems.

Equalization of Educational Opportunity Through Financial Support

During the past three decades there has been increasing recognition on the part of educators and economists of the wide variation among states and among local communities in their ability to support education and therefore the consequent wide variation in the quality of educational programs. The continued growth of geographical mobility of the population affects people and communities far removed from the locale of low-quality education. But the public and legislators have been slow to accept the facts and to take action that requires a broadening of the financial

14 William E. Amos, "A Study of Self-Concept: Delinquent Boys' Accuracy in Selected Self-Evaluation," *Genetic Psychology Monographs* (1963)
15 Deborah Partridge Wolfe, "The School's Role in Preventing Juvenile Delinquency," *Journal of Education Sociology* (October, 1962), pp. 87–88.

support of education. Now new emphasis has been given to these necessities by President Johnson and has been expanded to include a concentration of expenditures and efforts on culturally deprived neighborhoods.[16]

More adequate financial support by funneling money and "know-how" into culturally deprived communities can result in a concentration on those areas whose youth are most seriously in need of meaningful and useful educational experiences. Designed to combat problems of high dropout rates and deficiencies in preparation for employment, these measures should also do much to ameliorate juvenile delinquency that is closely related to leaving school early and unemployability. From whatever sources this additional money comes, it must be put to work as expenditures for the special and additional approaches and services outlined above and discussed further in more detail.

Quality Teachers

The pivot around which the success or failure of the school moves is the classroom teacher. The most appropriate curriculum, the most elaborate special instructional offerings, and the best staffed and most functional pupil personnel and guidance service are utterly dependent on the effective work of the teacher. It is the teacher who has the continuous contact with boys and girls, who largely determines their attitudes toward school and their progress in it, who understands and treats them as individuals or fails to do so, who utilizes special instructional services and pupil personnel and guidance services or who fails to do so, and who *is* the school in the eyes of the community.

Kvaraceus has described what the teacher is, believes, and will do in effective delinquency prevention and control in the following terms:[17]

1. Likes children, believes in them, and is glad to be with them, even when they are sometimes noisy, dirty, and annoying.
2. Knows each pupil as a person and develops a strong personal relationship.
3. Displays positive attitudes toward behavioral deviates as needing aid and understanding.
4. Remains free of emotional entanglements with the young offender, his peer group, and his family.
5. Differentiates and adapts curriculum to the varied interests and abilities of all class members.

[16] U.S. House of Representatives, "Education Program," Message from the President of the United States, 89th Congress, 1st Session, Document No. 45 (Washington, D.C.: U.S. Government Printing Office, 1965).

[17] William C. Kvaraceus, "Teachers and Delinquency," *NEA Journal* (November 1958), p. 523.

6. Works with a diagnostic point of view, always asking the key question: "*Why* this behavior?"
7. Uses available special services and resources: counselor, psychologist, school nurse, caseworker.
8. Participates in case conferences and treatment programs as part of the school-community team.
9. Maintains close liaison with the student's home.
10. Functions as a parent surrogate, offering a good (even exciting and glamorous) imitative example with which to identify.

Relatively few teachers today have the attitudes, preparation, time, reasonably sized classes, or administrative support to carry out such an ambitious program. In view of their basic responsibility to teach subject matter to a group of youngsters within the classroom, it must be recognized that until such time as increased financial support results in much lower pupil-teacher ratios and relief of teachers from onerous clerical chores, and provides more modern teaching aids, such programs will be mostly fiction with very little fact.

Although recognizing fully the limitations of time and facilities, it is well for teachers and all others concerned to remember that effective teaching is based on the personal relationship between a teacher and her pupils. Those teachers who possess and display an understanding of the heterogeneous mass of pupils in their charge and who demonstrate a warmth in their attitude toward their varied backgrounds and behaviors can accomplish much, even though opportunities for specific and differentiated services may be limited. In other words, although a "point of view" is not enough, it will go far with many youngsters in developing a feeling on their part that they are valued and, in general, understood.

An attempt to prepare school personnel for service to socially and culturally disadvantaged children in which the "school will emerge as the sole and major consistently stabilizing influence in their lives" is the notable Project Beacon of Yeshiva University.[18] A study of the characteristics of disadvantaged youngsters resulted in a division of training required for school personnel into the following three categories: home, community, and school analysis; child appraisal; and psychoeducational process and guided development.

Under the first category, Project Beacon points out that "The usual social class, economic group, and cultural system identifications of school personnel in the United States render most of such persons deficient in their knowledge and attitudes toward people and neighborhoods which constitute the families and homes of children from disadvantaged back-

[18] U.S. House of Representatives, Committee on Education and Labor, *Pioneer Ideas in Education*, 88th Congress, 1st Session (Washington, D.C.: U.S. Government Printing Office, 1963), pp. 75–83.

grounds."[19] Therefore, in order to correct the cultural biases common to those whose background is "American, white, middle class," teachers are helped to become aware of the factors influencing the behavior of pupils and parents from disadvantaged areas. These studies probe family disorganization and familial patterns; patterns of community disorganization such as poverty, delinquency, unemployment, migrancy, and illiteracy; cultural biases toward study, social advancement, postponement of gratifications, cultural loyalties, etc.; insight by teachers into their own backgrounds, abilities, and values that tend to create biases; and private and public community welfare organizations that attempt to meet human needs in deprived communities.

Project Beacon has used this analysis as a basis for the development of courses in the urban community, ethnic relations, social psychology of education, psychology of minority group children, and guidance services in education. These courses are supplemented by field work at the preservice level to improve the practicality and meaningfulness of the more formal studies. Project Beacon also provides a study of the school as an institution and of individual and group interaction in the classroom through classes, seminars, and lectures.

In the areas of child appraisal and psychoeducational processes, the approach is more traditional but with greater emphasis on the culturally disadvantaged than has been common to most efforts in measurement, diagnosis, and various phases of educational psychology in the past.

The recruitment of capable teachers for disadvantaged schools has been a problem for years. Teachers are reluctant to join the faculties of such schools because of the problems of student behavior, lack of professional stimulation and recognition, and a minimum of personal satisfaction from outstanding student successes. In order to facilitate the recruitment of capable teachers, imaginative programs must be developed. They may include these techniques:

1. Extra salary for teaching in disadvantaged schools.
2. Tuition-free graduate courses for in-service teachers and other appropriate staff development activities.
3. A plan to provide sabbatical leaves or rotation assignments after a period of several years.
4. Public and professional recognition of the efforts and successes of the staff.
5. The necessary supportive services, such as guidance counselors, psychologists, social workers, teacher aids, health services, and subject matter resource persons, which will allow the staff to plan and carry out the necessary remedial programs.

[19] *Ibid.*

6. Adequate staff, which will allow the number of pupils in classes to be limited.

Meaningful and Effective Curriculum

Orville Johnson has pointed out that a meaningful and effective curriculum must reflect the following:

1. The curriculum must reflect the characteristics of the child or group of children for whom it is designed.
2. The curriculum must take into consideration the educational, vocational, and social prognosis of the individuals.
3. The curriculum should reflect the environment of the individual in order that he will learn to live as effective a life as possible within that environment and eventually make changes to better it.[20]

In contrast to the above principles, we can ask ourselves what the actualities of the learning experiences provided in the typical American high school are and why more emphasis has been placed on enunciating these principles than on practicing them.

The dominant middle-class culture of the country, in contrast to that of the culturally deprived, is well described by the anthropologist E. Adamson Hoebel in four values that dominate the American way of life. They are reported by Wrenn[21] as follows:

1. *The notion of progress.* Material and social conditions are constantly improvable. There is an unceasing ferment to develop better laws, better education, and more satisfying ways of spending leisure time.
2. *A rational universe.* In general we prefer to apply the scientific method rather than to rely on chance or mysticism. In this, says Hoebel, we are exceeded only by Russia among the world's cultures. We act as if we believed that man directs his own destiny. We are a nation of doers, a people who believe in action ("there ought to be a law"), not merely contemplation.
3. *Equal opportunity.* Each person should have the opportunity to exercise his special abilities in a manner that is personally satisfying and socially useful. Among the consequences of this belief are the ideal of universal education, a distrust of authority, a fluid status system, and an intense drive to "succeed." Success is often symbolized by money, but the things money can buy may be valued less for themselves than for what they proclaim about a person's abilities and personal fulfillment.

[20] Orville G. Johnson, *Education for Slow Learners* (Englewood Cliffs, N.J.: Prentice-Hall, Inc., 1963).

[21] Gilbert C. Wrenn, *The Counselor in a Changing World* (Washington, D.C.: American Personnel and Guidance Association, 1962).

4. *Looking ahead.* The American value system is future-oriented. The "golden age" is always yet to be realized. We count on change, even though we may not be satisfied when we get it and tend to see real improvement as still ahead.

The American schools, especially the high schools, have been slow to adjust to the fact that they must become the schools of *all* the people. Those youngsters not bound for college have been devaluated by being shunted into the "general" course, little more than a watered-down version of the college preparatory course, or into vocational or commercial courses. The all too common basis for such segregation has been negative—the lack of ability or interest in the college preparatory program—rather than positive—the possession of potentialities to succeed in and profit from other school programs. The common question directed to students, "Are you going to college or not?" has served by implication to downgrade those who have not planned to pursue their education at the college level. It is only fair to recognize that this categorization into a positive-negative dichotomy has been due not entirely to an attitude of mind, but also to the lack of a term that adequately describes those planning to follow other activities than those related to college.

Another factor has been the strong opposition to preparation for employability within the school on the grounds that the proper function of the school is to prepare for citizenship and "the good life." The necessity to have the wherewithal to purchase "the good life" has often been ignored as well as the more realistic recognition by both youngsters and their parents that ability to earn a living is fundamental.

Pertinent is the following from the Senate Subcommittee to Investigate Juvenile Delinquency:

> The inquiry into the relationship between youth employment and juvenile delinquency has shown that in so many instances young people are not ready for employment. It has been shown that frequently when the curriculum needs of pupils are not met, they lose interest in their classwork and drop out of school as soon as the law will permit them to do so. These young people are not prepared to compete in employment placement. Either they do not find a job or they fail in job after job. Guidance personnel have pointed out that aside from the particular study programs which young high school pupils experience, those that failed were found to lack personality or character qualifications. They did not take advantage of their school opportunities. Frequently, those that failed in school then carry their personality problems with them to their jobs and fail again. There is a need for sound planning and constructive action in these areas.[22]

[22] U.S. Senate, *Interim Report of the Subcommittee to Investigate Juvenile Delinquency of the Committee on the Judiciary, Youth Employment and Juvenile Delinquency* (Washington, D.C.: U.S. Government Printing Office, 1955), p. 17.

To advocate courses that will make youngsters employable does not mean that all will be trained with specific vocational skills. The first requisite has been pointed out by Odell: "In such curriculum a heavier emphasis should be placed on basic knowledge required for successful job performance, such as reading, writing and speaking, basic mathematics, good work habits, and a sense of achievement through successful completion of prescribed tasks."[23] These imperatives have recently been recognized and implemented, interestingly enough, by the Federal Government, in the 1963 Youth Amendments to the Manpower Development and Training Act and the Economic Opportunity Act of 1964.

Another needed development is that of work-study programs at the secondary level. Such programs, now enrolling small numbers under the restrictions of the distributive education program with grants-in-aid from the Federal Government, would provide youngsters with the opportunity to try a variety of work situations through which they could not only earn income but also explore occupations and their own aptitudes and interests, observe and absorb good work habits and attitudes, and engage in some activities so meaningful to them that they would be more likely to accept gracefully the other more formal aspects of the school program not of immediate concern to them and continue longer in school.

A meaningful and effective curriculum that would more nearly meet the needs of delinquency-prone youths consists of more than preparation for employability as has been stressed in this section. The principles enunciated by Johnson extend our concern into other areas of youngsters' lives and call for differentiation of instruction based on individual differences, the cultivation of constructive leisure time activities, provision of opportunities to develop skills in democratic living, such as realistic types of student government, and capitalization on the curiosity of youngsters in developing intellectual interests and the appreciation of good literature. Moreover, Kvaraceus and Ulrich point out that "The curriculum is tailormade and planned to fit the general and special social, cultural, and economic needs of the local school-community."[24]

Special Instructional Services

These special services, which must be coordinated with and integrated into the total educational program, should reflect the particular needs and problems of the youngsters and the communities from which they come. Basically these programs fall into two categories. First, there are those that are an integral part of the regular classroom activities but are

[23] U.S. Senate, *Hearings Before the Subcommittee to Investigate Juvenile Delinquency, Youth Employment,* 84th Congress, 1st Session (Washington, D.C.: U.S. Government Printing Office, 1955), p. 53.

[24] William C. Kvaraceus and William E. Ulrich, *Delinquent Behavior—Principles and Practices* (Washington, D.C.: National Education Association, 1959), p. 88.

tailormade to meet the needs of a comparatively small number of students. They must lean heavily on the diagnostic, interpretive, and case-finding assistance of pupil personnel and guidance services to which they are closely related but of which they are not a part.

Following diagnostic evaluation and testing by specialists in the pupil personnel and guidance service, those who have difficulty in most of the subject matter areas, especially in basic skills, will receive special help from regular teachers. If youngsters have weaknesses in speech, reading, mathematics, sight, or hearing or have physical or emotional disabilities, they will be assigned to specifically prepared remedial teachers on a full- or part-time basis. Moreover, services for those restricted to the home with emotional disturbances or physical handicaps are often needed.

Secondly, there are those services that must prepare a child so that he may take advantage of the opportunities that the American public educational system offers. It has become apparent in recent years that by the time a child who comes from a deprived area enters the first grade he is so handicapped by his sterile environment that he is fighting an uphill battle that he never overcomes. His deprivation may not be apparent when he first enters school. However, as time goes on, the effects of his environment will increasingly retard his progress by limiting both his interest in and ability to deal with materials that have little meaning or relevance to his experience. Consequently, he will be labeled "dull." This will be accentuated by the fact that he may be noticeably slow, lacking in communication skills, inattentive, and have a short attention span. Sometimes he appears passive (the better to stay out of trouble), although inwardly he may seethe with hostility, or he may be a "troublemaker," acting out his hostility.

To preclude such occurrences, preschool programs for youngsters of deprived areas must be developed. Children may enter these programs as early as age three and are involved several hours a day. The child must be offered experiences that will insulate him against the negative environment to which he returns each afternoon. Instead of reinforcing the efforts of the home, the preschool programs, in many instances, must overcome them. Such programs would include reading sessions, field trips, group games, creative opportunities, films, and individual play. They would allow for the development of relationships with adults as well as other children and provide the opportunity for personal achievements as well as group successes.

The preschool program may be complemented by evening programs providing study space, library facilities, and tutoring services for the children in the regular school program. Few of the homes that these children come from can provide study space and reference materials. The school and the community must provide these services if a realistic effort is made.

Pupil Personnel and Guidance Services

To help meet the challenge of the complex and rapidly changing modern world and the variety of backgrounds and needs of youth, teachers need specialized assistance in providing educational services beyond the time and competency that they possess. Out of this need have grown special school services, unique to the schools of this country, to place emphasis on, constantly stress, and provide help to individuals as individuals—a differentiating function of education. This is in contrast to the group technique that traditionally has existed, and in a system of mass education, will continue to exist in an educational program built around the classroom teaching of subject matter. This is not to say that subject matter is the end and children only the means, that teachers are not obligated to understand, appreciate, and empathize with their pupils and make all possible provisions for individual differences and needs, or that they have no part to play in providing guidance and other individualized services to youth. However, their efforts must be supplemented, and they require special help in meeting the needs of the individual in the form of organized and professionally staffed pupil personnel and guidance services.

The need for and value of such services in all school systems has been recognized by educational authorities for years. However, budget limitations and lack of public support have limited the services that could be provided. Characteristically, the schools with the greatest need received the smallest allocation of available services because they had fewer local spokesmen. As a result, those schools in the more disadvantaged areas received only token service in most instances. If a meaningful effort is to be made in salvaging the thousands of youngsters who attend such schools, the necessary pupil personnel services must be made available beginning with the preschool programs, when these are available, and certainly no later than the beginning of the formal school program, generally at age six.

Pupil personnel services include child accounting and attendance services, psychological services, health services, and social services manned by educators, psychologists, physicians, nurses, and social workers, all of which is pointed up and molded together by guidance services conducted by school guidance counselors who are "general specialists" in education with strong backgrounds in psychology, anthropology, sociology, and economics through their basic professional preparation and experience in education.

Guidance services assist the individual *as an individual* in the process of his educational, social, and vocational development leading to wise choices and adjustments. This process includes the development of self-understanding and self-acceptance, the appraisal of the realities of the present and probable future socioeconomic environment, and the integration of these two variables. Their purpose is to focus the goals of education on the individual in order to further both personal satisfaction and socioeconomic effectiveness. Concerned with the welfare of all young people, the "essentially normal" as well as deviates and the disadvantaged, these services provide information about the needs and desires of students and about the realistic requirements of the socioeconomic environment necessary for the improvement of the educational system.

As to the prevention of delinquency, pupil personnel and guidance services, in close cooperation with teachers, school administrators, and the nonschool agencies of the community, assist in the understanding of the cultural patterns of deprived neighborhoods, encourage and help teachers and administrators to provide appropriate educational programs, develop and implement plans for early detection and counseling through group guidance techniques, contribute to the control of norm-violating behavior, and consult with and refer to nonschool agencies those whom the school can no longer serve. The staff involved in these services may provide a bridge between the home and the school, which will allow better communication to take place. They may also provide a stable male figure in the lives of youngsters who have never before experienced such a relationship.

Few guidance counselors and nurses, psychologists, and social workers who, along with others, compose the personnel of well-staffed pupil personnel services, possess the background of experience and professional preparation essential for dealing with culturally deprived youth. However, the preservice and in-service professional upgrading of school guidance counselors has made some progress since the enactment of the National Defense Education Act of 1958. Opportunities for pupil personnel specialists to pursue courses of the type previously outlined in Project Beacon would be helpful.

Although the quantity as well as the quality of school guidance counselors has been raised since the inception of the NDEA, many schools do not have effective pupil personnel and guidance services. Significant in this connection were the recommendations to Congress by President Johnson that supplementary educational centers and services should be provided both for public and private school youngsters.[25]

Coordinated Community Efforts

Characteristically, school administrators have been reluctant to become a part of a total community effort to alleviate a social ill if it has

[25] U.S. House of Representatives, The President's Message, pp. 5–6.

meant the weakening of their administrative authority and an increased role at the policy level for various citizen groups. This has been justified for the most part because the goals of many citizen or pressure groups are ill defined, emotionally motivated, and may be contrary to good administrative or educational practices. However, the schools have been remiss in their responsibility to the public to keep them informed and to consider the opinions, needs, and desires of all citizens in the operation of the public schools.

In the past few years, however, an increased willingness to be a part of the whole has been reflected by many school systems as they became involved in a comprehensive, unified effort on the part of a community to solve its social and economic ills. This increased cohesiveness has been reflected in some imaginative programs aimed at the disadvantaged, delinquency-prone child.

It is most essential that the school should assume leadership in the organization and operation of a community, delinquency-control program. No other public agency in our culture has the day-to-day responsibility for and contact with the child. The school is in a position to coordinate and distribute services that influence the total life span of the child. In order for the school to assume its rightful leadership role in this time of social protest and upheaval, it must reflect great sensitivity as well as fortitude and dedication.

The following are points of major importance in any such program:

1. School administrators have long been aware of the value of neighborhood schools and the integral part that they should play in the life of the child, the family, and the community. Unfortunately, the slum schools, with their decaying physical plants, operating with inadequate resources and being responsible for children with multiple problems and shunted into the background of the community consciousness, have been unable to carry out their responsibilities. As a result there have been increased efforts on the part of various pressure groups, particularly those representing various minority groups, to weaken the role of the neighborhood school in the battle to overcome de facto segregation. Usually this has meant the "bussing" of youngsters to other schools. Regardless of its good intentions or the sympathy we may feel for this action, there is limited evidence at this time that children benefit from such moves, and programs of this type will affect only a limited number of children.

What must be done immediately, besides such experimental programs, is to upgrade the quality of education and services in the neighborhood school until it becomes a local fortress in the battle against ignorance, crime, disease, and poverty. These schools must become centers of all community services. Representatives of the Departments of Welfare, Health, Recreation, employment services, and other social agencies must be housed here. Adult education programs must be available in the evening together with library services, tutoring services, and recreation facilities for the students. Cultural programs as well as civic activities should be centered here. The neighborhood school must become a radiating complex of services, resources, and encouragement to the various islands of despair and poverty that surrounds it.

2. To provide the kinds of services that are mentioned above, increased resources are needed. Various programs that are involved in the current war on poverty will contribute greatly, but this is not enough. There is a scarcity of outstanding teachers and pupil personnel. In the past, an unduly large percentage have been assigned to the schools in the more affluent areas. In the future, they must be assigned to schools on the basis of realistic need, a need that will allow a guidance counselor to be reassigned from a school where he was helping a middle-class youngster to select a college to a school where he may help a lower-class youngster gain enough hope and control to stay out of a training school. The auxiliary services that the families of our middle and upper classes have come to expect from school resources may have to be provided by the family and socializing agencies other than the school so that the school can concentrate on areas of greatest need.

3. The school in the past few years has not done an adequate job in training youngsters for available jobs. Industry must inform the schools of what type of skills it will need in the future, and the schools must be flexible enough to provide these resources. This entails the use of representatives of labor and management in curriculum development and advisory committees. The schools of our smaller communities must be willing to train young people of that area for jobs that will be available in other areas. No longer can the boundaries of the school district dictate the responsibility of a school system.

Administrative Structure

One of the principal purposes of any administrative organization or design is to provide a framework in which the program or operational elements can be carried out in an efficient manner. In developing programs to improve educational and related services in disadvantaged areas, each school system must analyze its administrative organization to insure that all available resources will be efficiently directed in those areas where the need is greatest. In those cities or urban areas where there is a specific target area or where the disadvantaged schools are, for the most part, physically located in one area, it may be advisable to designate a person at the assistant superintendent level to act as the superintendent or chief administrative officer for all schools located in the specific area. This would take the form of a special school district within a larger system. Washington, D.C., has recently initiated such a plan for the Cardozo area of the city. This places the responsibility for utilization of resources in the hands of one person. It also demands that this person have authority and administrative control of the resources that are available for use.

In those areas where there are scattered pockets of poverty and deprivation and where, as a result, there may be several target areas, it is more advisable to have a person either working the assistant superintendent level or functioning as a special assistant to the superintendent to coordinate the resources throughout the system as well as in the community and personally to keep the superintendent informed as to successes and problems. In either of these plans, it is imperative that the board of education, through the superintendent, given support to this program and direct what resources will be made available and what the lines of authority may be.

The resources of the entire community must be utilized, and a major responsibility for any administrator concerned with such a program would be to maintain direct liaison with other community agencies and organizations that may be in a position to provide services for the various programs. Such programs as part-time employment that will allow youngsters to stay in school should be coordinated with the local employment service offices. Child welfare services may provide necessary clothing and medical services. Various volunteer and private agencies may provide money for transportation and lunches where needed, as well as tutoring and motivational services. There are many programs throughout the country where volunteer groups are making significant contributions in various educational and motivational activities that are part of the regular public school program.

Conclusion

The school is one of the principal socializing agencies of our culture and has an unusual opportunity to influence the behavior of the young people in its charge. There has been much criticism of the schools during the past decade. Some of this criticism has been unfair, but much of it has been justified. The schools as a whole have not met the needs of the child from the deprived area. The services and the experiences that the school has offered have been influenced and molded by the middle-class values of our society.

In many of our schools, however, efforts are underway to design meaningful, long-term, comprehensive programs that will help overcome the problems that allow the lower class to contribute such a disproportionate number of juvenile delinquents. In order for these programs to succeed, they must be directed at the following:

1. The development of new value systems for children from disadvantaged areas.
2. The development within the school curriculum of programs to improve employability.
3. The provision of experiences that improve the self-concept of the delinquency-prone child.

\ In order for the schools to take effective steps toward providing the programs and experiences in the educative process that will allow these goals to be reached, the following steps must be taken:

1. More adequate financial support of education with special emphasis on the equalization of educational opportunity for culturally and financially deprived communities.
2. The professional preparation, recruitment, and rewarding of higher quality teachers who understand the culture, nature, and needs of the children of the community in which they teach.
3. The development and implementation of curricula that will be meaningful and effective in the lives of the children of the community.
4. The integration into the total school program of special instructional services.
5. The provision of pupil personnel and guidance services staffed by guidance counselors and other specialists who understand the culture, nature, and needs of the children of the community.
6. Leadership by the school in the organization and continued operation of coordinated community efforts on behalf of youths, including the prevention and control of delinquency.
7. Where existing administrative structures impede direct and effective services to youth, the recognition and organization of novel administrative structures that can attack the problem.

SELECTED READINGS

Amos, William E., "A Study of Self-Concept: Delinquent Boys' Accuracy in Selected Self-Evaluations," *Genetic Psychology Monographs*, LXVII (1963), 45–87.

Amos, William E., Marilyn Southwell, and Raymond Manella, *Action Programs for Delinquency Prevention.* Springfield, Ill.: Charles C. Thomas, Publisher, 1965.

Beck, Bertram M., "Delinquents in the Classroom," *National Education Association Journal* (November, 1956). Pages 485–487.

Burchill, George W., *Work-Study Programs for Alienated Youth: A Casebook.* Chicago, Ill.: Science Research Associates, Inc., 1962. 265 pages.

Conant, James B., *Slums and Suburbs*. New York: McGraw-Hill Book Company, 1961. 147 pages.

Gnagey, W. J., "Do Our Schools Prevent or Promote Delinquency?" *Journal of Educational Research*, LX (November, 1956), 215–219.

Goldman, Nathan, "School Vandalism—A Socio-Psychological Study," *Education Digest*, XXVI (December, 1960), 1–4.

Kvaraceus, William C., "Counselor's Role in Combatting Juvenile Delinquency," *Personnel and Guidance Journal*, XXXVI (October, 1957), 99–103.

Kvaraceus, William C., and Walter B. Miller, *Delinquent Behavior: Culture and the Individual and Principles and Practices*. Washington, D.C.: National Education Association, 1959.

Kvaraceus, William C., and William E. Ulrich, *Delinquent Behavior—Principles and Practices*. Washington, D.C.: National Education Association, 1959. 339 pages.

Moore, Bernice M., "The Schools and the Problems of Delinquency: Research Studies and Findings," *Crime and Delinquency* (July, 1961). Pages 201–212.

Morgans, Robert D., "What California High Schools Are Doing About Juvenile Delinquency," *California Journal of Secondary Education*, XXXIII, No. 1 (January, 1958), 461–465.

Nolan, E. G., "Secondary Schools and Juvenile Delinquency," *California Journal of Secondary Education*, XXX (December, 1965), 473–475.

Ojemann, R. H., "Forewarnings of Delinquency," *National Parent Teacher*, XLIX (March, 1955), 20–22.

Schreiber, Daniel, "Juvenile Delinquency and the School Dropout Problem," *Federal Probation* (September, 1963).

Smith, Philip M., "The Schools and Juvenile Delinquency," *Sociology and Social Research*, XXXVII (1952), 85–91.

U.S. Department of Health, Education, and Welfare, Office of Education. *Teachers of Children Who Are Socially and Emotionally Maladjusted*, Office of Education Pamphlet No. 11. Washington, D.C.: U.S. Government Printing Office, 1957. 92 pages.

U.S. House of Representatives, Committee on Education and Labor, 88th Congress, 1st Session, "Pioneer Ideas in Education." Washington, D.C.: U.S. Government Printing Office, 1963. 112 pages.

U.S. President's Committee on Juvenile Delinquency and Youth Crime, "Summaries of Training Funded Under P.L. 87-274" (September, 1963), mimeo.

Venn, Grant, *Man, Education, and Work*. Washington, D.C.: American Council on Education, 1964. 185 pages.

Walker, Clare C., "A Positive Approach to Delinquency," *NEA Journal* (October, 1958). Pages 466–468.

Wattenberg, William E., *Relationship of School Experiences to Delinquency*. Detroit: Wayne State University Press, 1960.

What P.T.A. Members Should Know About Juvenile Delinquency. Chicago, Ill.: Chicago National Congress of Parents and Teachers, 1957. 96 pages.

8 Prevention
Through Recreation

Sidney G. Lutzin
R. C. Orem

Although the ideal organized recreation service would provide all people everywhere all of the time with whatever resources they need for wise use of leisure time, recreation programs have in reality only begun to reach such a goal. Recreation, although expanding, does not yet exert a vital influence on the lives of millions of young Americans.

A review of the limited and somewhat indecisive research indicates that "old line" traditional recreation programs have not had much proven impact on juvenile delinquency prevention. However, some recreation agencies continue to imply that their programs are delinquency preventive; it remains for research to demonstrate such effects.

As part of community-wide efforts to prevent delinquency, many recreation programs, specifically designed to "reach out" to and draw otherwise unreached and unmotivated youths, are being developed. These programs are realistically geared to the interests and needs of those who are likely to become delinquent. By attracting and serving such individuals, constructive alternatives to delinquent behavior can be posed. Another trend in the field is the increased employment of "detached workers" who work directly with delinquency-prone youths "on the street" rather than wait for them to enroll formally in a program. These approaches hold much promise, and considerable success is claimed for them, but research is required to measure their effectiveness.

How can we define "recreation"? Although the term has many

150

different meanings it will be used in a broad sense in this chapter to include all that is recreative of the individual, community, or nation. Recreation thus embraces the physical, mental, and spiritual expression of man.[1]

As Joseph Prendergast has noted: "Recreation is what you do when nobody (and no social pressure) tells you what you must do."[2]

This "voluntary choice" aspect of recreation is emphasized by the District of Columbia Recreation Department:

> An individual engages in recreation during his leisure time because he wishes to do so. There is no outside compulsion of any type; recreation satisfies a personal desire to achieve immediate and direct satisfaction in enjoyable, creative activity, self-expression and relaxation. It is an activity engaged in for its own sake, not for any external rewards.[3]

The ideal objective of the public recreation movement in America can be described as "the promotion of the general welfare, through the creation of opportunities for a more abundant and happier life for everyone."[4] It is against this admittedly lofty objective that recreation programs must ultimately be measured.

Recreation can be analyzed in terms of an almost unlimited number of dimensions: individual preferences, degree of organization, sponsorship, amount of mental and physical activity involved, degree of individual and group participation, personnel employed, population served, type of facilities utilized, etc.[5] However, our aim here is not to discuss in depth the many implications of recreation as a conscious cultural ideal of the American people.

Nevertheless, it is of value to list some general principles of recreation for youth as a framework for further discussion:

1. Recreation is a vital and significant part of life, and it is essential in a democratic society. It can be a positive force in the lives of all, particularly young, people.
2. Recreation is a primary responsibility of every community and must be adequately provided to meet the needs of all youth, regardless of race, creed, or economic status.
3. Recreation must receive major attention in planning for the preserva-

[1] John Collier, "Recreation in Our Changing Times," *Recreation* (National Recreation Association, 1959), p. 414. From a 1933 National Park Service Report.

[2] *Ibid.,* p. 414.

[3] District of Columbia Recreation Department, Division of Neighborhood Centers, *Survey of Anti-Crime Activities* (mimeo.), p. 1.

[4] John Collier, *op. cit.,* p. 414.

[5] National Conference on Prevention and Control of Juvenile Delinquency, *Report on Recreation for Youth* (Washington, D.C.: U.S. Government Printing Office, 1947).

tion and development of youth and in the prevention and control of delinquency. Government provision for recreation is needed at the local, state, and federal level.

4. Community recreation demands the mobilization and use of all resources—human, physical, and fiscal; public, private, and commercial.
5. Youth services must be carefully planned and coordinated.
6. Recreation programs for youth require adequate legislation, funds, facilities, and the leadership of competent paid and volunteer staff.
7. Youth must have both planning and leadership responsibilities in such programs.
8. Recreation has therapeutic values as part of the "social treatment" of individuals and groups.[6]

In the *Conference Proceedings* of the 1960 Golden Anniversary White House Conference on Children and Youth,[7] forty-three recommendations relating to recreation are listed under such topics as Program Objectives and Philosophy; Federal, State, and Local Action; Youth Participation; and Community Programs. Although space limitations preclude even a summary of these recommendations, it is sufficient to indicate that they fit within the eight-principle framework given above.

Limited space also precludes a coverage in any detail of the historical development of the organized recreation movement in America, a development that has culminated in recreation's present position as an accepted function of government at local, state, and national levels.[8]

Positive Growth of Services

Some recent developments in the field of organized recreation, although holding great promise for services to certain segments of our population, show little prospect of much needed services for those who could perhaps most benefit from them.

In recent years there has been an expansion of services and an increasing professionalization of personnel, unprecedented in the history of the field. More communities are establishing recreation agencies; larger budgets are making more and better facilities possible; more well-trained leaders and program administrators are emerging. These things have been occurring during a period of sharp competition for contributions and for the tax dollar.[9]

[6] *Ibid.*, pp. 1–3.
[7] Golden Anniversary White House Conference on Children and Youth, *Conference Proceedings* (Washington, D.C., 1960), pp. 348–352.
[8] Sidney Lutzin, "The Place of Recreation in Preventing Juvenile Delinquency," *Recreation*, National Recreation Association (September, 1955), pp. 300–301.
[9] *Ibid.*

Negative Narrowing of Services

Of particular significance to recreation are the profound population shifts that are occurring in many of our largest urban areas. As family after family has climbed the socioeconomic ladder, the movement from the old established neighborhoods has become a mass migration to the suburbs and new sections of the cities. Their places have been filled by migrants—often the inept and the indigent—who encounter a critical shortage of services, including recreation.

Where are the neighborhood house, the boy's club, the Y.M.C.A., the Jewish Community Center, which once flourished in the old neighborhood? They have moved with their former clientele to the new neighborhood, housed perhaps in a new and imposing structure, serving their members with many activities of interest to youth, whose parents offer financial support.

Even if such centers haven't moved physically, only a small proportion of their clientele still come from the immediate neighborhood. The old day-care center is now the day camp; the homemaking groups in sewing and cooking have given way to classes in ceramics and art; stickball and sidewalk tennis, once played in front of the old settlement houses, have been replaced by baseball, golf, and tennis on the new spacious grounds outside and squash and health club activities on the inside. The old clientele have become solid middle class, and the old neighborhood agencies have moved up with solid middle class recreation services and are fast becoming, in effect, new exclusively middle-class clubs.

While the character of the neighborhood and of the voluntary agency has been changing, the administration of public recreation has also been having its renaissance. The public officials, recreators, and their commissions have been finding new groups concerned with and interested in public recreation. Organized groups requesting services from recreation agencies have become hard to ignore. In addition, it has been discovered that these groups are willing to pay a share, and sometimes all, of the cost of the services they require. Thus we have swimming pools with a fee and sometimes cooperatively owned under public auspices; golf courses run at a profit to the municipality; self-supporting little leagues, dance groups, art classes; and even personally paid insurance policies to protect the municipalities from their own negligence.

This kind of recreation is easy to administer because it is needed and wanted. No "hard selling" is required to develop the program and the participation, and the municipal fathers will sponsor activities for which the citizens are willing to pay even a portion of the cost.

So public recreation, like many of the voluntary services, is fast assuming the character of services for a fee, geared to the needs of our great middle class. Public or voluntary, it appears that organized recreation is in danger of becoming a middle-class monopoly.[10]

Review of Past Programs

As in any field as broad as recreation, there is an abundance of organizations and programs embodying particular philosophies, purposes, and policies.[11] Because a major aim of this chapter is to review those programs that directly and indirectly have attempted to prevent or reduce juvenile delinquency, we should ask at this point: "What does research tell us about organized recreation as a force for the prevention of delinquency?"

Witmer and Tufts, in their appraisal of the evaluative studies of programs for the prevention of juvenile delinquency, note that the term "delinquency prevention" can have three somewhat different emphases:[12]

1. promoting the healthy personality development of all children,
2. reaching potential delinquents before they get into trouble, and
3. reducing recidivism and lessening continuing illegal behavior.

In their report of the effectiveness of delinquency-prevention programs, delinquency is broadly defined as "behavior that is in conflict with the law, whether or not it has brought the child to the attention of the police and courts," whereas prevention refers to both "the forestalling of delinquent behavior and also to the reduction in its frequency and seriousness."[13]

Although there have been many surveys concluding that the quantity and quality of recreation facilities should be increased to help reduce delinquency and some studies showing that delinquency rates may be high where recreation facilities are scarce, Witmer and Tufts found only three pertinent evaluative studies in the recreation area.

Shanas and Dunning Study

This study compared delinquents and nondelinquents in their use of recreation facilities and users and nonusers of facilities in their commis-

---

    [10] Sidney Lutzin, "The Squeeze-Out," *Recreation*, National Recreation Association (October, 1962).

    [11] Arnold Green, *Recreation, Leisure, and Politics* (New York: McGraw-Hill Book Company, 1964).

    [12] Helen Witmer and Edith Tufts, *The Effectiveness of Delinquency Prevention Programs*, Children's Bureau Publication No. 350 (Washington, D.C.: U.S. Government Printing Office, 1954), pp. 2–3.

    [13] *Ibid.*, p. 5.

sion of officially delinquent acts in four slum areas and one middle-class area in Chicago. Approximately 15,000 boys and 8,000 girls, 10–17 years old, were involved in the 1938–1939 study. The conclusions are summarized as follows:[14]

1. A larger proportion of the nondelinquents than delinquents used the recreation facilities, regardless of the area of residence.
2. Delinquents more nearly equalled nondelinquents in recreation facilities used in slum areas than in higher economic status areas.
3. In all areas the younger boys (under 14) made more use of the facilities than older boys.
4. In all areas delinquent boys who did participate in recreation activities spent more time than did nondelinquent boys.
5. The delinquents did spend less time in closely supervised activities, preferring game rooms and competitive sports.
6. The total amount of time spent by any children in supervised play was small, ranging from 43 to 87.5 hours annually.
7. All boys spent about twice as much time at the movies as in supervised recreation.
8. During the year of the study, about 2 per cent of previously non-delinquent participants in the recreation program became officially delinquent, whereas about 5 per cent of the previously nondelinquent who did not participate in the program became delinquent (known to the court).
9. Ten per cent of the delinquents who used the recreation facilities continued their delinquent acts as compared with 16 per cent of the delinquents who did not use the facilities.

What are the implications of these conclusions? If these findings are typical of other communities during the late 1930's, not much could be expected of the traditional recreation programs of that era in preventing delinquency. They attracted relatively few children, especially of the older group, and only for a little time.

Although conclusions 8 and 9 may appear encouraging at first glance, Witmer and Tufts[15] note that their significance is dubious, for it may well be that these figures only show that delinquents and near-delinquents who use recreation facilities are the ones who are less likely to commit offenses.

Thrasher Study

Thrasher, whose work with gangs[16] is classic, studied the Boys' Club of New York between 1927–1931 to discover the effectiveness of the

[14] Ethel Shanas and Catherine Dunning, *Recreation and Delinquency*, Chicago Recreation Commission (1942).
[15] Witner and Tufts, *op. cit.*, p. 20.
[16] Frederic Thrasher, *The Gang* (Chicago: University of Chicago Press, 1927).

program in preventing delinquency and imparting desirable behavior standards. Some of the findings were:[17]

1. Although the club was set up to serve 4,000 boys, no more than 2,500 (approximately 60 per cent of capacity) participated at a time.
2. The club appealed to more older (14 and over) than younger boys.
3. Many of the eligible boys in 30 nearby city blocks did not enroll or participate. Of the 635 delinquents in that area, for example, 298 never enrolled in the club program during the whole period of the study.
4. There was a 33 per cent turnover in club membership in each of the four years covered, with only a small number of boys remaining year after year.
5. Of the total official offenses of Boys' Club members, only 18 per cent occurred before their joining the club. Twenty-eight per cent occurred after joining the club. With each year of continued membership, the proportion of delinquents increased.

Thrasher believed that the boys were subject to a gamut of negative influences that the Boys' Club was simply unable to neutralize but concluded that "we shall need many more boys' clubs in order to perform the function of crime prevention adequately."[18]

Despite Thrasher's conclusion, his findings do imply that club membership in the situation under study did not reduce delinquency and possibly may have increased it. Although this study is an historic one, it should be noted that the conclusions that were inferred from it are applicable primarily to the agency under study and to agencies similarly situated at the end of the 1920's.

Reed Study

In 1942 Ellery Reed examined the records of 50 young people selected at random from the April, 1940, files of the Cincinnati Juvenile Court and found that in only 14 cases had the children been registered with group-work agencies at any time during the three years preceding their court appearance.

To test the hypothesis that the agencies served children who were not very likely to become delinquent, a random selection—1,679 boys and girls who were members of group-work agencies and 246 who came before the juvenile court—was made, and the two groups were then compared:[19]

[17] Frederic Thrasher, "The Boys' Club and Juvenile Delinquency," The American Journal of Sociology, XLII (1936), 66–80.
[18] Ibid., pp. 79–80.
[19] Ellery Reed, "How Effective Are Group Work Services in Preventing Delinquency?" The Social Service Review, XXII (1948), 340–348.

1. A smaller proportion of the group-work children than of the court children lived in the poorest areas;
2. Within these poorest areas, the court children came from less stable and fortunate families than the group-work children; and
3. Group-work children were more likely than court children to be Caucasian, female, and under age 15.

It was concluded that group-work agencies serve a selected group of children and, by the nature of its program, attitudes, and methods, screen out and fail to serve the children who most need their service.[20]

Group-work agencies, it should be noted, are generally much more aware of their responsibilities to serve those whom Reed found "screened out" in his 1942 study. Although some agencies still reflect the conditions found by Reed, many others have been completely reorganized to better serve those who most need their services.

Robison[21] has reviewed briefly two other studies that focused on possible relationships between recreation and incidence of juvenile delinquency.

Truxal Study

In a 1925 study done in New York City for the National Recreation Commission, according to Robison, Truxal tabulated juvenile court cases by health department census tracts in the borough of Manhattan and compared them with the provision of recreation centers.[22]

Interestingly, his statistics "did not demonstrate that in areas with playgrounds and parks the rate of delinquency was lower than in areas without these facilities," but the study did have a number of methodological shortcomings.

Louisville Boys' Club Study

In this study, released by the New York University Center for Community and Field Services, changes in the official delinquency rates among boys of comparable age in the area served by the boys' club were compared with rates in two other areas differing chiefly in terms of provision of services for boys.[23] Robison notes that "although the ratio of delinquents in the boys' club area did decline appreciably in comparison

[20] Ibid., p. 348.
[21] Sophia Robison, Juvenile Delinquency: Its Nature and Control (New York: Holt, Rinehart & Winston, Inc., 1961).
[22] Andrew Truxal, Outdoor Recreation Legislation and Its Effectiveness (New York: Columbia University Press, 1929).
[23] Roscoe Brown, Jr., A Boys' Club and Delinquency (New York: New York University Center for Community and Field Service, Monograph 2, 1956).

with the control areas, the authors of the study refrain from claiming that the boys' club was responsible."[24] Because the influence of factors other than recreation remained unknown, any reduction in delinquency could not be ascribed to recreation.

The Children's Bureau used a questionnaire technique to study community programs and projects for the prevention of juvenile delinquency.[25] Only 107 of 258 community welfare planning councils returned the questionnaires in time to be included in the study. Seventy-four of the 107 reported some current activity in this area. Whereas some councils were engaged in "primary prevention" programs designed to forestall delinquency by early treatment, for example, most apparently concentrated on "secondary prevention" measures directed toward youths manifesting behavior that might lead to serious delinquency or toward those already adjudged delinquent.[26]

One such primary prevention program concentrates on extending or improving existing leisure-time programs or developing new ones for youth, such as the employment of "roving group leaders" or the establishment of new recreation or athletic programs.

The projects and programs were grouped in such broad categories as detached-worker services, area projects, intensive coordination of services, intensive group work services, and recreation programs.[27] The authors of the report note that the effectiveness of extending the usual organized recreation activities of the community in preventing delinquency is questionable, although such activities, by meeting the interests of youth generally, may indirectly serve as a delinquency-prevention measure.

Almost none of the programs studied was scientifically evaluated; many faced serious obstacles, including lack of staff, money, facilities, and referral sources; few new project methods were found.[28]

In reviewing this handful of studies most pertinent to our topic, it appears that the "usual sort" of recreation program offering the "usual sort" of service is not very effective in preventing delinquency or, for that matter, reducing it. Why is it that organized recreation has not fared better in the research findings concerning its effectiveness in delinquency prevention?

Wylie offers a number of reasons why public recreation programs fail the delinquent and potential delinquent: too much competition and skill required, need for fees, not enough active participation, lack of youth

[24] Sophia Robison, *op. cit.*, p. 479.
[25] Mary Novick, *Community Programs and Projects for the Prevention of Juvenile Delinquency,* Children's Bureau Publication on Juvenile Delinquency Facts and Facets, No. 14 (Washington, D.C.: U.S. Government Printing Office, 1960).
[26] *Ibid.,* pp. 2–3.
[27] *Ibid.,* pp. 3–9.
[28] *Ibid.,* pp. 9–11.

planning, too "boy slanted," lack of choices, too little family involvement, lack of year-round scheduling, not enough continuity, and inadequately trained staff who do not understand such youth.[29] In other
words, the programs are inadequately planned and administered, and they
do not fulfill the basic principles of sound recreation practice.

Goranson, writing in a similar vein, calls for public recreation agencies
to reexamine those policies that exclude "bad" youth, to train their staff
to understand the motives of rule breakers, to encourage "reaching out"
to contact hard-to-reach youth, and to establish working relationships
with other community agencies concerned with these youth, including
the school, church, health, and social services.[30]

As Kraus has noted, "education, recreation, family counselling, or
improvement of housing or job opportunities cannot work miracles when
taken *separately*. They must be combined in a meaningful, effective, team
approach, focusing on environment, family structure, and individual
personality. Recreation's specific role includes providing for the following basic elements: socially acceptable leisure outlets, understanding adult
leaders, family programs, involvement of youth in program planning, and
the use of "roving leaders" or "detached workers."[31] Essential components of an effective recreation service must include: adequate philosophy, planning, legislation, financing, facilities, and leadership. The needs
of the hard-to-reach must be represented in each of these components.

Paradoxically, and unfortunately, organized recreation has often been
supported by funds voluntarily contributed or tax-derived on the assumption that recreation, per se, prevents delinquency. This assumption, for
which there is no basis in research to date, is bandied about during fund-
raising campaigns of voluntary agencies and is advanced at budget
hearings at all levels of government. The community, in its frantic search
for a panacea for delinquency prevention, may too easily view recreation
as *the* program that will somehow make delinquency disappear.[32] After a
program is planned, funded, and implemented, and delinquency doesn't
"go away," frustration and disillusionment at "recreation's failure" may
follow.

The Unfulfilled Potential of Recreation

Whereas it is not our intention to condemn recreation for providing
greatly improved services to one substantial group in society or for

[29] James Wylie, "Can Community Recreation Meet the Needs of Youth?"
Recreation (November, 1963), pp. 406–408.

[30] Ernest Goranson, "The Unacceptables," *Recreation* (January, 1962).

[31] Richard Kraus, "Delinquency and Recreation: Fact and Fiction," *Recreation*
(October, 1965), pp. 382–385.

[32] Sidney Lutzin, "The Place of Recreation in Preventing Juvenile Delinquency,"
Recreation (September, 1955).

devising the policy of requiring those benefiting from certain kinds of special recreation facilities and services to help defray the costs, the fact is that another large and important segment of our population is being squeezed out of recreation programs, either because its members cannot or are unwilling to pay even minimal fees or because they are not being offered suitable, attractive programs and therefore stay away from recreation activities.

Is not the ultimate goal of recreation to provide the broadest possible recreation opportunities for the greatest possible number of people—regardless of age, color, creed, or economic station? Yet we are moving in a direction that neglects a large segment of our population to whom the role of recreation is most vital. The distribution of recreation services is becoming, in many areas, increasingly inequitable. The youngster most likely to become a delinquent, the one already enmeshed in unlawful acts, or the one who is a problem in other ways just as costly to society often receives but the shallowest token of services from organized recreation in his neighborhood.

Working with such youngsters is not an easy job of following up on requests for services from eager groups. It involves, first, the providing of real recreation opportunities in those neighborhoods that so many agencies have been ignoring in recent years. Second, it requires the devising of ingenious techniques and programs designed to attract and hold those youngsters who until now have been as oblivious of organized recreation service as it has been of them. Third, it demands of recreation leaders an enthusiasm for this special type of challenge; they must be trained to their responsibilities on the integrated team of community resources, which can provide some positive structure in the lives of these youthful misfits in our society.[33]

Reasons for Employing Recreation Group Work with Hard-to-Reach Youth

There are a number of reasons for recreation being uniquely suited for favorably influencing hard-to-reach youth.

Recreation, as an enjoyable experience, can function as the medium "luring" delinquent and predelinquent youths and holding them in an organized social setting, without compulsion or legal mandates.

The recreation situation can provide an ideal laboratory for observing an individual's behavior pattern in a regular social group. The participant is involved of his own volition, and in this setting he voluntarily associates with those of his own choosing. Therefore, it is possible to make a gross

[33] Sidney Lutzin, "The Squeeze-Out," *Recreation* (October, 1962).

diagnosis of certain personality problems based on observable attitudes and on the degree of adjustment within the social group he selects.

Recreation can provide an ideal situation for developing rapport between the leader and the child because, by its very nature, recreation fosters a close, favorable relationship between good leaders and youngsters in the program. Good rapport is basic to success in delinquency prevention.

Recreation can be used as a prescriptive element to satisfy many of the emotional needs of individuals. In this context, prescribed recreation activities can serve as the "therapy" selected by specialized leaders to provide the satisfying group experience or personal outlet that can help young people with certain emotional problems to better social adjustment.[34]

It remains for longitudinal studies to prove that recreation can indeed apply this rationale to function successfully with those youth not now being reached.

Locating "Problem Youth"

In the community there are numerous sources through which problem youngsters can be brought to the attention of the recreation agency: (1) police personnel; (2) probation officers and children's court personnel; (3) school personnel: principals, teachers, attendance officers, guidance staff; (4) clergymen; (5) public and private welfare agencies; (6) recreation staff members; (7) newspaper clippings; (8) social service exchanges or similar agencies; and (9) the recreation agency's registration form when it is designed in this type of program to cull "problem" youth on the basis of established criteria.

Programing for "Problem" Youth

What are the procedures to be followed after a listing of problem youth has been established? (1) Determine from analysis of program registrations who is already in the program and who should be attracted to it. (2) Develop listings for each of the playgrounds and other program centers, which will provide the leaders with the names of problem youth from that specific area who are already participating in the program and who require special attention as well as of those who need special attention but who are not coming to the recreation facility or participating in its activities. (3) Learn as much as possible about the youngsters involved and brief the recreation personnel who will be working with them. (4) Develop techniques and activities designed to attract the

---

[34] Sidney Lutzin, "Casework in Recreation," *The Community Courier* (Community Programmes Branch, Province of Ontario, 1951).

"specials" to the program without letting them discover this interest in securing their participation in the program. (5) Pursue a course of continuous follow-up to determine the success of efforts to attract the "vulnerable" youth or "specials" and to know who are not being reached, so that additional effort can be expended toward attracting as many as possible to the program. (6) Attempt to diagnose the problems of the individual child on the basis of all available information and provide activities designed to meet his specific needs or determine when there is need for more skilled services and referral to a qualified agency.

These techniques are particularly adaptable for dealing with youth problems in smaller cities and in neighborhoods either by public or voluntary agencies. It was first successfully introduced in 1936 at the city of Kingston, New York, a Hudson Valley community of about 30,000 population. Similar applications of the utilization of recreation services in dealing with delinquency-prevention efforts have been made in other communities. Frequently, a specialist trained in the field of delinquency prevention is employed to direct and coordinate this phase of the small community's public recreation program or the "reaching out" aspects of the settlement house or other voluntary agency program.

A Close Look at the "Detached Worker" Concept

The most widely known adaptation of this service is that employed by large city agencies, both municipal and voluntary, under a variety of job titles but utilizing similar techniques and directed toward the same goals. These are the "street club workers" of the New York City Youth Board, a municipal delinquency-prevention agency that functions with state financial aid from the New York State Division for Youth. Other large city youth boards in New York State operate under this same fiscal arrangement and utilize "detached workers" under contract with private agencies in Buffalo, Rochester, Albany, and in other large upstate cities. In Washington, D.C., during 1956, the "roving leader" became the specialized worker in the District of Columbia's Recreation Department in the area of delinquency prevention. Similar positions have been established or are currently under consideration in the recreation agencies of major metropolitan communities from coast to coast.

In most communities the detached worker program, whether operated by public recreation departments or voluntary agencies, is coordinated at a higher level by either a special municipal coordinating committee, such as the Commissioner's Youth Council in Washington, D.C., the municipal youth boards operating in New York State cities, or the associated agencies of Oakland, California. These coordinating agencies include representation from the principal organizations and municipal departments having basic responsibilities in various areas of the youth services. Whereas the detached worker is directly responsible to the individual agency that employs him, the policies governing his employment, his area of service, and the general policies under which he works are ordinarily determined at the coordinating agency level.[35]

Deciding to Use Detached Workers

In general practice the decision to utilize detached workers in a given community is decided at the coordinating agency level as part of an integrated approach and in response to the determination that certain problems exist that a service of this type can help to alleviate. Frequently, such a decision follows a crisis situation, such as gang wars, highly publicized vandalism, or a particularly bad crime condition involving youths, or follows the focus of attention on unattached youths, which comes from a newspaper series, a youth problems survey, or community planning project.

A joint board of agency representatives, having decided to launch such an effort, recommends that it be undertaken by the specific agency or agencies that it believes has the greatest capability of making it a success.

1. The recommendation is based in most instances on the character of the agency's responsibilities, and, therefore, the municipal recreation agency or a voluntary agency whose program is steeped in recreation ordinarily is designated.
2. The interest of the agency's board and its key staff personnel in dealing with the problem at hand is a factor involved in the final designation. An agency that does not see its responsibilities extending beyond the confines of its physical plants or beyond those who normally come to it cannot be effective in carrying out this program.
3. The ability of the agency to finance a detached-worker project without cutting back on its normal operation is sometimes, but not often, a determining element. In instances in which the agency cannot itself provide the funds, it is often possible to make financial arrangements through community chest, new municipal appropriations, demonstration project funds of foundations, federal grants or state aid, or the purchase of the detached-worker service from voluntary agencies on a contractual basis when such agencies are designated.

[35] See: John Nagy, "Ripe for Trouble," *Recreation* (November, 1962), pp. 445–446; *Youth Groups in Conflict*, Children's Bureau Publication No. 365 (Washington, D.C.: U.S. Government Printing Office, 1958); *Reaching the Unreached*, New York City Youth Board, second printing, rev., 1952 (pamphlet).

There are many examples of individual organizations or agencies independently providing detached-worker services other than through one or another of the integrated community approaches. Usually such efforts produce good results in bringing the organized program to additional clientele but can rarely produce the overall results accruing from a combined effort of many disciplines.

How Detached-Worker Duties Differ

The services of the detached worker differ from those of the regular staff member of a recreation agency in a number of ways:

1. The former works in a neighborhood and is not limited to any given facility such as a playground, community center, or settlement house. His initial contacts are on the street.
2. He utilizes all of the physical resources of the neighborhood he serves, conducting his activities in any of the facilities available in his area. His employment by a specific agency does not limit him to use of only those facilities operated or controlled by that agency.
3. He makes contact and works with youth who ordinarily would not come to organized programs of recreation agencies or any other organized program.
4. His services are individual and group-centered rather than activity-centered. He determines the direction and extent of his activities on the basis of the needs of the young people he serves and the level to which he has been able to bring them.
5. Although his lure is recreation activity, and the organized program toward which he attempts to lead his clientele is also recreation, he provides personal counseling as well as referral services to vocational agencies, social casework services, psychiatric and mental health agencies, and to any other service helpful to the youths over whom his responsibilities extend.
6. He personally maintains relationships with staff personnel of police, school, recreation, social service, and other agencies so that the resources they represent can be used most effectively with his group.
7. His hours of employment are irregular because he works when his group is active and is ordinarily on twenty-four hour call so that he can be available whenever conditions require that he provide leadership in situations involving his group or any of its members.

The Detached Worker on the Job

The detached worker makes his contacts on the streets of the neighborhood to which he is assigned. If he is dealing with gang problems, the specific gang with which he is expected to deal is ordinarily specified in his work orders. If his contacts are to be of a more general nature, he will frequently begin with one or two individual contacts and eventually develop a group of from eight to ten young people with whom his contacts will be concentrated.

Whereas he can hold out the promise of better opportunities for them, he cannot do that effectively until he wins their trust and reliance. He has to deal with them at a level they can understand and accept—most frequently this begins by making life less drab and unexciting by providing opportunities for them to do things they will find satisfying and enjoyable.

These opportunities are ordinarily recreation experiences, which can be introduced in the immediate neighborhood but which may frequently involve trips to amusement parks, camping areas, or other places. At this stage it is essential that the worker establish a relationship with his group that leaves no question of doubt that, although he can accept less than model behavior from them, he cannot close his eyes to violation of the law. Early experiences with some detached-worker programs that went to extremes of permissiveness created breaches with police and other community agencies leading to loss of confidence in the detached-worker program and proved conclusively that such extremes were completely unwarranted and dangerous.

The natural group leaders wield considerable influence on members of the group. Early identification of these individuals and greater concentration of them often effects quicker results with the entire group. The "bell cow" approach is an effective tool for the detached worker.

As work progresses with a group and as the skilled worker begins to identify the problems of the individuals, it becomes essential that he have the support of community resources necessary to treat the specific problems. The vocational counseling service, psychiatric clinics, family casework services are examples of primary resources that cooperate in the detached worker's team approach to his group. Good results in this area require that the worker first be fully informed of the resources available and second that, through his personal contacts with staff personnel of these agencies and through the work of the coordinating agency under whose auspices he is employed, easy channels of referral and prompt attention to his problem cases be effected. This is one point at which the involvement at the coordinating level of all community agencies related to youth services becomes a key to success. Participation at the top makes commitment to the assumption of responsibility at lower levels much easier.

One of the obvious objectives of the detached worker is to move his group from outside the influence of organized services to an initial point of contact with these services, to acceptance of the services, and then to voluntary participation in them. The time it takes to complete this cycle depends on the degree of maladjustment of the youngsters involved, the availability and effectiveness of the resources he can utilize, and his own inventiveness in providing the opportunities for satisfying experiences for his group.

In this process, he requires a home base. Generally, this is a recreation facility in the neighborhood. Here again the need to cross agency fences becomes apparent, because if the organization employing the worker does not have a facility in that neighborhood he must use the one available. In most instances, by prior arrangement, any needed facility is placed at the disposal of the worker, at least to a limited degree.

In the initial transitional step, when the group is first brought to an organized facility, regular operation of the agency's program could suffer considerable disruption because of the nature of the group at this stage. Therefore, arrangements are ordinarily made to introduce the group to the facility gradually, participating at times when regular programs are not in operation. When facilities are used in this way for the first time, it is worthwhile to take the time to orient the resident staff to problems that may arise and to create a favorable attitude toward the group.

It is not unusual that facilities suitable for use by a group during this period are not readily available in the neighborhoods served by a detached worker. Some kind of improvisation is often possible. One of these is the rental of a storefront as a headquarters. There is a hazard in this expediency because there is the danger that this or other groups may find it desirable to utilize similar facilities on their own and function without control or direction in such a "clubhouse." This could lead to new problems in the neighborhood.[36]

The detached worker must be able to recognize those signs that indicate the group members are functioning at a level mature enough to enable him to "ease off" at the proper time so that he can begin the process all over again with another group.

Detached-Worker Qualifications and Guiding Principles

Qualifications that may serve as criteria for employment of detached workers include:

[36] See: D. Maulmud, Paul Crawford, and James Dumpson, *Working with Teen-Age Groups: A Report on the Central Harlem Street Clubs Project* (New York: Welfare Council of New York City, 1950). *Prevention-Treatment-Control of Delinquency Through Group Work Services* (Proceedings of the Annual Spring Conference of the New York City Youth Board, 1959); David Austin, "What About Reaching Out—An Account of the Boston Youth Project," *The Round Table*, XIX (New York: National Federation of Settlement and Neighborhood Centers, 1955); Stanley Anderson, "A New Dimension in Recreation—Roving Leaders," *Recreation* (January–February, 1965); and *An Interagency and Community Approach to Youth Problems*, Western Interstate Commission for Higher Education, Boulder, Colorado (November, 1964).

1. Personality. The individual most sought after is the one who can relate readily to the young people with whom he will be working, who can develop good rapport with them, who will be able to secure their full confidence, and who has insight into their problems and potentials.
2. Education. College graduation is the minimum desired educational attainment although in some instances workers with less than a college degree have been successfully employed. Special training in the fields of recreation, social group work, physical education, sociology, or psychology are prerequisites in many places.
3. Prior job experience. Those people who have demonstrated particular skills required of the detached worker, in regular agency staff positions, are frequently moved into detached-worker positions. Prior work experience with agencies of the type involved in dealing with problem youth is considered an important asset.
4. Personal experience. Individuals who grew up in the cultural, economic, and physical milieu of the young people with whom they will be working are desired in detached-worker positions because of the assumption that they will have a better understanding of the factors involved in the problems with which they will be dealing. Many detached workers are indigenous to the neighborhoods they serve.[37]

Guiding principles that the detached worker can follow in carrying out his responsibilities with unattached youngsters include:

1. Get them where they are and stick with them.
2. Work with them at their own level.
3. Establish your own integrity toward them and toward the law.
4. Concentrate on their own leaders.
5. Know the available community youth services and how to utilize them effectively for the benefit of your group.
6. Be inventive in providing success opportunities for them as a group and as individuals.
7. Have a physical facility in the neighborhood that is prepared to accept them.
8. Help establish a relationship for your group with regular staff personnel.
9. Be able to recognize when to ease off and when to eventually let go.
10. As you let go, start working with the next group.[38]

[37] See: Mason Moton, "Role and Function of the 'Reaching Out' Youth Worker," Proceedings of the 42nd National Recreation Congress (New York, 1960); and L. T. Delaney, "Establishing Relations with Anti-Social Groups and an Analysis of Their Structure," The British Journal of Delinquency, V (July, 1954).
[38] See: Edward Thacker, "Roving Leaders Extend Our Reach," Recreation (April, 1960); Juvenile Delinquency Evaluation Project of the City of New York, Interim Report No. XIV, Dealing with the Conflict Gang in New York City (May, 1960); Gilbert Geis, Juvenile Gangs, President's Committee on Juvenile Delinquency.

Conclusion

The provision of adequate, broad-based recreation services that attract and hold young people may make a substantial, measurable contribution to the diminution of the problem of juvenile delinquency. To be effective, however, recreators will have to aggressively seek out and serve those who ordinarily would not come and, like the detached worker, be inventive and resourceful in developing the kinds of recreational opportunities to meet the challenging needs of today's complex and changing society. At the same time, recreators must be willing to admit that there are still many gaps in knowledge in such areas as how to obtain sufficient numbers of trained and qualified leaders; how to discover the extent of the delinquency problem and its implications for recreation agencies and other groups (police, schools, etc.) working in the field; how recreation workers can best use referral to other agencies; and how recreation can support and strengthen family life.[39,40,41] These are just a few of the perplexing "unknowns."

Recreation means different things to different people, including workers in the field. A broad definition of the term was selected in the beginning of this chapter.

It was noted that various publications of government agencies and recreation authorities contain impressive lists of principles and recommendations "justifying" a wide range of recreation programs. However, such lists are derived more from tradition and speculation than from the "hard data" of long-term research. In terms of available research findings there is still little reason, for example, for "selling" recreation programs strictly on the basis of a presumed power to prevent delinquency.

Organized recreation, although a relatively new field, has expanded greatly in scope and importance in recent years, and there is every reason to believe that it will continue to do so as increasing amounts of leisure time become available to increasing numbers of people.

Recreation, like other services in the health-education-welfare spectrum, must not only be flexible enough to stay abreast of rapid changes in

and *Youth Crime* (Washington, D.C.: U.S. Government Printing Office, May, 1965); and *Roving Leader Program* (Washington, D.C.: District of Columbia Recreation Department, n.d.). Various reports and mimeographed material relating to the Roving Leader Program are available from this agency.

39 Edwin Staley, "Critical Issues and Problems in Recreation," *Recreation* (January–February, 1965).

40 *Joining Hands for the Prevention and Treatment of Juvenile Delinquency*, Proceedings of the Second Governor's Conference on Juvenile Delinquency (State of Maryland, 1956), pp. 65–70.

41 Kenneth Kindelsperger, *Recreation and Delinquency, Recreation* (April, 1960).

population, housing, communications, and transportation that typify our complex society but also farsighted enough to anticipate and plan for the manifold recreation needs of diverse groups.

Recreation must have administrative, supervisory, and line staff willing to continually innovate, evaluate, and readjust policies and procedures, utilizing a coordinated research effort conducted with a background of unifying philosophy. It is hoped that other fields with which recreation must cooperate will do the same.

There is ample evidence that recreation (again, like the other social services) is only partially meeting its responsibilities to certain groups, including the so-called hard-to-reach youth. A number of writers offer a number of opinions concerning recreation's "failure" to meet the needs of delinquents and delinquent-prone youth, but it remains for research to validate these opinions.

A review of the available limited major studies pertinent to the evaluation of the effectiveness of recreation in delinquency prevention revealed that in no case could a reduction in juvenile delinquency be clearly ascribed to the preventive influence of organized recreation projects. At the same time, it is doubtful that any other allied fields can yet prove such cause-and-effect relationships, but this is surely little reason either for comfort or despair. Rather, both interdisciplinary research and coordinated programs must be conducted concurrently. Neither can wait for the other to provide final answers to the many pressing problems confronting the recreator. But a strong evaluation component must be built into new programs whenever possible—a practice altogether too rare in the past.

Present lack of knowledge concerning the relation of recreation to delinquency in general and to the prevention of delinquency in particular reflects a lack of firm understanding of the phenomenon of delinquency —its nature, causes, prevention, and control. This lack stems, perhaps, from the present state of development of the behavorial sciences. We cannot, for example, be sure about how a youth in a recreation program may learn not to become delinquent until we know a great deal more about the psychology of learning itself.

In the final part of the chapter, some of the qualifications and functions of detached workers were given as well as guiding principles for their work that have been formulated as more experience with this plan has been gained. Many communities are staking a great deal of hope on the possibilities of detached-worker programs.

SELECTED READINGS

Butler, G. D., *Introduction to Community Recreation* (2nd ed.), National Recreation Association. New York: McGraw-Hill Book Company, 1949.

Cavan, Ruth, ed., *Readings in Juvenile Delinquency*. Philadelphia: J. B. Lippincott Co., 1964.

Counter-Attack on Delinquency. Mimeographed by the President's Committee on Juvenile Delinquency and Youth Crime (September, 1963).

Kindelsperger, Kenneth, "Recreation and Delinquency," *Recreation* (April, 1960).

Kraus, Richard, "Delinquency and Recreation: Fact and Fiction," *Recreation* (October, 1965), pp. 382–385.

MacIver, Robert, "Juvenile Delinquency," *The Nation's Children: Problems and Prospects*, Volume 3, ed. by Eli Ginzberg, 1960 White House Conference on Children and Youth. New York: Columbia University Press, 1960. Pages 103–123.

Moton, Mason, "Role and Function of the 'Reaching Out' Youth Worker," *Proceedings of the 42nd National Recreation Congress* (New York, 1960).

Neisser, Edith, and Nina Ridenour, *Your Children and Their Gangs*, Children's Bureau Publication No. 384. Washington, D.C.: U.S. Government Printing Office, 1960.

New Directions in Delinquency Prevention: 1947–1957. New York City Youth Board (pamphlet).

Riccio, Vincent, *All The Way Down: The Violent Underworld of Street Gangs*. New York: Simon and Schuster, Inc., 1962.

Shivers, Jay, *Leadership in Recreational Service*. New York: The Macmillan Company, 1963. Pages 421–423.

Staley, Edwin, "Critical Issues and Problems in Recreation," *Recreation* (January–February, 1965).

Teenage Gangs. New York City Youth Board, 1957 (pamphlet).

Thacker, Edward, "Roving Leaders Extend Our Reach," *Recreation* (April, 1960).

9 Prevention Through
the Economic Structure

*Ivar Berg**

Teenage drunken driving in Darien, Connecticut, property damage at Long Island debutant parties, springtime riots in Fort Lauderdale, and the current debate over contraceptive pills at leading women's colleges remind us that juvenile delinquency is not restricted to the children of low-income groups. The number of Congressional Medals of Honor awarded to the sons of urban lower-class families however, gives testimony that virtue is not the monopoly of any single group.

In recognition of these facts, numerous recent volumes have been written to make sense out of the anomalous data on crime and delinquency, and voters and elected officials have sought to frame public policies that would reduce delinquency among our young. Unfortunately, public policy, especially economic policy, is not usually affected by the considerable research on delinquency. As two students of delinquency have said after a careful review of the literature:

> Delinquent behavior, like human behavior in general, involves a large number of interrelated personal, social and cultural variables, as well as a variety of idiosyncratic conditions; therefore, no single interpretation of delinquent behavior is possible. . . .[1]

Even the most popular traditional view, born of research investigations undertaken by students in the manner of the so-called Chicago

* Support from the Graduate School of Business, Columbia University, and to assistance of S. Prakash Sethi are hereby gratefully acknowledged.
[1] T. M. Martin and J. P. Fitzpatrick, *Delinquent Behavior* (New York: Random House, Inc., 1964), p. 83.

School, that delinquent behavior can be linked to economic and related
circumstances is now seriously questioned. After reviewing relevant data
and the numerous theories that have been deduced from it, Martin and
Fitzpatrick conclude:

> Simple poverty . . . is not the cause of delinquency; nor is
> neighborhood instability a satisfactory alternative explanation.
> Although many high-delinquency areas are unstable, some are
> quite stable in their social organization. . . .[2]

These authors continue, however, to provide a clue of no small
significance to the formulation of public policy in this area. Borrowing a
concept from an earlier work by Sutherland and Whyte, they point out
that some stable areas may be

> . . . breeding delinquency because they are "differentially organ-
> ized"—that is they are organized on a basis that is out of harmony
> with, or contradictory to, conventional standards.[3]

According to this logic, we may turn away from delinquent behavior to
the forces associated with "differential organization." By so doing, we
may recapture the role of economic circumstance that eludes us in an
examination of individual behavior. Clearly the "differential organization"
of a population group is not unrelated to its position in the social system,
and the correlates of class membership are among the best documented
findings in modern sociology.

In this connection we may note that the thrust of our national interest
in delinquency is toward the urban lower classes. We surely know more
about (and seem to be more offended by) delinquency among the young
in this group than about the "antics" of suburban youth or the white-
collar crime of upper-income adults. The reasons are well known: We
undoubtedly enforce the law more scrupulously in urban centers; we can
safely assume that the poor in large cities are less able, financially and
otherwise, to win acquittals than are middle-class deviants; and it is
further realistic to recognize that the poor have "differential opportunities" to embezzle large sums, to rig prices in the heavy electrical
equipment industry, or to participate in the "relatively safe deviation
. . . exemplified by the car-sex-alcohol syndrome . . . especially as
practiced by such privileged groups as college students. . . ."[4]

Our information, however, inadequate for the reasons enumerated,
indicates that there is substantial reason for concern. Thus Fleisher has
noted that ". . . The effect of unemployment on juvenile delinquency is

[2] *Ibid.*, p. 79.
[3] *Ibid.*, p. 79.
[4] *Ibid.*, p. 29.

positive and significant"[5] and that ". . . The effect of income on delinquency is not a small one."[6] He goes on to point out, from his rough calculations,

. . . That a ten percent rise in income may be expected to reduce delinquency rates by between fifteen and twenty-five percent when the income change occurs in a very delinquent area and is of the type that will reduce the number of broken families as well.[7]

It is clear from these two reports and from several others reviewed by Guttentag[8] that poverty by itself accounts for only part of the variance observed in the statistics on crime and delinquency. Thus Guttentag notes that delinquency rates are higher in industrialized than in so-called developing societies and that some researchers have found an inverse relationship between unemployment and delinquency. After exploring errors resulting from faulty statistical methods and from shortcomings in the data used by various researchers, she concludes that the apparent anomalies in the data can be explained by focusing on similarities in the experiences of population groups with a high incidence of crime and delinquency. She deduces, from two revealing studies of the concomitant variations occurring among factors associated with crime and delinquency, that it is necessary to bring back the "venerable concept of anomie." This concept seems most appropriate to characterize the shifting population and resulting normlessness, which are positively related to crime and delinquency. She goes on to state:

Conditions of employment and unemployment play a direct role in population shifts. If we examine conditions of employment and unemployment throughout the world, we will see that depending on their differential effects on population mobility and social change, employment patterns are related *both* to rises and declines in the rate of delinquency in different countries. It is possible to predict the direction of the effect by following the consequences of the employment pattern on the stability of the population.[9]

At the same time we know from other studies that geographic mobility is a common response to unemployment:

[5] B. M. Fleisher, "Unemployment and Juvenile Delinquency," *Journal of Political Economy*, LXXI, No. 6 (December, 1963), 53.
[6] B. M. Fleisher, "The Effect of Income on Delinquency," Working Paper No. 40, Center for Organizational Studies, University of Chicago (January, 1965), p. 28.
[7] *Ibid.*, p. 29.
[8] M. Guttentag, "The Relationship of Unemployment to Crime and Delinquency" (unpublished manuscript, Department of Psychology, State University of New York at Stony Brook, N.Y.).
[9] *Ibid.*, pp. 6–7.

In 1963 the migration rate for unemployed males was about 11 percent compared to 6 percent for employed males. Approximately 70 percent of migrants who were unemployed the previous year moved to look for work or to take a job. In contrast, only about one-half the employed and one-third not in the labor force migrated for these reasons. . . . Brian Perken's study of social security data shows that in times of recession there is an actual net inflow into the farm work force. Even in years of low unemployment, such back movement appears surprisingly high. . . . These findings are in accord with the "shuttling" pattern observed among Appalachian whites who move irregularly between their rural (although nonfarm) homes and big cities like Chicago, depending on the employment situation.[10]

These numbers take on added significance when we include the family members of the unemployed male in search of work. Geographic mobility "helps" a large number of citizens to disregard the norms that support conventional behavior among less mobile population groups.

We may say, therefore, that the economic factors that begin to fade in efforts to account for individual behavior and then vanish in efforts to comprehend the incidence of crime and delinquency among differentially situated subgroups reappear when the analyst controls circumstances that intervene between economic well being and social pathology.

Again, available data, middle-class sensibilities, and up-to-date thinking about delinquency among sociologists combine to indicate that our policy concerns have more to do with the "differential organization" and behavior of our low-income population than with upper-class deviance, delinquency in general, or the specifics of reforming the behavior of individuals.[11]

[10] M. Freedman, "The Social Accounts of a Mixed Economy," paper in preparation for Conservation of Human Resources Project (Columbia University, 1965).

[11] For an overview of the American position on crime, see D. Bell, "Crime as an American Way of Life," *The End of Ideology* (New York: The Free Press of Glencoe, Inc., 1960). Sometimes, indeed, criminality can, in Alice in Wonderland fashion, actually become a source of respectability. Thus it was rumored that Tino DeAngelis, perpetrator of a $150 million dollar swindle in the recent "salad oil scandal," was mixed up in the Cosa Nostra. Said an official of a major company extending credit to DeAngelis: "If he were backed by that kind of money, we would have known that he was good for all that he owed us." See N. C. Miller, *The Great Salad Oil Swindle* (New York: Coward McCann, Inc., 1965). It may be noted that we "socialize" (and thereby legitimize) upper-class crimes to a notable degree by allowing their perpetrators to deduct criminal fines from taxable income. Thus heavy electrical equipment manufacturers who defrauded hundreds of customers of millions of dollars deducted the fines they were obliged to pay in pursuance of antitrust proceedings as "ordinary business expenses." And bankers, who carelessly extended credit to the Salad Oil King, were casual about the exposure of Tino DeAngelis as a swindler because they were able to offset their losses by deducting them as expenses. Perhaps the most interesting commentary on our "differential attitudes" toward crimes among different populations was made by Judge Wortendyke who presided

This inference is reinforced by the related conclusion, drawn from field investigations, that "lower-class" delinquency may represent a range of responses that is not, sociologically speaking, altogether inappropriate.[12] Given the different opportunities confronting low-income groups, the delinquent behavior of urban youths may be regarded as a way of coping that, by the standards of the subculture in which it occurs, serves significant sociological functions. In many instances, these standards (e.g., status and success) are "borrowed" from the middle class by social groups lacking the means to achieve them.[13]

Delinquency as "Differential Response"

If we are attentive to both the preferences and probabilities indicated, then the problem of selecting among public policy options is simplified considerably. Putting aside problems of implementation, we need only to examine the conditions, arrangements, and institutional structures that reinforce the "differential organization" of our urban, lower-class population groups.

If deviant behavior is adaptive in some socioeconomic contexts, according to the logic implied in the foregoing discussion, then we may modify these contexts and thereby make the deviance maladaptive. The problem is to discover policies and programs aimed not at delinquency, per se, but at specific circumstances that provoke unacceptable social responses, with the objective of so altering these circumstances that delinquent behavior no longer serves "sociological functions."

Consider an illustration from a related problem area. We know that a very substantial proportion of Negro youngsters are reared in households headed by women,[14] a consequence of current occupational problems facing Negro males, welfare policies that discriminate in favor of widowed and deserted female household heads, and historical conspiracies against stable Negro family life rooted in the period of slavery. In light of

---

in the Salad Oil trial. According to Miller: "The judge gave a glowing account of Tino's business acumen and stated: 'You yourself, Mr. DeAngelis, have exemplified what can be achieved with only a little backing or influence, by courage and vision.' Tino's success in business provided proof that 'we have a workable democracy' the judge declared."

[12] See Martin and Fitzpatrick's account, in the first chapter of *Delinquent Behavior,* of the development of this view.

[13] See, for example, R. A. Cloward, and L. E. Ohlin, *Delinquency and Opportunity* (New York: Free Press of Glencoe, Inc., 1960). The analysis draws heavily on the well-known theoretical work of Robert K. Merton, Columbia sociologist.

[14] *The Negro Family: the Case for National Action,* Office of Policy Planning and Research, United States Department of Labor (Washington, D.C.: U.S. Government Printing Office, 1965) (March, 1965), p. 17. (This is the so-called Moynihan Report.)

these factors, the much discussed matriarchal pattern (that sometimes even pertains in a stable Negro family where the male head has few employment opportunities) is an adaptation to grim social realities that make middle-class family patterns irrelevant if not impossible. As with low-income delinquency, it would be almost useless to "reform" the low- or no-income *family*. If the matriarchal pattern is undesirable then it is the structural arrangements endowing it with sociological functions that need to be reformed.[15]

The same logic may be applied to the problem of urban delinquency by redefining it in terms of class behavior. Thus we link it to the economic plight of those among whom it is prevalent, and we may move to a consideration of public policy alternatives that could alleviate this plight.

Two cautions must be made before we review policies in this context, however. First we need not deny, as James Tobin, distinguished economist and former presidential advisor, has pointed out, that

The economic plight of individuals . . . can always be attributed to specific handicaps and circumstances: discrimination, immobility, lack of education and experience, ill health, weak motivation, poor neighborhood, large family size, burdensome family responsibilities. Such diagnoses suggest a host of specific remedies. . . .

But, Tobin goes on to say,

Important as these remedies are, there is a danger that the diagnoses are myopic. They explain why certain individuals rather than others suffer from the economic maladies of the time. They do not explain why the over-all incidence of the maladies varies dramatically from time to time—for example, why personal attributes which seem to doom a man to unemployment in 1932 or even in 1954 or 1961 did not handicap him in 1944 or 1951 or 1956.[16]

The second warning is implicit in the preceding discussion. We have repeatedly emphasized that national interest in delinquency focuses on urban lower-class youths. We must be aware of the implications of such selectivity. If we did manage, by astute policy decisions, to minimize the "differential organization" of American society, we would not necessarily eliminate deviance. In reviewing our most relevant policy options, therefore, we must make room for the possibility—or even the probability—that forms of delinquency among the young may change as more become

[15] See H. Gans, "The Negro Family: Reflections on the Moynihan Report" *Commonweal*, LXXXIII, No. 2 (October 15, 1965).
[16] J. Tobin, "Improving the Economic Status of the Negro," *Daedalus* (Fall, 1965), issued as XCIV, No. 4 of *The Proceedings of the American Academy of Arts and Sciences*.

"middle class." We may take some consolation, perhaps, in the fact that deviant actions among the middle class are less troublesome (certainly less often prosecuted) than those manifest in the so-called culture of poverty. Presumably the anxieties of the prosperous are "better" than the alienation of the poor, sex is better than violence, and LSD at Harvard Square is preferable to heroin at Times Square. Fortunately or unfortunately, public policy, generally, is biased in favor of a middle-class way of life, however shallow, criminal,[17] or stultifying it may often be.

There is an advantage in linking urban delinquency to class structure and in considering economic policy in the context of concern with the reduction of gross class differences. Whatever policies we elect to pursue and implement, the aim is ostensibly to extend the prosperity of the majority to larger numbers of families. The result, to judge from studies on family dissolution, psychotic crime, addiction, malnutrition, and other pathological conditions disproportionately prevalent among low-income groups should be salutary indeed,[18] however much residual deviance we must expect to find in other social classes.

The policy options that become relevant to our discussion, then, are the same as those continually offered by participants in the contemporary debate over ways to achieve more rapid economic growth, an expansion of economic opportunity, and a solution to the problems of those who cannot work for reasons of health, age, or domestic obligations. We may now review those policies.

Public Policy Options: The "New Economics" and "The Positive State"

It is probably not much of an oversimplification to argue that we are confronted by only two real economic policy alternatives in the United States today, and even these have a number of apparently similar components. Neither has very much to do with the extremes in policy that used to color debate over public policy. We may, in short, safely ignore the economics of the radical Left and the radical Right. The 1964 Presidential election indicated no significant urge in America to repeal the twentieth or even the nineteenth centuries. Whereas editorialists in the *Wall Street Journal* preach *laissez-faire*, the news columns in that paper remind us daily of business support for a host of government activities that benefit corporations, the "widows and orphans" who own them, and the socially conscious professionals who manage them.

The Left, meanwhile, is also making peace with its devils; it is, indeed, almost embarrassing to witness the tortuous efforts of old-line planning

17 See D. Bell, *op. cit.*
18 M. Freedman, *op. cit.*, in which the author, in collaboration with this writer, has made estimates of the social and economic costs of poverty.

enthusiasts to work comfortably with basic principles of modern cost accounting. Just as the Right stumbles over subsidies, government contracts, and the many facilities provided at public expense—roads, airports, and the like—the Left is trying to find an ideological way round the nettlesome problems of distribution and resource allocation. While the Right has tried to make room for individualism in large and efficient collectivist-type organizations, the Left has attempted to develop a concept of "socialist profit."

Entertaining as these ideological tergiversations may be, they hold little significance for policy today. Neither the Radical Right nor the Radical Left, it may be asserted, has offered us meaningful policies; neither can mobilize the support of large segments of the population. There remain the "new economics" and the economics of "the positive state" from which to choose. We will consider these in some detail.

According to the "New Economics," economic growth comes primarily from the private sector of the economy and from public policies that give confidence to businessmen and investors. These policies would include: restraints on the powers and demands of organized labor; welfare policies that, through their modesty, encourage people to be gainfully employed; tax rates and provisions that favor corporations and upper-income groups; public subsidies for a multitude of business activities needing indirect assistance or even direct price support; and the exercise of a light hand on the levers of government regulations and antitrust machinery. According to the logic of the New Economics, poverty and unemployment will be gradually eliminated by economic growth.

To this end "Keynesian" ideas have been accepted by erstwhile conservatives as long as the object of government spending is to increase confidence. Thus "deficit spending" has been accepted in principle—even by the President of the U.S. Chamber of Commerce—if, in practice, the spending directly aids business and upper-income groups and if the Federal "take" from these groups is gradually reduced. Low- and no-income groups, it is argued, will benefit indirectly by a "trickle-down process,"[19] as confident business leaders and investors make socially desirable decisions to expand their operations. Such decisions, it is concluded, must be enlightened by educated expectations that government will eschew actions that, by helping the low-income population directly, would surely lead to confidence-shattering inflation and inevitably intensify the gold problem.[20] The assumption is made that direct action

[19] For a most helpful analysis of this point see W. H. L. Anderson, "Trickling Down: The Relationship Between Economic Growth and the Extent of Poverty Among American Families," *Quarterly Journal of Economics*, LXXVIII (November, 1964), 511–524.

[20] Tobin, *op. cit.*, pp. 884–886. See also J. K. Galbraith, "Economics and the Quality of Life" *Science*, CXLV, No. 3628 (July 10, 1964), 117–122.

against the conditions of poverty and inequality in the distribution of income would "tighten" the labor market, weakening a needed constraint on prices. The point is also made that the rise in the price level, resulting from more liberal action of the government, would not be offset by "the real economic and social gains of higher output and employment" that come with full employment.[21]

The only direct action concerning the poor that adherents of the New Economics have favored consists in such programs, embodied in the Economic Opportunity Act of 1964, which provide no full-time jobs—at least in the long run—for the underemployed and unemployed. Much of the "war on poverty" is actually a series of skirmishes with the poor themselves: Programs like the Job Corps are designed in part to train and educate youths, the (gratuitous) assumption being that there will be jobs available for successful graduates who are not personally inadequate in one or more ways.

The reader will have little difficulty recognizing that the assumptions, logic, and arguments of the New Economics form economic policy today. They underlie the efforts of the government to participate in collective bargaining negotiations, to link wages to productivity in the goods-producing sector through the proclamation of "guide posts," to reduce taxes for middle- and higher-income population groups, to increase depreciation allowances for capital equipment, and to avoid disrupting the political consensus that has made a more comfortable relationship between business and the federal government.

It is perhaps fair to characterize some of the liberals who have joined the proponents of the New Economics as political realists. Although they rarely say so explicitly, they know that one of the most crucial issues is maintaining business confidence. They bow to the capacity of business decision-makers to fulfill their own predictions concerning the likely consequences of policies that would tighten the labor market, raise median incomes, or make life slightly more bearable for citizens who receive welfare assistance.

Such political realism is criticized by the heirs of the liberalism of the 1930's, who have remained ideologically loyal over the years and are proponents of the *positive* uses of the state. They argue that the New Economics takes almost no account of the social costs of poverty and deprivation. If these policies are politically realistic, goes the argument, they are not economically unrealistic. They object that we now spend vast sums on the symptoms of poverty while not doing enough to eliminate the disease. At the same time we spend increasing sums on a "trickle down" policy that yields only drops. They point to the alienation of the poor, the disproportionate contribution the poor make to delinquency, dependency, crime, mental illness, and innumerable other forms of "devi-

[21] Tobin, *op. cit.*, p. 885.

ance" and social pathology. Disregarding the political problems involved, they remind us that if we had an adequate system of social bookkeeping we would see that we pay so enormous a price for our poverty that it is our biggest and most malevolent national luxury. We lose the manpower, tax payments, and social commitments of a fifth of the nation although we must finance broken families, prisons, detention homes, urban police forces, and a significant percentage of the capital and operating costs of courts, hospitals, and housing. At the same time, we receive an inadequate return (in employment) on our investment in economic growth policies.

Proposing that the state be positive in promoting employment (by investing, for example, in our sadly neglected public sector—roads, hospitals, schools, and housing) instead of making unproductive investments in arrangements that prevent full employment and perpetuate maldistribution of income, modern liberals argue that we make too much of inflation and gold stocks and ignore the "social" savings (and the gains) that could result from higher output and employment.

Consider that it cost 11.4 million dollars in 1958 to operate 21 detention institutions serving jurisdictions totaling approximately 35 million people in 14 states. (Had the services been of standard, i.e., acceptable, quality, the figure would have been closer to 21 million.) Worse, the figures are twice what they ought to be, because about half the children in these institutions did not belong there. Adequate training schools would cost an estimated 80 million dollars; Americans spent $61.1 million to operate 139 training schools in 1957–58. In 1960 we spent nearly 20 million dollars for probation staffs serving juvenile courts. Had the quality of these services met acceptable standards, the salaries would have come to 58 million dollars in that year.[22]

Belton Fleisher, in a study cited previously, offers some idea of the direct costs associated with the apprehension and prosecution of criminals in 1960. His figures include those involving crime committed by youths:

U.S. Police payroll	$1,000,000,000
U.S. Police equipment	1,000,000,000
Cost of government lawyers (34,000 at $10,000)	340,000,000 (est.)
Full-time staff of federal and state prisons (42,387 at median male personal income)	174,253,000
	$2,514,253,000[23]

[22] "Comparison of Expenditures and Estimated Standard Costs for Selected Juvenile Delinquency Services," pamphlet prepared for the Department of Health, Education, and Welfare by Government Consulting Service, Fels Institute of Local and State Government (University of Pennsylvania, 1960).

[23] B. M. Fleisher, "Unemployment and Juvenile Delinquency," *Journal of Political Economy,* LXXI, No. 6 (December, 1963), 554.

Fleisher estimates the lost labor productivity of individuals because of criminal records, using 1960 income data, and concludes . . . "the resulting lost earning power (to be) about $800,000,000 per year."[24] But, more significant to our discussion, he also estimates some of the savings that could result from a reduction in unemployment:

> Suppose appropriate policies should reduce unemployment by half. According to the regression results (obtained in his study of unemployment and delinquency) such a reduction in unemployment would be accompanied by a decline in property crime of approximately 10 per cent. This would eventually result in a saving to the U.S. economy of around $100,000,000 per year at present levels of population and labor productivity.[25]

We note that Fleisher writes here only of property crimes and points out that "obviously not all theft is social loss, since much of it must be construed as a wealth transfer."[26] Even considering this, the figures are significant. In a later study of "The Effect of Income on Delinquency,"[27] Fleisher reports, as we have pointed out, that a given rise in incomes will reduce delinquency by a predictable amount.

Obviously these analyses are based on estimates that may be faulty because of the weakness in the data used. Thus, no serious student of social pathology has much confidence in the comprehensiveness, for example, of the FBI's *Uniform Crime Reports*. The figures are offered in good faith as illustrative, not definitive. The reader must remind himself that in a discussion of delinquency, crime, and their costs we only scratch the surface of the personal, community, and societal losses associated so disproportionately with poverty.

Proponents of the positive state refuse to play according to the rules of what I have called the "confidence game."[28] Their commitment to government spending goes far beyond the amounts and types of Federal expenditures contemplated in the New Economics. Most of them would agree, however, that poverty has a depressing effect on price levels; it takes little imagination to see the substantial number of employable poor as a factor in controlling organized labor's demands for improved wages and working conditions. But the positive statists regard this as a doubtful value, one that is more than balanced by losses in productivity, in foregone tax dollars, and in transfer payments (e.g., for welfare) resulting from poverty.

24 *Ibid.*, p. 554.
25 *Ibid.*, p. 555.
26 *Ibid.*, p. 554.
27 B. M. Fleisher, "The Effect of Income on Delinquency," Working Paper No. 40, Center for Organizational Studies (University of Chicago, 1965), p. 28.
28 I. Berg, "The Confidence Game," *Columbia University Forum*, VI, No. 1 (Winter, 1963), 34–40.

These "Newer Dealers" have even begun to argue against minimum wage laws and trade union pensions (which do not take the productivity of labor into account) and in favor of supplementary payments to no- and low-income groups. They would, for example, eliminate a means test for public welfare and replace it with a needs test. Thus, both Gans, a sociologist, and Tobin, an economist, point out that aid for dependent— and too often delinquent—children is not available if there is an able-bodied man in the household, even if he is unemployed. This welfare policy, goes the argument, is misinformed in its assumption that welfare recipients will be encouraged, by penurious payments, to "get off the dole." Instead, families dissolve, mothers are taxed for working at a rate of 100 per cent, and children are encouraged to drop out of school when the inadequacy of welfare affects their dress and their capacity to participate in school life.[29] The reader may profitably read Professor Tobin's article for the most brief and intelligible statement yet offered on the concept of the so-called negative income tax to which the positive statists have recently returned.* They offer a welfare scheme based on need rather than on means and recognize that current welfare arrangements in most jurisdictions are cruel and demoralizing.

The positive statists applaud recent efforts to help specific disadvantaged groups, but they point out that the real problem of the poor goes beyond discrimination against Negroes. For them the "real" problem is embedded in social arrangements and economic practices that guarantee inequalities in the earning capacities of large numbers of citizens. It must be recognized, as Tobin suggests in his discussion, that many of these inequalities result less from the personal inadequacies of the poor than from inadequacies in the demand for their skills and from self-serving judgments on the economic value of some jobs among those who are well compensated. Individual earning capacity, they argue, is the result of labor market forces that interact with social judgments. Both of these are, in the view of reformers, subject to change by public educational and other policies. Thus, as Tobin points out:

> Economists have long held that the way to reduce disparities in earned incomes is to eliminate disparities in earning capacities. . . . If machine operators earn more than ditch diggers, the remedy is to give more people the capacity and opportunity to be machine operators. These changes in relative supplies reduce the disparity both by competing down the pay in the favored line of work and by raising the pay in the less remunerative line.[30]

[29] M. Freedman, *op. cit.*

*Robert Lampman, former staff member of the President's Council of Economic Advisors, has completed a study for the Office of Economic Opportunity in which he recommends a somewhat different version of the negative income tax from that outlined in *Daedalus* by Tobin. Both plans are reviewed, in outline fashion, in *Business Week* (November 13, 1965), pp. 105–106.

[30] J. Tobin, *op. cit.*, pp. 888–889.

It is obvious that the public has a vested interest in modifying the shape of the skill structure, patterns of discrimination, union barriers, educational practices, and needlessly selective recruiting policies. It also has an interest in tightening the loose labor market that reinforces inequalities in earning capacity resulting from social arrangements and practices that a loose labor market helps obscure.

Most adherents of this school admit that the New Economics has indeed produced increasing numbers of jobs in recent years. However, they see limitations in the capacity of these policies to produce jobs in numbers adequate to employ our growing labor force. They might argue, with some justice, that the New Economics is politically realistic largely because of its (economically unrealistic) concessions to recent converts. In yielding to criticisms that a shift in government spending in favor of low-income groups would be inflationary, the positive statists argue that the New Economics fails to consider the social costs of poverty and unemployment, including the direct and indirect costs of urban delinquency.

It is not hard for positive statists to understand that a traditional and narrow cost-benefit analysis of public finance would be attractive to reconstructed conservatives: A surplus in the labor force has been regarded historically as a boon to labor negotiations, to personnel officers in upgrading the quality of recruits, and to managers concerned with managements' rights and with discipline in the place of work. Such interests, however, can easily obscure the more vicious, if more subtle, consequences of substantial unemployment and underemployment.

The positive statists, in short, would use the considerable resources of the federal government not only to help groups such as Negroes, who have been deliberately denied advantages available to others, but all who do not have equality in earning capacity. For them, the fundamental prerequisite for equality in earning capacity is a "tight" labor market to be achieved through government spending on socially needed facilities and services and through a system of welfare based on the logic that family and individual income must be maintained. These are necessary, they argue, if we are not to have the higher costs that can be linked to the numerous pathological and socially disruptive correlates of poverty and if we are not to suffer the lost social product of unemployed resources. They favor employment policies responsive to a tight supply rather than the costs—personal and communal—that grow from a demand for people that adjusts itself by discrimination and excessive educational requirements, to an excessive supply. They would have the public take up this slack in demand.

In addition, the positive statists sometimes write of the need to reconsider the spending that does take place within the framework of the

New Economics. Thus economists Harold Edelstein and Peter Bernstein have argued that accelerating depreciation rates (widely hailed by post-Keynesians as indispensable to the stimulation of investment) "is not only unnecessary but dangerously discriminatory . . . it violates . . . basic principles. . . ." and point out that ". . . if obsolescence is used as an excuse for allowing corporations (to write off capital equipment faster), we face the danger that the tax structure will be used to bail out entrepreneurial errors. A plant or machine capable of producing goods for which there is no market may be the victim of technological obsolescence, but more frequently it is the product of managerial miscalculations in projecting the strength of future demand."[31]

We may also note criticisms of government policies involving the expenditure of funds that appear only as efforts to deflect attention from basic problems, to raise false hopes, and to help industry undertake new lines of activity without risk and with subsidies for the manpower costs of new business.[32] In general, however, the positive statists are inclined to accept present policies quite uncritically[33] and ask simply for extensions of policy along the lines outlined in our discussion.

Conclusion

Our policy choice is a relatively simple one. Although the politics of the New Economics and the economics of the "positive state" offer no solution to the problem of delinquency, which is a by-product of experiences that have no class boundaries, they both offer solutions to the problem of unemployment. We need only select one of the two, with the expectation that in eliminating poverty and unemployment we will have modified the circumstances that provoke the *specific* forms of unacceptable behavior occurring in conjunction with urban poverty.

My choice is full employment, a prospect I cannot see without government policies that go beyond those in the New Economics and without tying strings to many of the policies that are part of the New Economics. Thus I would favor a greater investment in the quality of

[31]H. M. Edelstein and P. L. Bernstein, "The Case against Accelerated Depreciation," *Social Research*, XXVIII, No. 4 (Winter, 1961), 492.

[32] I. Berg and M. Freedman, "Job Corps: a Business Bonanza," *Christianity and Crisis*, XXV, No. 9 (May 31, 1965), 115–119.

[33] Thus Leon Keyserling, Chairman of President Truman's Council of Economic Advisors, at a recent Symposium on Youth Employment said that ". . . private enterprise has done a good job in becoming more efficient, and this necessarily eliminates jobs; therefore they have to be created somewhere else." He went on to say that residual problems must be solved, and that they are the province of the Government and should be dealt with by a modest expansion of public ventures in housing and the rest. See I. Berg, "Help Wanted," *Columbia University Forum*, VII, No. 4 (Fall, 1964).

American life, in addition to a review of present expenditures with emphasis on needed reforms in tax laws and current subsidy programs.

I may conclude with a lengthy citation from "Improving the Status of the Negro" by Professor Tobin. It is an especially interesting statement, because Mr. Tobin was, during "The Kennedy Years" and during the first year of the Johnson Administration, a member of the President's Council of Economic Advisors. I have made the statement applicable to this chapter by omitting references to the Negro that appear in the original text:

> The forces of the market place, the incentives of private self interest, the pressures of supply and demand—these can be powerful allies or stubborn opponents. Properly harnessed they quietly and impersonally accomplish objectives which may elude detailed legislation and administration. To harness them . . . is entirely possible. It requires simply that the federal government dedicate its fiscal and monetary policies more wholeheartedly and singlemindedly to achieving and maintaining genuinely full employment. The obstacles are not technical or economic. One obstacle is a general lack of understanding that unemployment and related evils are remediable by national fiscal and monetary measures. The other is the high priority now given to competing financial objectives.

I see little purpose in attacking delinquency, as it is typically construed, and what Professor Tobin neatly describes as "related evils," apart from the more general problems of economic policy. We simply will never know how much and what kind of delinquency results fron noneconomic factors until we control the basic economic situation. Fortunately, our choices are not cluttered by great numbers of technical problems. It is therefore possible to recognize that the way to a sensible choice is blocked only by the debris of old ideas that makes debate on ideological issues perpetually difficult.

SELECTED READINGS

Arnold, T., "The Folklore of Capitalism." New Haven, Conn.: Yale University Press, 1938.

Bernstein, P., and R. Heilbroner, *A Primer on Government Spending.* New York: Random House, Inc., 1963.

Burns, A. F., "Our Largest Expansion," *Tax Foundations Tax Review,* XXVI, No. 11 (November, 1965).

Burns, E., "Where Welfare Falls Short," *The Public Interest,* No. 1 (Fall, 1965), pp. 82–95.

Butter, J. K., L. E. Thompson, and L. L. Hollinger, *Effects of Taxation.* Harvard University Graduate School of Business Administration (Boston, 1953). Pamphlet.

Cloward, R. A., and L. E. Ohlin, *Delinquency and Opportunity.* New York: Free Press of Glencoe, Inc., 1960.

Eckstein, O., *Public Finance,* Foundations of Modern Economics Series, Englewood Cliffs, N.J.: Prentice-Hall, Inc., 1964.

Federal Expenditure Policy for Economic Growth and Stability (Joint Economic Committee, U.S. Congress, 1957). Washington, D.C.: U.S. Government Printing Office, 1957. See especially papers by Frazer Wilde and Walter Heller.

Galbraith, J. K., "Economics and the Quality of Life," *Science,* CXLV, No. 3628 (July, 1964).

Guttentag, M., "The Relationship of Unemployment to Crime and Delinquency." Unpublished manuscript, Department of Psychiatry, Yale University.

Martin, T. M., and J. P. Fitzpatrick, *Delinquent Behavior.* New York: Random House, Inc., 1964.

Shonfield, A., *Modern Capitalism: The Changing Balance of Public and Private Power.* New York: Oxford University Press, Inc., 1966.

Tobin, J., "Improving the Economic Status of the Negro," *Daedalus* (Fall, 1965), issued as XCIV, No. 4 of *The Proceedings of the American Academy of Arts and Sciences.*

10 Prevention Through the Police

A. F. Brandstatter
James J. Brennan

The problem of juvenile delinquency in contemporary American society is inescapably serious. The latest FBI statistics[1] show that almost one million of our youth conflicted with the law during 1964, and the epidemiological rate for juvenile (age 18 and below) offenses increased 17 per cent in that year.

Unfortunately there is a certain superficiality in the public's attention to social problems, and delinquency is no exception. Public interest is maintained when the problem warrants headlines. Today delinquency, tomorrow a new problem arises, a new crisis fills the papers, and public attention is diverted from one to the other. Preventive measures directed at removing or ameliorating basic causal factors are neglected.

National conferences are held and remedial programs are proposed by sociologists, psychologists, and clerics. There are the advocates of stern retributive measures—those who would cure the problem with floggings, imprisonment, or hard labor. There are others who would solve it with so-called soft treatment, aimed at therapy. Determinists deny the force of intellect and will and claim that delinquents act as they do because of social conditioning. The problem continues, with untold cost in economic loss and human misery.

Confusion surrounds society's efforts to prevent delinquency in its

[1] *Uniform Crime Reports for the United States, 1964* (Washington, D.C.: U.S. Government Printing Office, 1965).

young. One can almost sympathize with some of the lay public's lack of understanding, apathy, and emotionalism. There are conflicts in facts, in theories of causation, and in theories of prevention and control. Some people blame world tensions, the aftermath of war, lack of educational facilities, lack of recreation, slums, and family disintegration for the increase in delinquency. However, other people are doubtful. World tension exists for all juveniles, but all are not delinquent; the same is true of war's aftermath. There is considerable doubt over the efficacy of traditional education. We are the most affluent country in the world, with less real hardship, and yet we have the most delinquency. Lack of recreation? Many children in areas without such facilities are not delinquent, whereas others are delinquent who enjoy ample recreational opportunity. Slums, large families, unemployment, ill health, lack of education and vocational training also exist for many more than those who are delinquent.

People are confused. They believe that to have 3, 2, or even 1 per cent of our youth committing delinquent acts is a national waste—morally, economically, socially. The public observes a change in the character of delinquent acts that frightens them. In juvenile killings, rapes, robberies, and vandalism they sense a moral depravity or psychopathy that is difficult to accept but tragic to see as it spreads more and more among our young.[2] People see a serious breakdown in social and individual morality and in respect for law and order.

The concerned public is no longer impressed by the often conflicting statistics, the conferences upon conferences, the seemingly studious avoidance of coming to grips with the problem while many specialists continue to study obscure social theories and rationalizations. These people, concerned about the young and their value and worth to themselves and society, are seeking a means to articulate a deep conviction. When it is expressed, it will call everyone to the battle, and at the same time it will be a tolling bell for the faddists and fashionists, the dwellers in libido, the particularists, the scientists who are not scientific, and those who would sacrifice more youth while temporizing and trying to discover more remedial programs that do not remedy.

One force that can respond to the needs of the bewildered and to the cry for help from those who want help, one force that can do much—but not all—to stem the tide of delinquent behavior is the police of our communities throughout the country.[3] Policemen bind themselves by oath to protect the lives and property of the people they serve. Fre-

[2] Walter A. Lunden, *Statistics on Delinquents and Delinquency* (Springfield, Ill.: Charles C. Thomas, Publisher, 1965), pp. 10–11.

[3] George W. O'Connor and Nelson A. Watson, *Juvenile Delinquency and Youth Crime: The Police Role* (Washington, D.C.: Field Service Division, International Association of Chiefs of Police, 1964), pp. 4–7.

quently, police officers sacrifice their lives in the performance of duty. Most policemen are aware of the value of youth; they realize that young people are worth all the time, talent, devotion, and sacrifice they can give. If the police protect and preserve the young, they protect and preserve our way of life, our democratic society, and our nation. Many police departments throughout the nation have accepted the challenge to do all in their power to understand, diagnose, and prevent juvenile delinquency. The dedicated and professional police officer, available twenty-four hours each day, is an indispensable agent of society in the prevention and control of juvenile delinquency.

Police and Social Problems

There is almost a universal stereotype of police as repressive agents concerned only with enforcing law and with apprehending violators. The patrolman who tries doors to see that they are secure and tickets illegal parkers, the "cop" who responds to fires and ambulance calls, accepts a bribe, and chases the kids—these form the stereotype.

That police could be concerned with social problems is difficult for many to appreciate. Yet crime and delinquency are themselves manifestations of personal and social disorganization and dyscontrol.[4] The breakdown of the family, the acceptance of materialistic over moral values, the inadequacies of education, the mobility of people, "big city" phenomena create problems that directly concern the police. To understand and cope with them, policemen must learn to understand the human relations problems that result from group living.

The role of the police is complex and difficult in today's urban society, especially in the "inner city." Police cannot be effective if they isolate themselves from the community or stand silent. They must articulate their problems if they are to gain understanding and support; they must join forces with responsible elements of the community if they are to minimize lawlessness and disorder, whether it emerges as minor delinquency or as adult criminality.

No longer can police departments be content with advances in transportation, communication, criminology, identification, and investigation as tools to apprehend the killer, the thief, and the vandal. Now police must understand and be concerned with racial prejudice, minority conflict, labor strife, juvenile gangs, addiction, alcoholism, and a host of other communal problems that, far more than challenging mere ordinances and statutes, threaten the very foundation of a democratic society. Policemen, now more than ever, must be "social practitioners," students of social and

[4] Karl Menninger, *The Vital Balance* (New York, The Viking Press, Inc., 1964).

psychological phenomena, if they are to fulfill their responsibility to promote the common good of our communities and nation. A knowledge of law and arrest procedures is no longer sufficient for even the lowest police "rookie."

The social aspects of police service can be expanded most directly through delinquency-prevention work. This must be developed and enlarged through imaginative and creative programs. The growth of the police function is necessary in a pluralistic, mobile society. To be static, to be isolated, to blindly pursue traditional practices is to ignore the social responsibility of police service and can only result in tragedy and wasted human resources.

The police is the agency around which the community can and often does rally when acute social problems must be solved. The traditional response of the police force is no longer completely adequate, and it must be supplemented with other means of developing and maintaining tranquility in the community; police can no longer stand by and wait to act until an easily anticipated incident has occurred with tragic consequences. The current emphasis and focus is on the prevention of delinquency and crime, and the police acknowledge this as one of their principal responsibilities. The public, in part, realizes this also but seemingly does not know how to respond. Therefore, by default, it falls upon the police to initiate positive action and to develop programs that will involve elements of the community in the preventive aspects of police work. In this way the community may find some solutions or amelioration of its complex problems. Social disorder and injustice are found within the community and can only be eradicated at their sources. By assuming a preventive leadership role, the police can assist the community to accept its responsibility in seeking solutions to the many complex social issues and stresses that threaten our society with anarchy and injustice.

The police must broaden their ability to meet the challenges of modern society: They must change their own image, increase their learning, and develop their capacities. Change must also come from the public, which, once vitally involved in policing the community, has surrendered the job completely and relegated it to paid public servants. People who are "police problems" are also problems for the entire community—for families, schools, welfare agencies, correction agencies, hospitals, and youth shelters.[5]

Much can be done when the police extend their role, and when the responsible citizenry cooperate there is no greater force in the community. An interesting example is the positive results of the National Police and Community Relations Institute, conducted since 1955 at

[5] O. W. Wilson, ed., *Parker on Police* (Springfield, Ill.: Charles C. Thomas, Publisher, 1957), pp. 11–17.

Michigan State University under the auspices of the School of Police Administration and Public Safety. This yearly institute has led to the formation of many local and regional programs through which police and other people of the community have worked together to solve difficult community problems. The institute has focused attention on the leadership potential of the police in the community and on the force of aroused public opinion.

Regionally, institutes on police-community relations have been held in the Northeast, Southeast, and Southwest. Each is of four or five days' duration and attracts participants—police and other community leaders— from several area states. For example, the institute at Texas A. & M. University has been held annually for seven years, with participants from Texas, Louisiana, Oklahoma, and Arkansas. State institutes have been held in twenty-one states, each of one or two days' duration, many of them on an annual basis. At the local level a wide variation in types of programs and projects exists—from highly organized, well-financed, crime prevention-oriented programs, such as in St. Louis, San Francisco, Washington, D.C., Baltimore, Philadelphia, and Chicago, to localized one-day institutes dealing with specific topics such as police relations with Puerto Rican citizens, police-press relationships, or the attitudes of youth toward law and authority.

The concepts discussed here reject the premise that a police department is only as good as the community wants it to be. This premise is based on a defeatist and negative attitude, and no police official needs to accept it. Admittedly, some elements in the community may favor such "laissez-faire" attitudes. The police officer is the symbol of law and order, and if this symbol is to be preserved, no enforcement agency can afford to succumb to negative community pressures. The heritage of freedom and "equal justice for all" is the reward for positive action. The visible representative of the power of the state must assure its citizens of this reward. No price is too great for the preservation of these principles.

Police and Delinquency

Delinquency is probably one of the primary social concerns of the police that cannot be corrected entirely by legal procedure.[6] The police can by no means do the job alone, but they can perform a vital service in delinquency prevention and control. Many public and private agencies must join forces to help young people develop, but no other single agency has been assigned a clearer responsibility than the police. All police are charged with the prevention of crime, and intelligent crime

[6] Sophia M. Robison, *Juvenile Delinquency, Its Nature and Control* (New York: Holt, Rinehart & Winston, Inc., 1961), pp. 207–226.

prevention must begin with delinquency prevention. Prevention of delinquency is not to be confused with crime suppression. Prevention, as Lejins has indicated in Chapter 1, is of a different character and must attack the contributing factors to delinquency and the motivations that precipitate delinquent behavior.

Delinquency prevention has been a recognized part of police work since the turn of the century. There has been scattered public, and even professional, appreciation. Long before any organized effort was made, there were policemen, who, avoiding indiscriminate arrests, gave advice and counsel to erring youth and were frequently rewarded by seeing these youngsters become worthwhile citizens. All too often, however, police were exposed to the frustrating experience of seeing delinquent youth grow into hardened criminals. Despite arrests, court appearances, and institutional commitments, the same young people at various ages were again recidivists, threats to the community, and problems to the police.

Throughout the country, various police efforts were made to warn and admonish youth, to avoid unnecessary arrests, to protect young girls, and to suppress conditions contributing to delinquency, but these early efforts were sporadic. Many police department administrators were unresponsive: To them it seemed to be "social work," not police responsibility. However, the movement toward prevention and control continued to develop slowly. Some police interpreted suppressive action to be strictly crime- and delinquency-preventive. Some opposed dissipation of police effort, already inadequate, to areas of peripheral concern. However, the crime wave of the 1920's compelled further attention and effort; since 1930 there has been a definite attempt to develop such programs in police departments. Some still object; others claim to be involved without actually being engaged in delinquency prevention and control; but many large and small departments are moving courageously ahead.[7] There is great need for enlightened leadership from police executives in this connection.

There have been, and still are, criticisms of police delinquency-prevention programs. Some are justified; others are not. Many criticisms are suspiciously allied to vested-interest concern rather than to the interests of youth. Professional titles and academic degrees do not necessarily qualify one to work constructively with youngsters in need of redirection. In general, however, steady progress is being made and public support is increasing for police involvement in prevention and control of delinquency and crime.

Numerous studies have been made of police work with juveniles, but

---

[7] *Police Work with Children,* Publication No. 399 (Washington, D.C.: U.S. Department of Health, Education, and Welfare, Children's Bureau, 1962), p. 5.

little evaluation has been made of these efforts. The bibliography appended to this chapter contains some references to such studies and provides for more extensive reading.

One of the earliest studies made on the police role in delinquency prevention and control was completed by Brennan[8] in 1952. This extensive research project involved 168 police departments throughout the United States, and reported many and varied activities in connection with delinquency and crime prevention under three basic functions. Whether the program is in the hands of one officer, as many are, or conducted by a specific unit in a larger organization, certain activities are directed more to control, others to the handling of the individual delinquent, and still others to community organization work.[9]

Not many departments conduct all three operations with equal vigor. The first function—control—is shared by the entire department, although certain conditions may best be dealt with by specialized units of the department such as vice squads, narcotics bureaus, patrols, detectives, and juvenile units. The second function—securing treatment for the individual offender—is a new concept of police administration and is handled with varying success in the many departments. The third function—community organization work—is less frequently attempted, but police are beginning to recognize its tremendous potential for delinquency prevention and control.

These, then, are the basic operations or functions of police in delinquency-prevention programs. Each will now be considered in greater detail.

The Control Aspect
of Police Delinquency-Prevention Work

There are persons, places, and socioenvironmental conditions in every community that can and do contribute to delinquency. Some of these exist in violation of law and are thus subject to police action or to control by licensing agencies. Others, however, are not amenable to a legal approach and can only be dealt with adequately by an aroused public opinion. Unfortunately, it is difficult to arouse such opinion and more difficult to focus it on a particular situation that must be eradicated. Better community organization is required to achieve this objective, with support from *all* sectors of society, not just those in the social welfare realm.

[8] James J. Brennan, "Police and Delinquent Youth," *Journal of Criminal Law, Criminology and Police Science*, XLVI, No. 6 (March–April, 1956).

[9] O'Connor and Watson, *op. cit.*, p. 52.

The "Fagin," the sex pervert, the promoter of prostitution, the drug pusher, the tavern owner who sells to minors, and all who contaminate the youth of our communities should be dealt with promptly and adequately. Such individuals must be prosecuted when they violate laws, especially when the moral and social welfare of youth is at stake.

Most communities have both licensed and unlicensed places, frequented by youth, which require supervision and control. Pool rooms, junk shops, secondhand dealers, movie theaters, and dance joints have legitimate reasons to be in business. But all too frequently economic gain looms more important to proprietors than the morality of boys and girls; in some instances, where laws are violated, vigorous police intervention is necessary. In situations where legal action is impossible, regulatory efforts must be attempted by other public and nonpublic agencies, such as the press. Close cooperation among these groups can have salutary results.

Parks, beaches, playgrounds, and public buildings are highly desirable for health and recreation, but unfortunately these, too, can be perverted by antisocial persons into liabilities rather than assets. Preventive work by the patrol force in such areas is mandatory.

The police responsibility for continuous surveillance of such persons, places, and conditions is not primarily that of the juvenile officer or juvenile unit. Specialization within some police departments gives the juvenile division, for example, sole responsibility in some instances involving youths. Usually, the need for continuous observation and for immediate action, when necessary, requires close coordination and cooperation of all police including patrol, traffic, detective, and juvenile units.

In all instances, however, officers assigned to youth work should maintain a special interest in all such potential trouble spots within their community. They should make it their responsibility to follow through on all cases until such conditions are eliminated or suppressed.

Police can only secure evidence, make arrests, and present their cases in court. Prosecutors, judges, and jurors must do their respective jobs with scrupulous care to guarantee the legal rights of the accused. There must be an accompanying zeal to protect the minds and bodies of youth and to promote the public welfare.

In addition, those forces that create delinquency also can act on the police and produce the enigma of every police department—the "crooked police officer." We cannot now evaluate the influence this role model has on juveniles, but obviously it must contribute to the rejection or neutralization by some juveniles of the norms of society. The absence of these norms is believed by many to be a precondition to consistent deviate behavior. We feel that this regrettable problem, though it is rarely faced, is a significant obstacle to police effectiveness in delinquency prevention. Society must create a more useful and meaningful role for the police, community opinion and resources must be mobilized in their support, and better pay and work conditions provided if police corruption is to be reduced and an effective attack is to be made on the larger problem of delinquency prevention. It is this ideal condition that we will consider in the following section.

As indicated earlier, not all community health and moral hazards are amenable to legal action. Some conditions detrimental to youth can only be remedied through aroused public opinion and concerted community action. Society will not favor a police force of inordinate size or power (this will be considered when discussing community organization). Both law and social pressure must be utilized to make communities socially healthy places for all children, where social disorganization does not occur in the form of "not enough" education, housing, food, recreation, and employment.

The Individual Delinquent

As stated previously, there is much confusion in the proposals for handling delinquents. Some would excuse all such acts as motivated by physical, mental, emotional, and social stresses beyond the individual's moral and social responsibility. Other proposals demand severe retributive punishment with no regard for various contributing factors, which, if they do not handicap the individual in exercising his social responsibility, at least tend to impel him to antisocial, destructive acts.

The children's court, which came into existence at the turn of the century, is meant to sustain the responsibility of youth and, at the same time, to delve into the surroundings, formative influences, and institutions to determine the assets and liabilities in a young offender's background and experiences. It is hoped that evaluation of such factors will lead to ways of increasing the assets and reducing the liabilities in each case to help develop a morally and socially responsible individual. In addition to the court, a variety of services—psychological testing, probation, clinics, rehabilitation institutions—has been developed to further this end.

In reality, we know that many youngsters, though legally delinquent, are fortunate enough to receive help without recourse to actual court appearance with its possible traumatic result. Social agencies, mental health and child-guidance clinics, youth clubs, recreation programs, and the schools have worked and are working with many such youngsters, with much success.

The police are the first social agency through which many delinquents are brought into contact with both executive and judicial functions. Frequently, because of the minor or initial nature of the offense, there may be only a police warning and a referral to parents. This is believed to be a desirable use of police discretionary power. Most first offenders never reappear on police records.

The apparent singleness of objective, both of court and probation procedures—the redirection of the erring youngster into a socially desirable way of life—demands the use of any and all facilities to accomplish or initiate such help. Neither extreme of ignoring the offense or indiscriminately arresting and charging all juvenile offenders is recommended. Enlightened police procedures call for wise discretion in the use of police power to apprehend, transport, retain in custody, and charge juveniles involved in delinquent acts.

Awareness of this fact has encouraged police to develop programs designed to achieve an understanding of the young and to secure adequate help for those in need of attention.[10] If a juvenile, guilty of a minor offense, receives intelligent and sympathetic consideration—neither authoritative nor condoning—factors contributing to his behavior may be discovered and an effective use made of community resources to help him solve his problems. This is essentially what social work is meant to accomplish.

Police who are attempting to do effective work along these lines appreciate the depth of this undertaking. They realize that basing action solely on the seriousness of the offense is actually treating surface "symptoms" and not basic causes. They are beginning to understand more and more that you cannot treat larceny, malicious mischief, or incorrigibility because these are only definitions in law books and reveal nothing of the character, personality, and compelling motivations of the offender, however unreal and distorted they may be.

There is an acute awareness in the better police programs that the police cannot initiate treatment, as such. What they want to accomplish is a gross or rough diagnosis that provides for an intelligent referral for treatment. In addition, the police want insight into the basic causal factors (which are always plural in number) which predispose many persons to antisocial conduct; only from such knowledge may a preventive crime program be designed.

This work requires superior education. There is a need to understand the nature and development of personality and character in the individual. Such professional scientific training is becoming more and more available throughout the country. Michigan State University, for example, through its School of Police Administration and Public Safety, offers both a bachelor's and master's degree with a major course of study in delinquency prevention and control. Curriculum requirements include ele-

[10] O. W. Wilson, *Police Administration*, 2nd ed. (New York: McGraw-Hill Book Company, 1963), pp. 321-353.

mentary and advanced courses in sociology, psychology, and social work, as well as a practicum in intensive field training.

For those already engaged in police work with social applications, various institutes and short-course programs are available. Michigan State regularly offers such training on both basic and advanced levels. Other universities and colleges also provide such training. Information concerning courses may be secured from the International Association of Chiefs of Police, 1319 Eighteenth Street, N. W., Washington, D.C. 20036.

This, then, is an overview of the new police concepts regarding the juvenile delinquent. There is nothing in this concept that condones or excuses a delinquent from responsibility for his actions. It is directed toward identifying the potential delinquent, determining by scientific diagnosis the help needed, and then making appropriate and timely referrals, with some followup to assist the referral agency if necessary and to assure that the planned program of rehabilitation and adjustment is functioning optimally.

Community Organization

By its very nature, the prevention and control of delinquency cannot be the sole responsibility of any one agency, public or private, judicial or nonjudicial. Many other agencies and persons in the community—parents, the church, social and recreational agencies, the school, local government, the press, and others—have equal responsibility. Delinquency is the expression of the dynamic forces that interact within a community. Both primary and secondary social institutions, so important to moral and social growth, are found there. What is required is more individual and collective awareness of the need for involvement of all agencies and social forces in the community to do everything possible for the good of its youth. Our basic institutions—home, school, and church—need serious reevaluation of their roles and functions.

The homes of many delinquents are deficient in love, affection, security, and discipline, and parents too frequently let neighborhood practice rather than firm moral ideas of right or wrong or common sense guide their decisions. This is particularly noticeable in such matters as steady dating for fourteen- or fifteen-year-olds, the uncontrolled use of cars, and the way both boys and girls dress.

It has been alleged by uninformed critics that our schools lack moral content in their educational program and that lack of school discipline leads to the further breakdown of respect for authority. They claim that students during twelve years of attendance are given little sense of moral and social responsibility and consequently will make a poor showing as future parents. Citizens tend to charge the school with responsibility for the moral training that primarily must reside in the home and church. Most schools work hard at instilling moral values and respect for persons and property. It is well-known that the quality of education varies greatly among communities. That the schools are doing a good job with the support they receive is proven by the great majority of graduates and even of dropouts who do adjust to life and become good citizens. There is room for improvement, which will come when society provides the schools with better tools to do this vital work. The question is not whether society can afford good schools: The question is whether society can afford *not* to have good schools.

Few people recognize the tremendous importance of religion in providing the spiritual element so necessary for man to achieve his true purpose of living. Many delinquents either lack such training or have had only a superficial exposure to it; few delinquents have a firm religious belief. Psychiatrists state that religious orientation is a source of great strength to ward off mental illness.

There are other institutions that must reexamine the part they play in the lives of youth. Government at the national, state, and local level must be vitally concerned with the welfare of youth: It must provide the facilities for physical, mental, and social development. Government agencies should make every effort to improve the moral and social climate of the community for our growing youngsters. Federal legislation has appropriated vast sums of money for education, vocational training, and antipoverty work on a scale never before attempted. The police of every community have the responsibility of enforcing the law; to a certain degree they regulate social conduct. The example they set is a powerful force for good or evil, and, if even a few are dishonest or brutal, these few can do much harm. The press and other mass media are likewise important in establishing the moral climate of our communities. All service agencies are committed to work diligently with youth. Commercial vendors of recreation must constantly be on guard lest a desire for profit lead them to acts detrimental to youngsters.

All of the above should be consciously concerned with the welfare of youth. Unfortunately, this is not always the case. Power, both legal and extralegal, must be exercised to bring about such concern. Good community organization can provide the means to identify problem areas. Whether it is a matter of comic book sales, the display of questionable magazines and movies, graft, corruption, or parental indifference, an active community organization can propose, demand, educate, and continue to arouse public opinion to make the community a healthier place physically, socially, and morally.

What is essential and most frequently lacking is a means of bringing together all of the moral and social agencies of the community, of stimulating them to action, of coordinating their activities, of determining the need for additional services, and of concentrating attention on the problems that must be solved. The difficulty in this is that most agencies and institutions serve others besides delinquents. They may want to help, but they often believe that it is not their specific responsibility to work for a united, organized program.

Police, on the other hand, are in a unique position to initiate such a program. They are not social agencies or institutions, per se: They are neutral in terms of social service, but not in objectives. They have a direct responsibility to prevent crime, and this involves preventing delinquency. If intelligently stimulated, the public will support such a program, and social agencies will support such a police initiative. A word of caution is in order: Some communities will not favor police involvement in "social work"; here the ground must be prepared carefully before police commitment is attempted.

As indicated earlier, this is an area few police departments have entered. It is an approach with great potential for successful control and prevention of delinquency, although some failures have been reported. Where such police initiative was unsuccessful, there may have been a lack of understanding of how to organize and develop programs and how to activate groups in the community without imposing undesirable controls under police auspices. One individual telling a stationer or drugstore proprietor to clean out the "muck" on his bookshelves will get nowhere, but a community, aroused by general awareness and determination, will soon accomplish more than the provisions of the penal law.

With the full support of the community and its resources, young people will feel important without headlines. Their need for guidance and direction will not receive secondhand, meager treatment. There will be a sufficient number of trained social workers, probation officers, and court facilities. For serious cases requiring institutional care, there will be the kind of institution and staff both able and willing to use therapy, not punishment, in salvaging youthful offenders. There will still be young people with problems and young people who fail to adjust to the demands of social living, but they will not be lost through the neglect of needed preventive measures on the part of those to whom their welfare should be of primary importance.[11]

An encouraging example of effective police-community cooperation is the Police School Liaison Program in Flint, Michigan. Here is a model of official agencies and parents working together to resolve a difficult situation involving teen-age crime. Prior to the development of this

[11] A. H. Chapman, *Management of Emotional Problems of Children and Adolescents* (Philadelphia: J. B. Lippincott Co., 1965), p. 143.

program, in a certain city area one child for every thirty-six public school-age pupils was involved in delinquency. After the program had been in effect one year, only one pupil in every 280 was involved. The results in that single year were convincing enough to continue and extend the program to other parts of the city. It consists in the full-time assignment of a police officer to the schools: He becomes an integral part of the school personnel and works with the teaching staff, administration, students, and parents. The officer is also a member of a "regional counseling team" consisting of a registered nurse, a qualified teacher, the junior high school dean of students, and the elementary school principal. The team's function is to identify a juvenile problem at the predelinquent or early delinquent stage and to make a proper referral for treatment.

Some Guides for Good Police Programs in Delinquency Prevention

A study of effective police programs for delinquency prevention and control has revealed that such programs were developed on sound principles, with excellent organization and administration. The purpose here is not to give a detailed procedure for such organization and administration: It consists in brief observations on some essentials believed necessary for success.

Preliminary Survey

The establishment of such a program should be preceded by a survey to determine the extent of the problem—the number of delinquents, their age and sex, and the type, location, and severity of offenses. A study of police records of complaints and arrests, of court records, and recommendations from police officers for several preceding years will provide this information.

The resources available for the treatment of individual delinquents should be surveyed. These include churches, schools, social agencies, child-guidance clinics, and health and recreation agencies. All facilities that can help to redirect the erring youngster should be investigated. It is equally important to know the liabilities of the community—the places, persons, and conditions that can or do contribute to delinquency.

Authority for the Program

Most police programs for delinquency prevention and control are established by order of the chief administrator of the department. Some, however, have been authorized by local ordinances. Before such a legal step is enacted, there are hearings at which the police program should be well described, its responsibilities established, and its relationship to other agencies of the community defined. When a departmental order is the source of authorization, efforts should be made to enunciate the details of policy, responsibility, and relations with other public and private services. This has been found imperative in order to avoid misunderstandings and malpractices by all concerned.

Determination of Policy

Police should establish policy for their own prevention program, and it should be extended to the entire department. Policy decisions should clearly specify standard operating procedures (SOP) for such matters as the age and sex of offenders to be handled by the prevention unit, the type and nature of offenses acceptable for diagnosis and referral to agencies, and the type and nature of cases that usually go to court. Where police discretionary action is permissible, it should be specified. Another question to be resolved is whether the police officers assigned to prevention work will keep under surveillance those places that could encourage delinquency. The duties of all police officers in respect to juvenile infractions also require definition, both for recruit and in-service training. In making such decisions, the recommendations of police commanders and supervisors, juvenile or probate judges, probation officers, and others who may be involved in the program should be invited.

Relation of Prevention Unit to Other Agencies of the Community

As indicated above, the police program should be explained to the youth-serving agencies of the community. The respective agencies should be asked to define their own areas of special concern and to indicate the cases they will accept on referral. They should be requested to advise the police-prevention unit on the continuing status of all referred cases and on when and what disposition has been effected and why, and a final report should be filed on each case in the police department's records.

Position of Prevention Unit in Departmental Structure

The delinquency-prevention unit should be independent and directly responsible to the chief of police. The nature of prevention work and the community relations that must be promoted necessitate a flexibility and opportunity for growth that should not be encumbered by subordinating the program under another police activity.

Personnel

EXECUTIVE DIRECTOR   The executive director may be chosen from within or without the department. It would be preferable to have an experienced police officer assigned to head the unit. Rank is important in large prevention units, but the rank of patrolman is satisfactory in smaller programs. It is important that the best man be chosen in terms of his education, personality, interest, and motivation. Salary and other desirable aspects of assignment to the preventive unit should be based on ability and experience, not merely on assignment to the unit. This will avoid the possibility of persons without interest or qualifications seeking this assignment solely for its material advantages.

OTHER MEMBERS   The number of personnel assigned, both policewomen and policemen, should be determined by the work load and by other demands on the department. A policewoman can handle girls' cases and those of boys under ten years of age. Academic experience, policework background, personality, adaptability to the work, and interest in the program are the overriding criteria to be used in selecting the staff. Seniority should have no consideration in selection.

REMUNERATION AND RECOGNITION   Specialized police work, especially in the detective division, frequently receives both extra remuneration and rank. Successful prevention work is as important as any other police activity, and the work of those who apply themselves in the prevention unit should be appropriately appreciated and recognized. However, personel should not be assigned to specialized police functions merely to gain promotion or more desirable work conditions.

TRAINING   In addition to a strong academic background and a minimum of experience, there should be initial indoctrination in the philosophy, procedures, and objectives of the unit. More extensive training in related social-science areas can be developed with the cooperation of local educational institutions. Staff meetings can be developed into training sessions. Personnel from the courts, social and health agencies, welfare, and the schools can be invited to discuss their programs. In-service training should be a continuous process, focused on both immediate and long-range deficiencies as they are identified.

Advisory Boards

Carefully selected civilian advisory boards can help to develop the program, to interpret the work to the community, to prevent undue pressure on the unit, and, from time to time, to help evaluate the effectiveness of the work. These boards do not necessarily become obstructionist unless poorly selected or administered. Lay counsel is often of great value in this connection.

Community Organizations

Organizing or participating in the establishment of a community organization or coordinating council is one way the police department can extend the effectiveness of the social and recreational facilities of a community. Such organizations can prevent duplication of effort, stimulate existing agencies to a better performance, and help determine the need for new facilities. The direction and continuous motivation of such groups requires understanding and a willingness to have individuals, other than police, propose programs for the welfare of the youth of the area.

Complementary Programs

Police delinquency-prevention programs should be concerned with:

1. Suppressing or eliminating persons, places, and conditions contributing to delinquency;
2. Identifying predelinquents and delinquents, determining their needs, and referring them to suitable remedial facilities; and
3. Engaging in effective community coordination and cooperation aimed at eliminating the causal factors of delinquency and at promoting the moral and physical welfare of youth.

Social-service activities, whether in social work, recreation, or rehabilitation, are not specific police responsibilities. If the lack of such agencies and facilities requires police to do such work, this should be temporary, conducted by the best personnel available, and confined to the limited area of absolute needs. As soon as possible, police operation should be terminated in favor of more professional programs.

Forms and Records

Forms and records should be at a minimum. These should include:

1. Referral cards, 3 in. by 5 in., to be carried by the entire police force to facilitate the referral of cases. The card should provide the identification of the individual, his age and sex, the complaint and the name of the complainant, the location and circumstances, and companions of the offender.
2. An information form to be used by the prevention unit to record additional information needed for diagnosis, referral, and follow-up, including disposition.

204 A. F. Brandstatter and James J. Brennan

3. Central filing to facilitate checking on individuals to determine whether or not they are "repeaters." A few communities have central files containing all delinquent cases, whether originally known to private agencies, courts, or the police. These records should be kept strictly confidential for police or court use only, and a "need to know" must be established for all users. When the juvenile becomes twenty-one, with no additional charges against him, the record should be destroyed. This prevents a childhood offense harming an adult who has become a good citizen.

4. Spot maps to help determine areas of delinquency concentration. They can also be used to designate resources as well as to point out conditions contributing to delinquency.

5. Monthly and yearly reports to show the number of cases handled, their source and disposition, agencies to whom referred, and number of repeaters. Age, sex, and offense classifications are also important.

Evaluative Studies

There is no excuse for perpetuating poor practices. Police delinquency-prevention work should be constantly evaluated. Records can give some evidence of the accomplishments of the program. Case loads, number of repeaters, and number of arrests can all be used to determine work efficiency and the need to change direction or to expand activities.

Evaluation by professionally trained, objective observers is most desirable. Colleges and universities can help here. Further, reports on cooperative studies by police prevention units and on research findings by colleges and universities can contribute to the general fund of knowledge concerning this complex social problem.

Public Relations

The need for sound public relations in all social-action programs involving the cooperation of groups as well as of individuals is self-evident; police delinquency-prevention programs are no exception. Many individuals and groups must come to mutual understanding and cooperate if the program is to be successful. There are always "blind spots" in thinking, fixed attitudes, resistances, prejudices, and other barriers to communication that must be considered.

Some of the individuals and groups of particular importance to police work with juveniles are: all members of the police department; the personnel of the prevention unit; complainants; delinquents; parents of delinquents; public and private agencies; and other prominent individuals of the community whose cooperation is needed. All these individuals and groups must gain an understanding of the program and of its objectives and goals, and efforts should be made to secure mutual cooperation and acceptance. For this purpose, brochures, discussions, meetings, and informal gatherings are useful. In dealing with individuals, the most important method to secure cooperation is personal communication, based on friendly personal relations. Everyone, including the policeman on the street, the delinquent and his parents, the complainant, public and private agencies, and the general public, should be made aware of what is being done, how it is being accomplished, and what objectives are sought.

Conclusion

Some years ago a police officer assigned to juvenile work in an eastern city spent a very uncomfortable evening. He was watching a clock move very slowly toward 11:00 P.M. A twenty-two-year-old lad, whom he knew, was to be electrocuted at the state prison. The boy came from a home that lacked everything a home should have: There was no love, no affection, no security, no moral training. He had been arrested many times, with several convictions and a few commitments. There was never an intelligent understanding of his needs or a real attempt to help him. This is not a maudlin, sentimental wail for a convicted murderer. It is an indictment of the ineffectual ways in which some young people are handled.

The same police officer could recall another incident of a young man becoming a member of his police department. This young man had made mistakes as a juvenile, but in his case police understanding, through a delinquency-prevention unit and through community help, had proved effective. This new police officer had a serious concern: He hoped that in his years of service he could help straighten out one "kid."

Police throughout this country who are concerned about youth can do much in the area of delinquency prevention and control. Police pose no threat to others engaged in serving youth. Police prevention work does not resort to "mollycoddling," and police power is never surrendered. Instead, it is reinforced with other approaches and techniques of great importance in deterring children from a collision course with crime.

Police have much to learn to do their jobs well, just as other agents of society must learn to do their jobs. Police *can* measure up to societal needs. They need opportunity and encouragement to grow professionally, and, above all, they need to see the false walls of "professionalism" and vested interest broken that separate so much potential support from them. Together with others equally concerned with the escalation of lawlessness, they can help to stop the tide of delinquency that sweeps throughout our country, ravaging many youths with moral and social cancer.

SELECTED READINGS

Brandstatter, A. F., "New Frontiers for the Police," *Police* (November–December, 1962).

Brecher, Ruth and Edward, *The Delinquent and the Law*. New York: Public Affairs Committee, Inc., 1962.

Brennan, James J., *Juvenile Delinquency: A Radical Approach* (monograph). New York: American Viewpoint, Inc., 1958.

——, "Police and Delinquent Youth," *Journal of Criminal Law, Criminology and Police Science*, XLVI, No. 6 (March–April, 1956).

Cavan, Ruth S., *Juvenile Delinquency*. Philadelphia: J. B. Lippincott Co., 1964.

Chapman, A. H., *Management of Emotional Problems of Children and Youth*. Philadelphia: J. B. Lippincott Co., 1965.

Holman, Mary, *The Police Officer and the Child*. Springfield, Ill.: Charles C. Thomas, Publisher, 1962.

Kenney, John P., and Dan G. Pursuit, *Police Work with Juveniles* (3rd ed.). Springfield, Ill.: Charles C. Thomas, Publisher, 1965.

Lohman, Joseph D., *Juvenile Delinquency*. Cook County, Ill.: Office of the Sheriff, 1957.

Lunden, Walter A., *Statistics on Delinquents and Delinquency*. Springfield, Ill.: Charles C. Thomas, Publisher, 1964.

Matthews, Robert A., and Lloyd W. Rowland, *How to Recognize and Handle Abnormal People—A Manual for the Police Officer*. New York: National Association for Mental Health, 1964.

Menninger, Karl, *The Vital Balance*. New York: The Viking Press, Inc., 1964.

Mulherne, Henry J., *Handbook for Police Youth Bureaus* (Division for Youth, State of New York, Albany, 1958).

Myren, Richard A., and Lynn D. Swanson, *Police Work with Children*. Washington, D.C.: U.S. Department of Health, Education, and Welfare, Children's Bureau, 1962.

O'Connor, George W., and Nelson A. Watson, *Juvenile Delinquency and Youth Crime: The Police Role*. Washington, D.C.: International Association of Chiefs of Police, 1964.

Police and Young Offenders. New York State Youth Commission. Albany, N.Y.: New York State Youth Commission, 1954.

Police Services for Juveniles. Washington, D.C.: Department of Health, Education, and Welfare, Children's Bureau, 1954.

Police Work with Children. Pennsylvania: Department of Public Welfare, Office for Children and Youth, 1963.

Robison, Sophia M., *Juvenile Delinquency, Its Nature and Control.* New York: Holt, Rinehart & Winston, Inc., 1961.

Uniform Crime Reports for the United States, 1964. Washington, D.C.: Federal Bureau of Investigation, 1965.

Vedder, Clyde B., *Juvenile Offenders.* Springfield, Ill.: Charles C. Thomas, Publisher, 1963.

Wilson, O. W., ed., *Parker on Police.* Springfield, Ill.: Charles C. Thomas, Publisher, 1957.

————, *Police Administration* (2nd ed.) New York: McGraw-Hill Book Company, 1963.

Winters, John E., *Crime and Kids: A Police Approach to the Prevention and Control of Juvenile Delinquency.* Springfield, Ill.: Charles C. Thomas, Publisher, 1959.

11 Prevention
Through the Judicial Process

Gary Bellow

There are several perspectives from which to view the functioning of the courts and the judicial process[1] in dealing with the problems of crime and delinquency. This chapter will deal with (1) the mechanisms of control available to the judicial process; (2) the failure of those mechanisms, as currently employed, to reduce the degree and scope of the crime problem; and (3) the changes in the handling of these mechanisms that could produce more substantial results.

The Judicial Process as an Instrument of Social Control

The judicial process functions in several ways as an instrument of social control. It affects values and attitudes toward law in our society and reconciles grievances and disputes between the state and the individual and among individuals. In addition, it directly exercises the power to define and punish unlawful behavior. Although each of these functions is interrelated, each involves somewhat differing mechanisms and ap-

[1] The term "judicial process" is used in this chapter to include all agencies concerned with the handling of the offender, i.e., the police, prosecutor, adult and juvenile courts, and correctional institutions. The term distinguishes the concerns of the chapter from the "legislative process" and the agencies involved in it. The chapter focuses on no particular jurisdiction or court system but rather seeks to find issues and problems common to the general administration of justice in this country. It will remain for later writing to refine and perhaps to refute some of the observations with respect to particular systems and areas.

proaches. It is the nature and implications of these differences with which
we must initially be concerned.

The Judicial Process and the Power to Punish

The most visible and, to many, the most important function of the
judicial process is the exercise of power to punish the guilt or involvement in unlawful acts. In this function the courts and the auxiliary
machinery that surround them have been vested with enormous authority
and a wide range of choices. They may mediate and withhold or impose
sanction with relatively little review or limitation of their judgment.[2]
They may sentence an offender to imprisonment, condition release on
any number of courses of conduct,[3] impose financial liability, or refrain
from imposing any sanction at all. In some jurisdictions the courts may
still impose the penalty of death for certain offenses.

The courts are not alone in their capacity to exercise such power. The
police, the prosecutor, and the probation officer also make judgments on
whether or not sanction is to be imposed or, to some degree, on the form
it will take. When a police officer allows a speeder to go on his way or
escorts a drunk home rather than to the precinct, he is exercising a very
real judgment on the seriousness of the unlawful act and how it should be
handled. When the probation office determines to refrain from seeking
revocation despite the probationer's later misconduct, there is further
mediation and modification of the scope of the original sanction.[4] Any
sophisticated analysis of discretion reveals that decision-making is fundamental to almost every stage of the process. Nevertheless, it is before the
judge and jury that the decisions concerning the accused offender become final, and it is here that the power of punishment most completely
resides.[5]

[2] There has been consideration given in recent years to the extension of legislative
or appellate limitations over this power. See Garhard Mueller, "Penology or Appeal:
Appellate Review of Legal but Excessive Sentences," 15 *Vand. L. Rev.* 671 (1962);
note, "Appellate Review of Sentencing Procedure," 74 *Yale L. J.* 354 (1964). See also,
Commonwealth v. *Green*, 396 Pa. 137, 151 A. 2d 241 (1959); *Leach* v. *United States*,
334 F. 2d 945 (D.C. Cir., 1964).

[3] Judah Best and Paul Birzon, "Conditions of Probation: An Analysis," 51 *Geo.
L.J.* 809 (1963).

[4] There has been a growing literature concerning the exercise of discretion in the
administration of criminal justice. Joseph Goldstein, "Police Discretion Not to Invoke
the Criminal Process: Low Visibility Decisions in the Administration of Justice," 69
Yale L.J. 543 (1960); Harold Dwight Lasswell, *The Decision Process* (College Park,
Md.: University of Maryland, 1956); Louis B. Schwartz, "Federal Criminal Jurisdic-
tion and the Prosecutor's Discretion," 103 *U. Pa. L. Rev.* 1057 (1955); Samuel Dash,
"Cracks in the Foundation of Criminal Justice," 46 *Ill. L. Rev.* 385 (1951); Donald
Newman, "Pleading Guilty for Considerations: A Study of Bargain Justice," 46 *J.
Crim. L.C. and P.S.* 780 (1956).

[5] None of the other discretionary stages of the process have the effect of relieving
the offender from subsequent reinstigation of the charge. For discussion of the limits

This power has several dimensions and tends to be interrelated with the court's control over jurisdiction and with the operation of other government agencies. In administering these other functions, the sanction power is further developed and enlarged. For example, the jurisdiction of the court system, beyond its structural outlines, is limited theoretically by the designation of the legislature of actions that come before it. The legislature may intend that a particular act or series of acts be treated in the courts as criminal, and it may promulgate a statute to that effect. However, it is the courts that ultimately control this judgment to a considerable degree. Every "criminal" act is partially defined as well as handled by the courts. In so doing, the courts may enlarge, modify, or nullify legislative determination. For example, the definition of disorderly conduct, criminal "intent," or criminal "negligence" is unspecified in the statutes. The delineation of the specific acts that fall within legislative definitions determines whether particular kinds of behavior will be brought into the judicial process at all and therefore whether the legislative sanction will be available to deal with it. The legislatures have, almost through necessity, invariably left this to the courts.

This power of definition has become even more significant as psychiatric knowledge has opened new approaches to criminal behavior motivation. The power of the court to define "responsibility" for criminal conduct gives the judicial process the final judgment on the way crime is not only to be handled but conceptualized.[6]

In addition, the courts set limits on the power and methods of other attempts to deal with deviant behavior. The courts, even beyond their definitional powers, may flatly declare a legislative definition of criminal conduct unconstitutional[7] or prohibit or limit law-enforcement techniques directed toward investigating the acts in question.[8] The courts have functioned, in a sense, as an arbiter of the entire process of social control. The ability of social agencies to set conditions for the receipt of assistance,[9] the power of mental health institutions to hospitalize those in

---

on the double jeopardy clause, see A. Whalen, "Resentence Without Credit for Time Served: Unequal Protection of the Laws," 35, *Minn. L. Rev.* 239 (1951); Kenneth Van Alstyne, "In Gideon's Wake: Harsher Penalties and the Successful Criminal Appellant," 74 *Yale L.J.* 606 (1965).

[6] David Bazelon, "The Concept of Responsibility," 53 *Geo. L.J.* 5 (1964); Learned Hand, "Insanity and the Criminal Law—A Critique of *Durham* v. *United States*," 22V. *Chi. L. Rev.* 317 (1955).

[7] *Robinson* v. *California*, 370 U.S. 660 (1962).

[8] See, e.g., *Escobedo* v. *Illinois*, 378 U.S. 478 (1964); *Mallory* v. *Unites States*, 354 U.S. 499 (1975). For an excellent review of such constitutional limitations, see Broeder, "*Wong Sun* v. *United States*—A Study in Faith and Hope," 42 *Neb. L. Rev.* 483 (1963).

[9] Charles Reich, "Individual Rights and Social Welfare: The Emerging Legal Issues," 74 *Yale L.J.* 1245 (1965).

need of treatment,[10] and the capacity of law-enforcement agencies to question suspects or search for evidence fall within the range of judicial scrutiny. Even the control of the courts over its own processes—the kind and sufficiency of evidence, the competency of witnesses, the availability of legal counsel—affects the actions that can be reached by legal sanction and the individuals upon whom such sanctions may be imposed. In evaluating the impact of sanction and punishment on crime and delinquency, it is necessary to recognize the less visible aspects of the process in which such decisions are made.

Beyond Sanction—Other Judicial Instruments of Social Control

The power to assume jurisdiction over offenders or to define the offense itself is not the sole way in which the judicial system functions as an instrument of social control. In a less direct manner, the judicial process performs other roles involving control of social behavior. These roles relate to the court system as a purveyor of values and attitudes and as an arbiter of disputes and grievances. In a population of 190 million people, thousands of cases are handled by trial courts every year. The greatest demands on the "law job" and the source of its greatest impact are found in the day-to-day workings of the lower-court system and in the image it projects to the public at large.

THE JUDICIAL PROCESS AS A PURVEYOR OF ATTITUDES   First, the judicial process is a purveyor of attitudes and values. As pointed out by Judge Bok, in a democratic society that functions without the trappings of a significant degree of ritual and tradition, the judicial process becomes a repository for the faith of the citizenry in the stability and justice of our entire legal system and in the validity of the law.[11] The trial becomes a source of recreation, a reaffirmation of the values of conforming conduct, and a teacher of the fundamental assumptions that lead to the resolution of dispute through law. The number of television shows, motion pictures, and books on the "lore" of law and lawyers is some indication of the public's fascination with the role and mechanics of law.[12] Although difficult to validate empirically, there is some evidence to support the notion that contact with and perceptions of the legal process affect the actions of significant numbers of people.[13] As long as the law is *con-*

[10] For a survey of similar problems, see Jerome Carlin and J. Howard, "Legal Representation and Class Justice," 12 *U.C.L.A. L. Rev.* 381 (1965).

[11] Curtis Bok, *Star Wormwood* (New York: Alfred A. Knopf, Inc., 1959).

[12] (E.g., "Arrest and Trial," "The Trials of O'Brian," "Night Court," "The Defenders," "Perry Mason.")

[13] Joseph Dean Lohman, *The Police and Minority Groups* (Chicago: Chicago Park District, 1947); De Beryhe, "Stereotypes, Norms and Interracial Behavior," *American Sociological Review*, XXII (1957), 689.

sidered just, speedy, and certain its effectiveness as an instrument of social control is undoubtedly far more persuasive than its actual impact on individual offenders. Likewise, if it is perceived as available to vindicate the rights and interests of persons who believe themselves aggrieved, it is more likely to command the respect and allegiance of the general public.

THE JUDICIAL PROCESS AS AN ARBITER OF GRIEVANCE Second, the judicial process functions as an arbiter of disputes in society. There are many other institutions of arbitration, public and private, that function to reconcile disagreement among members of society. Nevertheless the court system often stands as the final arbiter for a whole range of public and private issues. In the criminal process the imposition of sanction is an arbiter, not only of the victim's dispute with the offender but also of the public's potential for "mob" response to crime.[14] In the civil process the court lays down rules and procedures that mediate a whole range of economic, social, or political relationships among groups and individuals. Insofar as grievances can be channeled into the legal system and resolved within a range of acceptance, the judicial process acts to control significantly the most potentially violent kinds of lawless behavior.

The Failure to Control Crime and Delinquency

An examination of the empirical data and experience of the last ten years indicates that there has been a failure to control the growth of crime and delinquency in the United States. To what degree this must be blamed on failures of the judicial process is a question relatively unanswerable in light of the complexities of causation and of the relation of lawless behavior to the entire institutional fabric. Nevertheless, the last several years raise questions as to the adequacy of the judicial process' performance of its functions in social control and, more fundamentally, of the assumptions that underlie those functions.

The crime rate has expanded six times as fast as the population since 1958, with an enormous increase in the number of young persons having contact with law-enforcement agencies.[15] Almost 75 per cent of the persons arrested in the United States were under 25 years of age, and 62 per cent were under 21.[16] In the District of Columbia the number of referrals of the Youth Aid Division of the Metropolitan Police Department doubled as compared to a 12 per cent increase in the juvenile age population as a whole.[17] Demographic projections for the District of

[14] Symposium, "Violence in the Streets," 40 *Notre Dame L. Rev.* 497 (1965).
[15] *Uniform Crime Reports* (Washington, D.C.: Federal Bureau of Investigation, 1964), p. 3.
[16] *Ibid.*, p. 24.
[17] *Annual Report, Metropolitan Police Department* (Washington, D.C., 1965), p. 44.

Columbia, which predict (from 1960 to 1970) expansions of 44 per cent in the population age 15 to 19 and 52 per cent in the population age 20 to 24 as compared to an overall increase of 19 per cent in the population as a whole, foreshadow acceleration of these trends.[18]

In addition, offenders who have had previous contact with the judicial process seem to exhibit little change in behavior as a result of such contact. In a recent study of 1,015 male offenders released from a federal institution, 35 per cent had previously been incarcerated. In the same study, the author estimated that in a sample of 114 men, relatively few benefited in any way from educational or vocational experience in prison in maintaining or finding postrelease employment.[19] Other studies on recidivism support the finding that one-third of those released will be returned.[20]

The apparent ineffectiveness of the judicial process is even more dramatic with respect to youth. Youths released from the Youth Institution in Englewood, New Jersey, were convicted of later crimes in 41 per cent of the cases, and youths from the National Training School failed to avoid law violations in 44 per cent of the cases.[21] In the Juvenile Court for the District of Columbia, 59 per cent of the referrals by the Youth Aid Division had been referred more than once in the same year.[22] Of 60 youthful offenders studied in Lorton by the Department of Corrections, over 90 per cent had been arrested as juveniles, 65 per cent had been previously incarcerated once, and 25 per cent had been incarcerated two or more times.[23] Perhaps most disturbing are the results of the PICO experiment in California by the California Youth Authority, which suggests that intensive counseling with the most difficult delinquent youth may not only be ineffective but conducive to further delinquent, rebellious behavior.[24] It is difficult to lend any support to the dispositional choices and to the administration of sanctions by the courts generally in light of this data.

In addition, experience suggests other failures in the techniques of

[18] *Financial and Statistical Report, 1964, A Supplement to the Annual Report of the District of Columbia* 134 (Washington, D.C.: District of Columbia Government, 1965), p. 134.

[19] Daniel Glaser, *The Effectiveness of a Prison and Parole System* (Indianapolis: The Bobbs-Merrill Company, Inc., 1964).

[20] *Ibid.*

[21] Donald Clemmer, *Composition of Inmate Population of Youth Center* (Washington, D.C.: District of Columbia Department of Corrections, 1965).

[22] *Annual Report, Metropolitan Police Department*, p. 17.

[23] Donald Clemmer, *op. cit.*, p. 21.

[24] Peter White, *Submission to Department of Health, Education, and Welfare, Program for the Control of Crime and Delinquency* (Washington, D.C.: United Planning Organization, 1965); see also Bowning C. Tact, Jr., and Emory F. Hodges, Jr., *Delinquents, Their Families* and *The Community* (Springfield, Ill.: Charles C. Thomas, Publisher, 1962).

social control available to the judicial process. By and large, the courts have experienced a lessening of community support for the judicial process. In slum communities this is characterized by an unwillingness of the community to cooperate with the police, by a hesitance to appear as witnesses, and by a growing hostility and rebelliousness toward the law-enforcement process. Attacks on police officers and interference with arrests, the proliferation of criminal conduct, and the tendency to violence are only evidence of the gap between the population and the police that the law-enforcement process now faces in dealing with urban crime.[25]

In other segments of society there is also evidence of a growing distrust of the court process as a way of coping with crime and delinquency. This may be seen in some measure in the intensity of the attacks on recent judicial decisions dealing with law enforcement, in the attempts to limit judicial authority through legislation,[26] in the sanction and support of police misconduct in light of what are considered "unreasonable" rules, and perhaps in the growing incidence of delinquency and "white collar" crime in middle-class society.[27]

The judicial machinery has not been able to maintain its accessibility as an arbiter of disputes. Studies of delay in the courts indicate that litigants must wait years for redress and absorb extensive costs in the process.[28] The expense and complexity of legal work has virtually priced out most of the poor and a large segment of the remaining population of effective use of the legal process.[29] In addition, some civil and criminal process is subject to political and economic pressures, further subverting the effective use of the courts. Lawyers are not employed or are not available to a substantial number of the population, and the procedures are too rigid and complex to meet the demands of decision-making in modern urban society.

[25] Joseph Dean Lohman, *Violence in the Streets; Its Context and Meaning,*" *Notre Dame L. Rev.,* XI (1965), p. 497.

[26] See, e.g., 108 Cong. Rec. 7026–31 (1965) (remarks of Senator Eastland); "Note, Congressional Reversal of Supreme Court Decisions, 1945–1957," *Harv. L. Rev.* LXXI (1958), p. 1324.

[27] For a treatment of the latter phenomenon, see Harry E. Barnes and Negley L. Teeters *New Horizons in Criminology* (Englewood Cliffs, N.J.: Prentice-Hall, Inc., 1959), p. 4; Edwin H. Sutherland, *White Collar Crime* (New York: Holt, Rinehart & Winston, Inc., 1961); Herbert A. Bloch and Gilbert Geis, *Man, Crime and Society: The Forms of Criminal Behavior* (New York: Random House, Inc., 1965), pp. 379–408.

[28] Hans Zeisel, *Delay in the Courts* (Boston: Little, Brown, and Company, 1959).

[29] Junius Allison, "Poverty and the Administration of Justice in The Criminal Courts," 55 *J. Crim. L.* Criminology and P.S. 241 (1964); Jerome E. Carlin, *Lawyers on Their Own: A Study of Individual Practitioners in Chicago* (New Brunswick, N.J.: Rutgers University Press, 1962); Erwin O. Smigel, *The Wall Street Lawyer: Professional Organization Man?* (New York: Free Press of Glencoe, Inc., 1964).

However complex the reasons for these failures, it seems evident that the judicial institution has not been able to make a significant impact on the control and reduction of delinquent and criminal behavior. It is suggested that some of this failure can be understood only in the context of understanding the limits of law, the inadequacy of resources available to the courts, and the absence of innovative use of the resources actually existing.

The Limits of Law

Fundamental to an analysis of the deficiencies in judicial control of delinquency and crime is an appreciation of the limitations of the judicial process as an agency of control. The discussion in the first part of this chapter analyzed the functions of the judicial process in dealing with unlawful conduct. It did not fully explore other functions of the law and court system or delineate similar roles and functions performed by other institutions in society. This is left to other chapters of this book.

Nevertheless, the judicial process must be briefly set into the context of these institutions if its own deficiencies are to be identified. Crime, in this author's view, is a response to the failure of several institutions—economic, social, and political—and can be dealt with only in that context.[30] The judicial process, which necessarily focuses in some measure on the offender rather than on the environmental process of crime, can never adequately deal with criminality. The dispositional process, which returns a man to the same deprivations and pressures that contributed to his original violations, is doomed to failure no matter what remedial ends were achieved in the correctional process. As Professor Frank Allen points out, certain patterns of behavior represent adequate adjustments within some segments of society, even though they are labeled criminal.[31] It is only through change in the institutional and social structure that produces or reinforces criminal behavior that any alternatives to crime and delinquency can be generated. It is only through the marshaling of a large segment of the community's resources and through the stimulation of active participation and involvement of the community that any meaningful impact will be made. Although there have been failures in the judicial process to respond in this matter, this is a problem of many institutions and forces and a "legal" problem primarily in terms of the way law allocates resources and shapes social policy. In the last

[30] There is considerable controversy over this statement, particularly in relation to institutional breakdown. See *Report of Washington Action for Youth*, United Planning Organization (1964); Mabel A. Elliott, *Crime in Modern Society*, 1st ed. (New York: Harper & Row, Publishers, 1952), p. 383.

[31] Francis A. Allen, *The Borderland of Criminal Justice* (Chicago: University of Chicago Press, 1965).

decade, these functions have become more and more the responsibility of the legislative rather than the judicial branch of government.[32]

The Limits of Resources

Within this context, the sources of some of the limitations of the judicial system itself in coping with crime and delinquency can still be documented. Like other institutions, whether educational, political, or economic, the judicial institution has failed to demand and acquire the resources necessary to carry out its functions.

Throughout the country there is a woefully inadequate number of trained personnel to do the job that properly falls in the jurisdiction of the institutions concerned with the administration of justice. The number of police have fallen far behind the rising population and crime rates, and salary, conditions of employment, and status have not improved sufficiently to ensure the recruitment and training of an adequate number of skilled professionals.[33] In the lower criminal courts, hundreds of thousands of misdemeanors are handled by a relatively small number of judges who cannot adequately investigate all the facts relevant to guilt and disposition. In the civil field, the backlog of cases involves years of waiting and usually the compromise or failure of just claims. Probation and parole facilities are equally undermanned. In the federal system, a probation officer can spend an average of two hours per month on each of the cases for which he must provide counseling and supervision.[34] Other writers have documented the shortage of prison personnel, of inmate training and educational facilities, of psychiatric resources available both to the courts and the correctional process, and of staff and resources for postrelease and prerelease counseling.[35] The shortages in the juvenile court process of intake officers, probation officers, judges, and dispositional facilities raise questions concerning the whole conception of the "benefits" available to the child.[36] Even within the limitations of an individualized approach to the offender, little can be achieved if the entire administration of justice

[32] [E.g., Manpower Development and Training Act (1962); Economic Opportunity Act (1964); Elementary and Secondary Education Act (1965); Juvenile Delinquency Prevention and Control Act (1962); Housing and Urban Development Act (1965)].

[33] Harry E. Barnes and Negley K. Teeters, *op. cit.*

[34] Kenneth Pye, George Shadoan, and Joseph M. Snee, *A Preliminary Report on The Federal Probation System* (Washington, D.C.: Georgetown University Law Center, 1963).

[35] See, for example, *Of Prisons and Justice, A Selection of the Writings of James V. Bennett*, Subcommittee on National Penitentiaries, Committee of the Judiciary, United States Senate (1964).

[36] Oram Ketcham, "The Unfulfilled Promise of The Juvenile Court," *Justice for the Child, The Juvenile Court in Transition*, ed. Margaret Keeney Rosenheim (New York: Free Press of Glencoe, Inc., 1962), p. 38.

must be handled in response to full calendars and impossible demands on staff. It is the particular problem of volume in the criminal courts that intensifies the lack of enlightenment in arrest and prosecutorial decisions, the responses of the courts to external influence, the lack of coordination among the components of the administration of justice, and the abuse of legal limitations on police treatment of offenders.

The Limits of Adaptability

In addition to the failure to demand or acquire resources, and perhaps most fundamental to the failure of the court systems in this country to deal with crime and delinquency, has been their inability or unwillingness to adapt to the new demands of a complex urban environment and to new approaches to the problems such as environment engenders. In the past fifty years there have been enormous advances in the social sciences and in the level of understanding of the psychiatric and sociological dimensions of group and delinquent behavior. The relationship of economics, psychiatry, sociology, and medicine to crime, although still inadequately understood, have begun to be considered fundamental to an understanding of crime and rehabilitation. Nevertheless, the judicial process has remained relatively insulated from such knowledge. Legal concepts of responsibility for crime largely still reflect antiquated notions of human behavior.[37] The sentencing and correctional processes still function without the use of much information relevant to understanding and dealing with the offender. Even court rules concerning coercion of confessions, admissibility of evidence, and the definition of crime are still created with little reference to the relevant social-science data on the subject.

In addition, the agencies of the judicial process do not render decisions on the basis of all the facts available to them. Although there could be some argument that the adversary process, despite its fact distortion and withholding of evidence, can be justified at the trial level, it is difficult to defend such a process with respect to sentencing, probation, and parole decisions or even with respect to pretrial detentions. Nevertheless, in most cases the judicial system has not adapted to the need for more facts and data in decision-making.

More fundamental, the judicial process has remained less a process than a series of isolated institutional components often functioning with conflicting or contradictory policies. A legislatively or judicially declared policy to be rigorous in the enforcement of certain laws may still be nullified by the unilateral decisions of the police, the prosecutor, or the correctional institution. Conversely the prosecution of a particular case

[37] See Ibanez, "Bridging the Gap on Concepts of Mental Illness," 1 *Crim. L. G.* 23 (1963); and David Bazelon, "The Dilemma of Punishment" (Brandeis Memorial Lecture, 1960).

may be dismissed by the court or the sentence suspended despite the declared policy of the law-enforcement agency. Training of personnel and articulation of policy have not been carried out with an overview of the purposes and goals of a philosophy.

Finally, the judicial process has not been able to adapt its institutions to make full use of the existing facilities in the community. The courts and their subsidiary institutions function in semi-isolation, treating cases as they are brought in and crises as they arise. There have been few attempts to involve large numbers of lay people in the law-enforcement process or to use the educational, social, or even the political institutions of the community as supports in handling offenders. Despite the continuing debate over crime and law enforcement, judicial institutions have remained relatively unconcerned with gaining widespread support from the community as a whole. This is carried further by an even more pervasive tendency to ignore the problem of support from the low-income communities in which most of the crimes occur.

These failures, as much as the inadequacy of resources and the limitations of law, have contributed to the lack of effectiveness of the judicial process in the control of crime and delinquency.

The Potential for Change

An examination of the failure of the judicial system in the control of crime and delinquency suggests modifications and changes that could be made. Such changes cannot alter the economic, political, and social readjustments that must be the basis of any fundamental change in the nature and scope of the crime problem, nor can such changes be substitutes for the enormous needs for new and greater resources. If substantial alterations of resources in the form of personnel, technical equipment, or facilities were made, the focus of these suggestions would be considerably different. Nevertheless, there still remain areas in which existing institutions and structures can be adapted to deal with some of the failures we have discussed.

The Utilization of the Community Resources

Basic to the failures that have been examined has been the inability of the legal system to function as an integral part of any overall utilization of the community's resources in dealing with crime and delinquency. This takes many forms. The judicial process has not developed new alternatives in handling an offender or a delinquent outside of the correctional or institutional structure. The war on poverty, urban renewal, federal and state social welfare legislation, and scientific advances are all producing new resources in the community available to the legal process in exercising control. Unless the sentencing process, the police or prosecution's decision to charge, and the administration of probation use these resources, the total resources of the judicial system will always be inadequate. The number, variety, and complexity of the problems continue to be too extensive for the judicial system to function in the semi-isolation that has characterized its approach to the offender. For example, it has been demonstrated that employment is fundamental to the stability needed by the convict to handle release from convict status.[38] There is some evidence to indicate that recidivism is directly related to the ability to find steady and satisfying employment in the first two months of release from prison.[39] The judicial system must utilize the job development and training programs and existing employment opportunities available within the community. The legal system as a rehabilitative agent can be an extremely effective source of referral within the community's substantive programs in these areas. Without such a concern, the offender can be "assisted" only through institutionalization or through a probation and parole system that do not have the time and resources necessary to provide the guidance and supervision required for realistic rehabilitation.

The handling of the particular offender or delinquent is only one aspect of the need and possibilities for involvement of community resources. The use of existing health, employment, and educational facilities involves only one segment of the community. The total community must be directly involved in the application of sanctions and must understand and support enforcement practices if the legal process is to be effective. This is particularly true for the residents of the slum ghettos of our cities.[40] The involvement of these groups offers the greatest potential for reaching the delinquent or criminal offender and for providing the day-to-day support needed in working with such individuals. More fundamental, such involvement offers one of the only avenues for influencing the attitudes and perceptions of such groups toward the law-enforcement process and for marshaling support of the legal system. It is now apparent that the largest number of urban crimes occur within the populations of slum ghettos and with the sanction even of its law-abiding members. Achievement of some commitment to law compliance and mediation of the hostility that now exists between law-enforcement personnel and the people of such areas will depend on the degree of

[38] Daniel Glaser, *The Effectiveness of a Prison and Parole System* (Indianapolis: The Bobbs-Merrill Co., Inc., 1964).

[39] *Ibid.*

[40] William C. Kvaraceus and Walter B. Miller, *Delinquent Behavior, Culture and the Individual* (Washington, D.C.: National Education Association, 1959), and Walter Cade Reckless, *The Crime Problem* (Washington, D.C.: Washington Juvenile Delinquency Project, National Education Association, 1959).

constructive personal contact and mutual support that can be developed between them. The hiring and training of neighborhood people as police, probation, or clerical aides who can perform many of the administrative and other jobs involved in the legal process, the development of probation teams from the neighborhood who could assist in the support and supervision of probationers, and the inclusion of the poor on policy-making or advisory committees of institutions devising programs all offer the possibility of not only relieving the work-loads of already burdened staffs but also of affecting the way in which the residents of slum areas relate to the legal process. Law enforcement and law observance are both the responsibility and the problem of the entire community; they will not receive the allocation of resources or make any significant inroad on the problems of crime and delinquency without such involvement. It is essential that the judicial process be perceived by the public and, in fact, operate as part of the entire system of social control and direction.

The Coordination of the Components of the Judicial Process

As has been indicated, serious inefficiencies have been introduced into the judicial process by the inability of its various components to coordinate their policies and decisions. This is particularly true in the criminal process although similar problems exist with respect to domestic relations and other civil courts. Part of this problem is the result of the statutory creation of each component as a separate, identifiable, and fully independent entity; part of the problem is the political nature of the selection of personnel, whether as judges, police, or prosecutors; and part resides in the failure of the courts or any of the other components to take the leadership in developing consistent policies in the administration of justice. Change in this area will require considerable thought and willingness to experiment. It may mean the creation of state or even national academies to explore and to rationalize policies and approaches in the administration of justice.[41] It may necessitate the creation of crime commissions to develop empirical data on the operations and interrelationships among segments of the legal system. It may require legislation unifying the selection of judges and the operation of the court system as well as eliminating the jurisdictional frictions and overlappings that have characterized police and prosecution organization.[42] Certainly it will require more concern and study by the law schools and other academic institutions than has previously been afforded. In only a few studies has

[41] There is current legislation pending before Congress seeking creation of such an institution. Georgetown University has recently received a grant of one million dollars for the establishment of an Institute of Criminal Justice.

[42] See, for example, Bruce Smith, *Police Systems in the United States* (New York: Harper & Row, Publishers, 1960).

the need to coordinate the agencies involved in the administration of justice been explicitly recognized and examined. Whatever form such reexamination of justice takes, it must reflect some rational and consistent approach that is shared and developed by the various institutional agencies of the system.

The Redefinition of Function

Perhaps most fundamental to the relation of the judicial system to the control of crime and delinquency is the question of definition of role. As indicated, the judicial system uses varying methods and performs several functions as an instrument of social control. These have already been described. Clearly the most relied upon is the power of the system to impose sanction for deviance. The theories of retribution, deterrence, and prevention all implicitly rely on the presence of such power. Even judicially imposed limitations on the law-enforcement process assume the ultimate effectiveness of sanction as the primary instrument of social control.

It could be suggested that this emphasis is misplaced. If the legal system is effective at all in the control of crime and delinquency, it is probably more as a purveyor of values and as an arbiter of grievances than as an instrument of punishment. At least the failure of the prior emphasis on sanction in the last several decades suggests the need for a different approach or an intensification of efforts in other areas. The suggestions already made with respect to the coordination of existing agencies and the involvement of the community follow this approach.

Such a change in approach could include several other dimensions. Efforts must be made to make the judicial system more accessible to the community. The law must be a source of protection as well as a promulgator of sanction. It must provide redress for grievances and a channel within which abuses can be identified and dealt with. The extension of legal services to the poor, the decentralization of legal aid facilities, and the concern for law reform in areas affecting poverty are steps in this direction.[43] Although these are in the civil-law field, their impact is certainly not limited to "civil" fields of law. It seems clear that the dichotomy between civil and criminal problems has been overemphasized. The accused offender, his family, and the community from which he comes face problems, legal or nonlegal, civil or criminal. Their attitude toward the law and perhaps their receptiveness to law observance may be directly related to the ability of the legal system to cope with these problems. In addition, concern must be given to the accessibility of the courts to the witnesses and the victims of crime. Witnesses find them-

[43] Patricia Wald, *Law and Poverty* (Washington, D.C.: Office of Economic Opportunity, 1965).

selves inadequately compensated for days missed from work, for being forced to wait for hours before being called to testify, and for being uninformed of continuances or changes in the status of the case. Is it any wonder that most people are reluctant to become involved in the judicial process or to offer relevant information concerning an offense? Victims likewise find themselves caught in a process that is inconvenient and inadequately explained to them. It may be that compensation must be paid to witnesses for their time and to victims for the injury suffered. Whatever the specific choice, the emphasis again must be on creating a relationship between the judicial system and members of the community that will guarantee their support and participation.

It should also be noted that a new definition of the role of the courts and a reorientation of the privacy of sanction would involve reconsideration of the definition of crime itself. The enormous problems of volume and enforcement created by the current methods of handling alcoholism, drug addiction, and sexual deviance and the essential social and psychiatric nature of such behavior would suggest that they be better handled outside the criminal process.[44] The mental abnormality connected with much deviant behavior could likewise support the handling of many offenders through civil commitment rather than through the criminal process. Again, whatever the particular choices, the limits of resources available to the judicial process seem to require a new examination of what problems should or must be handled entirely within the administration of criminal justice or the legal system.

Finally, the judicial system must be accessible to new fields of knowledge and more factual data than has been available for decision-making thus far. It is suggested that the adversary process, particularly in the dispositional stages of the judicial process, could well be reexamined. Certainly the restrictions on discovery to the defendant prior to the trial and to the sentencing process are not consistent with achieving more breadth and flexibility in the ability of the system to use all relevant facts. More important, it is essential that the choice made reflect as broad a factual base as possible. The use of psychiatric and social-science data and testimony, the provision of opportunity to be represented by counsel in parole and probation revocation proceedings, the active participation of the court in seeking information relevant to disposition, and the recording of all proceedings to facilitate appellate review add to this purpose. The judicial system cannot function creatively, fully involve the community's resources, or even be perceived as fair and accessible without these other mechanisms aimed at improving decision-making in all stages of the process.

[44] Richard C. Donnelly, Joseph Goldstein, and Richard D. Schwartz, *Criminal Law: Problems in the Promulgation, Invocation and Administration of a Law of Crimes* (New York: Free Press of Glencoe, Inc., 1962).

Conclusion

The foregoing can only provide a framework within which to evaluate the role of the judicial process in the control of crime and delinquency. The functioning of this process, its apparent failures, and even the suggestions that have been made are only meaningful in terms of an appreciation of the limits of law itself and of an understanding of the relationship of the function of the legal system to the function of innovations in land use, education, health, and housing.

We have not concentrated on the juvenile court as a separate institution. Although there are special considerations relevant to the philosophy and functioning of the juvenile court as a source of control and innovation in this area, the role of the entire judicial process with respect to the crime problem was more fundamental. The juvenile court, as part of this process, has special problems, but it also functions as part of the system of justice, and the matters discussed here are equally relevant to its organization and administration. As with the other agencies of the judicial process, it is the degree to which it can be operated as part of the whole system of justice, in relation to and supported by the institutions and members of the entire community, as well as the extent to which it can remain flexible and accessible to new knowledge and full factual investigation that its value as a significant instrument of social control will be measured.*

SELECTED READINGS

Allison, Junius, "Poverty and the Administration of Justice in The Criminal Courts," 55J, *Crim. L. Criminology and P.S.* 241 (1964).

Bazelon, David, "The Concept of Responsibility," 53 *Geo. L. J.* 5 (1964).

Best, Judah and Paul Birzon, "Conditions of Probation: An Analysis," 51 *Geo. L. J.* 809 (1963).

Bok, Curtis, *Star Wormwood.* New York: Alfred A. Knopf, Inc., 1959.

Carlin, Jerome E., *Lawyers on Their Own: A Study of Individual Practitioners in Chicago.* New Brunswick, N.J.: Rutgers University Press, 1962.

Carlin, Jerome, and J. Howard, "Legal Representation and Class Justice," 12 *U.C.L.A. L. Rev.* 381 (1965).

Donnelly, Richard C., Joseph Goldstein, and Richard D. Schwartz, *Criminal Law: Problems in the Promulgation, Invocation and Administration of a Law of Crime.* New York: Free Press of Glencoe, Inc., 1962.

* Much of the content and approach of this chapter is attributable to the thoughtful and time-consuming work of Peter White, Deputy Director, Delinquency and Crime Control Division, United Planning Organization and the Delinquency Prevention Program of the United Planning Organization as presented to the Department of Health, Education, and Welfare.

224   *Gary Bellow*

Goldstein, Joseph, "Police Discretion Not to Invoke the Criminal Process: Law Visibility Decisions in the Administration of Justice," 69 *Yale L. J.* 543 (1960).

Hand, Learned, "Insanity and the Criminal Law—A Critique of *Durham* v. *United States*," 22V *Chi. L. Rev.* 317 (1955).

Ketcham, Oram, "The Unfulfilled Promise of the Juvenile Court," *Justice for the Child, The Juvenile Court in Transition*, Margaret Keeney Rosenheim, ed. New York: Free Press of Glencoe, Inc., 1962.

Lohman, Joseph Dean, *The Police and Minority Groups* (Chicago: Chicago Park District, 1947).

Reich, Charles, "Individual Rights and Social Welfare: The Emerging Legal Issues," 74 *Yale L. J.* 1245 (1965).

Smigel, Erwin O., *The Wall Street Lawyer: Professional Organization Man?* New York: Free Press of Glencoe, Inc., 1964.

Symposium, "Violence in the Streets," 40 *Notre Dame L. Rev.* 497 (1965).

Wald, Patricia, *Law and Poverty*. Washington, D.C.: Office of Economic Opportunity, 1965.

Zeisel, Hans, *Delay in the Courts*. Boston: Little, Brown and Company, 1959.

12 Design for Community Action

Melvin B. Mogulof

New Analyses and Interpretations of an Old Problem

"Central Harlem ranks extremely high on six of seven indices of social pathology. Its rate of juvenile delinquency, over a ten year period, has consistently been twice as high as the city rate, and has been increasing more rapidly than the city. For the past seven years, the proportion of habitual narcotic users has been from three to eight times that of the city as a whole. Its rate of venereal disease among youth is six times that of the city. Infant mortality is twice as high. Proportionately three times as many youth under the age of 18 as for the city as a whole are supported, wholly or in part, by aid to dependent children funds. The homicide rate of the community is over six times as high as that for the city."[1]

The above "tangles of pathology" were part of the community analysis in the proposal submitted by Harlem Youth Opportunities to the President's Committee on Juvenile Delinquency in 1964. Had the proposal continued the dismal liturgy, it might have noted that high rates of delinquency keep statistical company with poor housing, high birth rates, broken families, high percentage of minority group residents, low rates of voter registration, schools with few resources, high unemployment, low incomes, low levels of adult education, low levels of medical expenditures per capita, etc.

[1] "Youth in the Ghetto" (New York: Harlem Youth Opportunities, 1964), p. 156.

The beginning student of statistics learns that association and causation are vastly different concepts. It is all too easy to impute a causal relationship to related phenomena, particularly when our values or our theories are satisfied by the posed relationship. A recent attempt to examine the linkage of social class (at least that part of it measured by economic status) to deviant behavior ought to caution those who think causally without reference to empirical evidence. Robins, Gyman, and O'Neal suggest that one of the *consequences* of being reacted to as a delinquent is a negative impact on the economic choices of the delinquent's family.[2]

In an action-oriented society, the concept of "cause" is of the greatest importance. If we know what causes things, we have an immeasurably greater amount of control. An example from some of our continuing efforts in public housing, with its presumed impact upon juvenile delinquency, is instructive. We know empirically that high rates of delinquency and poor housing have an unfortunate association. Logically and sequentially, we believe that poor housing precedes delinquency, and, if it precedes, it is not a farfetched step to say that it causes. As a consequence, we act to improve housing with the hope that the betterment will break the chain of causation and diminish delinquency.

The equation looks this way: bad housing (leads to) delinquency. If bad housing is eliminated, therefore, delinquency stops. However, consider the following proposition:

Bad housing and delinquency are really part of a syndrome. Their association is an overpowering one because they are *both* the products of a third factor—X. The new equation looks this way:

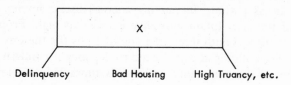

In this model, the removal of the bad housing may have little or no effect on delinquency because the causal chain between X and delinquency is not broken.

Let us pursue the logic further. If the researcher questions the "causal" nature of the previous association, he begins to look for phenomenon X, which may be "causing" both delinquency and bad housing. He may argue that X is "broken family life." If he can hold the quality of family life constant, he may be able to say important things about the

---

[2] "Social Class and Deviant Behavior," *American Sociological Review*, XXVII, No. 4 (August, 1962), 480–492.

association between delinquency and bad housing. By statistical manipulation, he may then present the following two sets of data:

(a) Where family life is intact, there is *no* relation between bad housing and delinquency.

(b) Where family life is broken, the association between bad housing and delinquency becomes even stronger.

At this point, an action-oriented society may begin to concentrate on broken families instead of (or, hopefully, in addition to) bad housing. But the process may not end here. Another researcher may show that good schools are a substitute for intact families in breaking the chain between delinquency and housing; or an even more creative researcher may be able to show that delinquency can be logically considered a "cause" of bad housing. In truth, one may never know final causation, but to be overwhelmed by that thought is to give way to a sterile relativism. To use research as a rationale for doing nothing because one can never know "final" causes is to surrender to a blind universe.

It would be difficult to infer from the resources expended for youth in our society that we have succumbed to a "sterile relativism." These expenditures lend themselves to classification under the broad terms "prevention" and "control." These two categories were of major concern to the 87th Congress when it passed the Juvenile Delinquency and Youth Offenses Act of 1961 (Public Law 87–274). This Act stated that it was

> the policy of the Federal Government . . . to assist in developing techniques for the prevention and control of juvenile and youth offenses, and to encourage the coordination of efforts among governmental and non-governmental educational, employment, health, welfare, law enforcement, correctional, and other agencies concerned with such problems.[3]

In categorizing agencies of education, employment, health, and welfare, as concerned with the problem of juvenile delinquency, Congress was pointing to those societal institutions whose task is to prepare youth to live in such a way that their behavior will not involve them in the process of being delinquent. Presumably, where these major institutions function well, the youth they work with will possess the knowledge and attitudes necessary for socially sanctioned behavior, and society will provide these youth with the opportunities and incentive for such behavior. If one now returns to the "tangle of pathology" enumerated previously, we see the evidence that, at least with some of our youth, these preventive agencies have failed. The reasons for this failure are somewhat less apparent, although most reasons seem to be geared toward blaming the individual rather than our institutions. Thus, the dropout

[3] 75 Statute 572, Public Law 87–274 (1961).

becomes evidence of the youth's failures, not the school's. The unemployed are viewed as malingerers and parasites, not as evidence of an economy that is unable to provide employment for all of our citizens. The unwed mother is seen as a degenerate, not as a possible victim of social situations that provide little opportunity for her to be a wed mother.

Our national bias toward individual rather than (or in addition to) social responsibility for failure has led to a pattern of therapy or punishment (the boundaries between them are sometimes indistinguishable) as a response to the deviance of youth. In effect, we say that the individual has chosen his affliction. We will punish him so that he does not choose that way again, or we will offer him therapy so that he need not choose to act "irrationally." For the youth whose behavior has been formally labeled delinquent, the correctional process becomes the embodiment of our ethic of individual responsibility. The delinquent's social rehabilitation may include a probationary process whose dual functions are surveillance and guidance or a term in an institution whose former title of reformatory is now in disrepute. Presumably, the disrepute springs from its rather notorious failure to reform. This is statistically illustrated by evidence that a term in a correctional institution is the best predicter that a youth will again appear before a court.

With regard to our correctional apparatus, the failure to rehabilitate deviant youth amounts to a disaster of very large proportions. The increasing number of our nation's youth whose behavior leads to apprehension by the police and adjudication by the court and the failure of our correctional system to correct were implicitly noted by the 87th Congress in passing the Juvenile Delinquency Act of 1961. In addition to calling for demonstration programs, which might make a contribution to delinquency prevention, the Act stated that "delinquency and offenses occur disproportionately among school dropouts, unemployed youth faced with limited opportunities and with employment barriers, and youth in deprived family situations."[4]

In an area well marked by the failure of numerous projects, the Juvenile Delinquency Bill of 1961 represented the first federal effort to provide leadership and money to a program concerned with the *prevention* of delinquency. One could infer from the language of the legislation that Congress saw a linkage between delinquency and failure in school, limited opportunities and discrimination in employment, and growing up in a deprived family. Nevertheless, the Delinquency Bill, as written, gave its administration wide latitude in selecting the types of projects to support. It can be argued that the failure to make the delinquency legislation specific was a failure of national policy. A program that resorts

4 Public Law 87–274.

to supporting demonstration projects with little to specifiy what the projects should include can be considered as acting from ignorance. Painful as it may be to admit, ignorance is the best characterization of our knowledge about the prevention of delinquency.

Could the first national delinquency prevention program have funneled its resources into more intensive police work? An effective police force is a crucial local defense against delinquency, but what of the evidence that police tend to disproportionately label lower-class youngsters as delinquents or the argument that one of the best means of diminishing reported delinquency and the consequent large number of youth who are forced to consider themselves "delinquent" is to curtail the way police relegate youth to the status of delinquent.

On the other hand, those who have argued for prevention as the first line of defense against delinquency may favor a national policy giving additional resources to our many youth-serving, recreation agencies. But such a national policy would need to confront the *lack* of evidence that such agencies, as presently constituted, are a deterrent to delinquency and, even more important, that most youth agencies have moved away from working with the most difficult youngsters or from those population groups whose youth appear disproportionately as delinquent.

A national policy of increasing the counseling and psychiatric help available to youth in trouble may be popular. But here again, such a policy would have to confront the evidence that the individual helping professions rely on verbal technologies, which seem ineffective with many youth in our delinquent population. Even more crucial, a national policy giving primary support to individual helping strategies would have to consider the mounting evidence that the motivation for delinquent behavior derives from the expectations of the social situation that many young people confront as well as from their individual psychiatric problems. The accumulated evidence points to a public health approach to delinquency as more strategic than our previous (and continuing) clinical efforts focused on rehabilitation. In delinquency, as with lung cancer, perhaps the time has come to "shut down the well."[5]

Negative arguments similar to the foregoing can be offered for each prevention or control strategy that could be made the focus of a national policy to battle delinquency. The evidence to date is that each of these strategies is partial, and a national program tied to any particular one of them would be in vain.

The delinquency legislation of 1961 directed the Secretary of the

[5] In commenting on the correlation between lung cancer and smoking, the Surgeon General of the United States cited a classic incident in public health in which a European community treated an epidemic by closing the source—a contaminated well.

Department of Health, Education, and Welfare to consult with the President's Committee on Juvenile Delinquency on matters of general policy. Thus it was the President's Committee that confronted a problem to which there were many answers, each answer embodying as much uncertainty as certainty. Therefore, a policy was formulated to support demonstration projects that would attempt to plan for and implement many of these partial answers as part of a comprehensive, coordinated group of programs. Following this, the President's Committee made a series of decisions that were derived logically from the nature of delinquency in America. First, the program would deal directly with local communities where the problem of delinquency was most keenly felt and where the available resources were least. Second, it would not dictate to a local community as to what methods should be used in that community's plan to demonstrate effective approaches to delinquency. The President's Committee would only say that there were many partial approaches and communities would have to combine some of them in a way that was pertinent to the nature of the problem and to the organizational skills in that community and that the approaches taken must be rational, based on logic, experimentation elsewhere, and recent theoretical development.

This emphasis on a locally developed plan for delinquency prevention must be viewed in relation to other criteria established by the President's Committee. Central among these was the conception that delinquent behavior could be viewed as a product of current societal arrangements in which the display of delinquent behavior was normative for particular situations. Thus an Office of Juvenile Delinquency[6] policy statement read:

> The youngster whose delinquency is primarily rooted in his social situation lived in an environment marked by inadequate opportunities for conforming behavior, and inadequate means of preparing for those opportunities which do exist. These inadequacies, which have their source in certain current social arrangements, are the conditions of life for many lower-economic, minority group youth. As long as these conditions, and the sources that give rise to them prevail, our society will be confronted with a block of its youth vulnerable to delinquent behavior. *This assumption undergirds the demonstration program policy of seeking to support those actions aimed primarily at changes in social arrangements affecting target area youth rather than changes in the personality of the individual delinquent.*[7]

[6] The administration of the Juvenile Delinquency Act of 1961 was lodged in the Office of Juvenile Delinquency and Youth Development. This office worked closely with the President's Committee in the determination of program policy.

[7] Policy Guides, Office of Juvenile Delinquency and Youth Development (Washington, D.C.: Intra-agency publication, 1963, mimeo.), p. 3.

This policy statement also pointed to inner-city slums as the logical place for a delinquency-prevention program whose primary focus was situational rather than personality change. Thus a supportable demonstration would have to be focused on a target area in an inner-city slum for "that delinquent behavior which is believed most amenable to a strategy of social situation intervention, has its locus in the decaying inner core of our cities."[8]

The specification of target populations reflecting high rates of social pathology was consistent with the notion that delinquency was more than inappropriate individual response. Intervention focused on target groups in target areas resulted from the theoretical position that delinquency could be viewed as *patterned behavior*, which was normatively supported by particular groups in particular environments.

As demonstration programs were planned for action, and as the President's Committee refined its policy, a number of assumptions were made that became central to these efforts at delinquency prevention:

(a) Programs dealing with social conditions that can be conceptualized as causal to delinquency rather than programs of individual rehabilitation and control will be more effective in the long run.

(b) Lower-class youth, dwelling in the slums of our great cities, represent the population of greatest risk. It is this population in which delinquency is most amenable to strategies of social change rather than psychotherapy.

(c) Because youth, like other human beings, live in a variety of social situations, efforts aimed simultaneously at a variety of these situations will be most effective in facilitating conforming behavior.

(d) While a comprehensive program seeks to create opportunities for conforming behavior, it also must seek to increase the skills and motivation of youth to enable them to perform satisfactorily in the situations confronting them. It is the dual attempt to *raise* skills and to *create* new opportunities that will be most effective in dealing with the problem of delinquency.

(e) Programs must seek to enhance the competence and concern of local community residents so that they become a more potent influence on the lives of their youth. Such competence will lead to a diminution of the problem of delinquency in the neighborhood.

[8] *Ibid.*, p. 4.

The Planning of Community Demonstrations and Foci for Action

In the very way it awarded its grants, the President's Committee made a significant contribution to the idea that intelligent action that can have relevance to a problem must be preceded by planning. With delinquency (as with the problem of getting to the moon) the planning of action that would relieve the problem was a painstaking process, painstaking because each of the means considered relevant were only partially so, and in some instances these means entailed possible negative consequences. Each of the means selected by a particular community to deal with the problem of delinquency must, in itself, represent a social "good" about which there could be some consensus. Thus, programs like teaching children to read and training youth for employment could be goals in themselves, and, if they served to reduce delinquency, so much the better.

In each of its seventeen planning grants, the President's Committee sought to allow a period of time in which a particular community could select means about which there was a working consensus and which would contribute to the prevention of juvenile delinquency. Although specific programs and rationales differed among communities, the plans emerging from the President's Committee projects produced remarkable agreement as to the relevant areas for an attack on delinquency. The key areas selected for action were education, youth employment, neighborhood organization, courts and corrections, group services, and services to families.

Education

Each project viewed its schools as key institutions in the preparation of American youth for responsible adulthood, but in each community the schools were found wanting. For certain groups of youth, the period of mandatory schooling was only a holding operation, with such youth slipping farther behind, academically, each year. It was not clear whether the schools cared about these failures, but, even if they did, their response was more often "we tried, but the material we work with is poor."

The demonstration projects maintained that failure in school was crucially linked to failure as an adult, and such failure had important correlations in juvenile and adult crime. Program plans in the area of education placed emphasis on new techniques for reading instruction, new curriculum materials more sympathetic to cultural differences among students, new methods of dealing with a youth whose school behavior is disruptive to himself and other students, early educational efforts to help youngsters from families whose home environments handicap them in keeping up in school, new attempts to involve the families of youngsters in depressed areas with their child's school experience, new ways to help teachers become familiar with the families and the particular strengths of youngsters who might be culturally different, new efforts to raise the aspirations of lower-class youngsters so that they could see the school as a place to succeed, and new ways to develop expectations by teachers and administrators that such youngsters could succeed.

Youth Employment

In surveying its community, each demonstration project found a frighteningly large block of minority group youth who were out of school, unemployed, and had few apparent skills that could place them in any but the most menial jobs. With many such youth, projects found pathetic aspirations for achievement, with few skills or opportunities that could make achievement possible. Our knowledge of human behavior is sufficiently clear concerning the consequences of an unbridgeable gap between aspiration and opportunity: At best, such a gap results in wasted lives—at worst, it threatens the basis of society.

Here again, the consensus was clear in the delinquency demonstration programs. Plans were made for increasing the *employability* of youth through the provision of vocational skills and basic education. Equally important, plans were made for developing *employment opportunities* for these youth.

Neighborhood Organization

Many of the demonstration projects attempted to develop programs in neighborhoods having little apparent formal organization. Such communities were largely abandoned by political organizations, which, in past years, sought to "trade off" local benefits for the promise of votes. Political machines had not been replaced by locally based groups that could deal with "city hall." Cut off by a lack of working connection with the machinery of city government, the needs and problems of such communities were engulfed by apathy or became issues for local "firebrands." The delinquency projects revealed evidence that organized communities were often more interested in and capable of applying informal controls to the troublesome behavior of their youth.

Although the possibility of an organized, effective local community was not accepted with equanimity in all quarters, projects secured initial consensus that neighbors should be brought together to deal with their common problems and helped to confront the larger community with these problems when they could not be handled on the neighborhood level. It was clear in these projects that planting flowers in window boxes does not make the neighborhood beautiful: Organizations of neighbors in a delinquency-prevention program must deal with problems like employment, landlord-tenant relationships, legal services, etc., if they are to be relevant to the real problems of neighborhood residents.

Courts and Corrections

In many communities, the planning period revealed that probation efforts did not meet national standards, youth were sent to correctional institutions (which not only failed to correct, but seemed to vastly increase one's chances of being caught again) because the court had no alternate choices, youth who returned after imprisonment needed community help if they were to "make it," and communities were only prepared to act when it was appropriate to punish youth, not to use the initial contact of youth with the law as a means of preventing future contacts.

In the face of this evidence, the demonstration projects planned to strengthen probation systems by providing experimental alternatives to incarceration, establishing "half-way" measures to help youth returning from institutions to gain a "toehold" in the community, and formulating methods whereby initial police contact would result in preventing future contacts.

Group Services and Recreation

Concerning the popular "wisdom" that the panacea for delinquency is more recreation, programs supported by the Juvenile Delinquency Act of 1961 devoted a minimum of resources to this area. In many communities, the problem is not inadequate recreational services but their failure to make contact with many youth from inner-city slum areas. The various demonstration projects became key forces in negotiating the return of group services to children in inner-city areas.

Services to Families

In each project, the planning of programs to deal with delinquency inevitably led to efforts for strengthening the family. The statistical correlations between youth misbehavior and inadequate family life are too overwhelming to ignore. Many projects provided for the establishment of neighborhood service centers—agencies where families could get help for a range of problems from their landlord to their psyche. These neighborhood service centers were considered as more than referral resources: They would be prepared to accompany their clients to sources of help if necessary and to intervene on their behalf with public agencies that controlled critical resources (e.g., housing authorities, welfare departments, hospitals, legal services, etc.). In some of these projects, the provision of neighborhood-based legal services became an important instrument in the effort to help families procure the aid to which they were legally entitled.

The demonstration projects found that families most in need of services often did not know such services existed or did not have the "know-how" to go about getting them. Thus, a key strategy in services to families was the role of "social-broker"—the delinquency project as an intermediary between those in need and the public and private agencies controlling the resources to meet those needs.

Prototypes of Community Action Organizations

The foregoing program patterns were by no means utilized by all seventeen projects that received planning grants to develop comprehensive demonstration programs. In some projects there was an inability to develop access to critical organizations, such as the schools or the employment services; in other projects there was not sufficient expertise to develop programs that were attractive to supportive organizations. These failures should be studied by those who plan future community action programs. At this point, what is of greatest interest is the creation in each of these projects of a central mechanism to plan action programs and to supervise their implementation. In each city, with one exception, the organization created had not previously existed in the community. The structure of these organizations had to enable the fulfillment of the legislative mandate that called for the coordination of efforts among a variety of governmental and nongovernmental forces. Because the concern of these new organizations was a major social problem, delinquency, rather than the particular function of any single agency, they needed to make their program plans relevant to the presumed etiology of the problem rather than to what was feasible within the community's existing organizational framework. In addition, each of these planning mechanisms had to build or develop access to professional competence, which would aid in evaluating program success or failure.

The building of organizations with the competence to plan programs in a variety of functional areas and with the capacity to evaluate them has offered a model to American communities through which they can mobilize to deal with a variety of social problems. These delinquency demonstration programs have become the prototype for the community action programs provided for in the Economic Opportunity Act of 1964. Because these organizations seem to offer so much potential for social planning and for more rational community action, some ideal types, as found in the demonstration projects, are presented:

(a) The strong Mayor model:

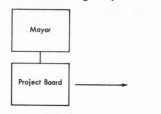

Appointed by and responsible to the Mayor. Includes "elite" (voluntary) leadership plus key figures in those agencies relevant to the development and implementation of a plan.

(b) The government coalition model:

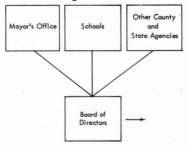

Separately incorporated and autonomous in policy. Composed primarily of key public agency figures. In communities where voluntary welfare was powerful, the coalition became mixed, involving private and public forces, and the Board included agency professionals as well as "elite" leadership.

(c) The cause-oriented voluntary model:

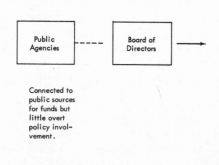

Boards generally a "mix" of those oriented to action on the problem plus major representation from public and voluntary agencies who were controlling resources critical to the project's success. In a number of communities, when this model proved itself viable, the organization was adapted by the Mayor as an action instrument. Such adaption was generally followed by certain Board changes to assure greater responsiveness to city hall.

In each of the demonstration cities, projects roughly constituted from one of the above ideal-typical models secured a professional staff to enable it to pursue the task of developing plans for action aimed at the prevention of delinquency. In addition, each project developed an internal research function or contracted an academic source for such purposes. Generally, it was the research function that developed an overview of the way in which that particular project understood the problem of delinquency. It was intended that this overview point to certain areas of action where implementation could be viewed as a test of the project's delinquency-prevention program. It has been previously noted that, despite differences in rationales for action, there was a remarkable consensus among these projects as to the appropriate areas for action. These areas were education, youth employment, courts and corrections, services to families, group services, and neighborhood organization. The emerging plans in each of these projects were the basis for a reorganization of services to areas of high social pathology, so that youth in these areas would have greater skills, motivations, and opportunities for behavior less apt to be considered deviant by the larger society.

Hopefully, the comprehensiveness of these designs has discounted all the single-minded slogans of those who press their own particular functions as the panacea for delinquency prevention. At the bottom of these community action efforts is the implicit notion that there was a growing lack of connection between the slum populations of our great cities and our increasingly large middle-class society. This disconnection is marked by differences in the availability of opportunities and resources to the residents of slum areas and by the growth and persistence of a slum-area youth culture in which normative patterns place the actions of such youth in constant jeopardy of being labeled delinquent.

The efforts of these demonstration projects to alter the pattern of those social arrangements assumed to support slum-area delinquency have been well summarized in the words of the research coordinator of the Cleveland project:

> (A comprehensive demonstration program) "is complex, because we dare to cut across many levels of government. Complex, because we are bold enough to cut across the sanctified boundaries of the public and voluntary services. Complex, because we dare to link community-wide organizations of great power, with the people of the small area with little. Complex, because we deal with juvenile delinquency, a subject on which every man is an expert, yet few stir themselves to action. Complex, because we are poised over and grapple with some of the most controversial issues in American society today. Complex, because we attack this problem in many ways which must be brought into mutual, meaningful focus. Complex, because we are not bystanders, but are in the arena."[9]

[9] Robert McCargar, "Some Comments on Comprehensive Demonstration Programs," Cleveland Action for Youth (Unpublished project paper, Cleveland, 1964), p. 1.

Designs for Neighborhood Action

In each of the demonstration cities, projects attempted to involve affected populations in their policy formulation and, in *some measure*, to organize the citizens of their target areas so that they could influence the policies of agencies that controlled resources crucial to local area residents. Thus we return to the previously noted ideal-typical models of board formation and note that in a number of projects neighborhood residents occupied policy-making positions on a level with key political and voluntary welfare figures. In other demonstration projects, target area residents in previously formed groups (such as area councils) or in newly formed groups were made a formal part of the advisory or sanctioning functions of these projects.

There was no legislative mandate for this involvement of those who had been consigned in the past to the caste-like role of client. This involvement of target area residents was aided by the fact that most of these projects were new ad hoc arrangements, lacking authority and legitimacy. They needed a constituency to be able to influence existing agencies to attempt new programs. In the search for a constituency, the client population emerged as a likely source. In those projects where the target area residents were largely Negro, projects found a powerful ally in the Negro civil rights movement. In some cities where the project was not quick to recognize this ally, the leaders of the Negro community found ways to inform the project that they were not willing to be planned *for* once again.

The involvement of area residents did not end with policy making. In fact, such involvement often began by the employment of target area residents as agents of the project. The rationale for such involvement is clear and sound: Certain area residents can be far better contacts with their neighbors because there is a smaller gap culturally; employment of area residents has the advantage of creating jobs; and professionals in the human services and the funds to employ them are simply not available in adequate supply.

Policy involvement and employment of area residents were important achievements in these community action demonstrations. However, it is the way in which certain antidelinquency projects endeavored to insure continuing involvement of neighborhood residents, independent of project philosophies or federal legislation, that is the subject of the last in this chapter.

Because these demonstration programs were time-limited, they had to deal with the prospect that their idea of involving neighborhood residents would not always prevail. Equally important was the possibility that, with the demise of the demonstration, pressure for reorganization of social arrangements would lessen. Thus each project elected to put a portion of its resources into the development of *competent* neighborhood communities, which eventually would not be dependent on project support in taking action.

What is a competent community? It is a place where the leaders are from the people and are powerful in affecting the decisions of all those agencies that furnish resources to that community. In communities of the poor, it is a place where people have representatives who know how to deal with the police and the courts and how to make their public schools aware that the price of continued failure with their youth will be very high and where the welfare department, housing agencies, etc., know they are not dealing with a supine mass. Given this focus on community competence, some of the delinquency demonstration projects established groups of area residents who could remain powerful after projects departed and whose autonomy would be protected while the project was in existence.

A clear example of this intention is embodied in New York City's Mobilization for Youth proposal:

> Attempts to deal with the aspirations of delinquents and low income youth generally should also include an orientation toward social change. Opportunities for collective social action should be incorporated into any large scale delinquency program . . . If opportunities for the constructive expression of alienation can be organized and employed, the problem of delinquency can be correspondingly reduced. The task is to direct the expression of alienation against the social structure which is its cause and to discourage its expression in delinquent acts. In this way, these discontented may help to alter the very inequalities which oppress them.[10]

In its program of organizing the "unaffiliated," Mobilization for Youth states the following objectives:

1. To increase the ability of local residents to participate in and influence the social and political life of their community. This will have the further objective of providing an example for adolescents of a means of handling alienation constructively.
2. To identify, document, and dramatize community needs.
3. To widen channels of communication between lower-class persons and institutional personnel or decision makers, and thereby to increase both the institution's responsiveness to lower-class

[10] "A Proposal for the Prevention and Control of Delinquency by Expanding Opportunities" (New York: Mobilization for Youth, 1961), p. 69.

needs and the residents knowledge and use of community resources.

4. To increase community integration and the effectiveness of social control.

5. To improve the confidence of the leaders to deal with grievances and to defend their constituents' rights and privileges.[11]

Mobilization for Youth understood the pressures that would result if such programs of recognizing the "unaffiliated" were effective. Their proposal notes:

> The uniqueness of our approach to community action is the encouragement of autonomy among lower-class participants. There is, of course, a contradiction inherent in the proposal to establish lower-class community organizations under Mobilization sponsorship. Mobilization is responsible to a wide variety of groups. Issues with which lower-class organizations deal may threaten some of these groups. Unless they are formed spontaneously under the impetus of an inflammatory issue, lower-class groups cannot be organized without the financing and support of such established (i.e., middle-class) organizations as Mobilization. The fact that Mobilization constitutes a new structure partially mitigates the problem of control. So, too, does the Mobilization intent to protect the organizations' independence from both outside pressure and Mobilization's own opinions about their mistakes. This is no real solution, however; it will be necessary for Mobilization to divest itself of responsibility for the project as soon as feasible. Encouraging the organizations to raise their own funds will be a step in that direction.[12]

Conclusion

A design for community action toward the prevention of delinquency must flow from the multicausal nature of the problem. In the community action programs discussed in this chapter, a major concern was the inclusion of efforts that would change the social arrangements by which youth in inner-city slums are motivated as well as the way in which they are taught skills and given the opportunities to use their skills. In these community action programs, new organizations were created with the skill and capacity to cross governmental and organizational lines in the development of programs relevant to delinquency prevention among youth in those areas of highest social pathology. In these efforts to reorganize community services, delinquency demonstration programs

[11] *Ibid.*, pp. 328–329.
[12] *Ibid.*, pp. 136–137.

reflected a consensus that the critical areas were education, youth employment, group services, court and corrections, services to families, and neighborhood organization.

In seeking to organize neighborhood groups for self-help and social action, demonstration projects recognized that competent neighborhood communities must continue to act effectively on behalf of their youth. At the roots of such action is a continuing base for the redress of services and opportunities in the most deprived areas of our great cities. It was hypothesized that as neighborhoods developed competence in dealing with their environment they would also become better able to exercise controls on the behavior of their youth.

The foregoing designs for community action seem complex (and perhaps elusive) when compared to previous efforts at delinquency prevention. The major parts of this design are:

(a) The creation of a central community mechanism, which can plan and secure resources to implement programs affecting the motivation, skills, and opportunities of our most deprived youth and their families.

(b) The reinforcement of local neighborhood communities so that they may become a relevant force in influencing the allocation of resources to their neighborhoods.

(c) The development of the capacity and concern of neighborhoods and families to transmit expectations and to exercise controls that would influence their youth's behavior to diminish the risk of their being labeled delinquent.

These have become the referents of action aimed at the prevention of social problems. They have proved viable concepts in the demonstration programs sponsored by the President's Committee on Juvenile Delinquency. Of greater significance, the basic idea of community action, with its focus on comprehensiveness, neighborhood involvement, and situational change, seems a better "fit" to a society that is discovering the social and cultural basis of behavior defined as deviant.

SELECTED READINGS

Adrian, Charles, *Social Science in Community Action*. East Lansing: Michigan State University Press, 1960.

Agger, Robert E., Daniel Goldrich, and Bert E. Swanson, *The Rulers and the Ruled*. New York: John Wiley & Sons, Inc., 1964.

Alinsky, Saul D., *Reveille for Radicals*. Chicago: University of Chicago Press, 1946.

Banfield, Edward C., *Political Influence*. New York: Free Press of Glencoe, Inc., 1961.

Banfield, Edward C., and James Q. Wilson, *City Politics*. New York: Free Press of Glencoe, Inc., 1963.

Banfield, Edward C., and Martin Meyerson, *Politics, Planning and the Public Interests*. New York: Free Press of Glencoe, Inc., 1955.

Cahn, Edgard and Jean, "The War Against Poverty: A Civilian Perspective," *Yale Law Journal*, LXXIII, No. 8 (July, 1964).

Gurin, Arnold, "Factors that Influence Decisions in Community Planning," *Journal of Jewish Communal Service*, XXXVIII, No. 1 (September, 1961).

Lippitt, Ronald, Gene Watson, and Bruce Westley, *The Dynamics of Planned Change*. New York: Harcourt, Brace & World, Inc., 1958.

Litwak, Eugene, "Voluntary Association and Neighborhood Cohesion," *American Sociological Review*, XXVI, No. 2 (April, 1961).

Miller, Walter B., "The Impact of a Total Community Delinquency Control Project," *Social Problems*, X, No. 2 (Fall, 1962).

Mogulof, Melvin, "Delinquency Intervention Based on Person and Situation," *Social Work*, IX, No. 2 (April, 1964).

Morris, Robert, and Martin Rein, "Goals, Structures and Strategies for Community Change," *Social Work Practice, 1962*. New York: Columbia University Press, 1962.

Polsby, Nelson, *Community Power and Political Theory*. New Haven, Conn.: Yale University Press, 1963.

Ross, Murray, *Community Organization: Theory and Principles*. New York, Harper & Row, Publishers, 1955.

Rossi, Peter H., "Community Decision Making," *Administrative Science Quarterly*, I (March, 1957).

——, "Power And Politics: A Road to Social Reform," *Social Service Review*, XXXV, No. 4 (December, 1961).

Silberman, Charles E., "Up From Apathy—the Woodlawn Experiment," *Commentary*, XXXVII, No. 5 (May, 1964).

Sower, Christopher, *et al.*, *Community Involvement*. New York: Free Press of Glencoe, Inc., 1957.

Warren, Roland L., *The Community in America*. Skokie, Ill.: Rand McNally & Co., 1963.

Wilensky, Harold, and Charles LeBaux, *Industrial Society and Social Welfare*. New York: Russell Sage Foundation, 1958.

13 Summary and Conclusions

Charles F. Wellford
William E. Amos

In this final chapter we will indicate what we believe is the central proposition that has emerged in this book, and discuss the place of this proposition in the historical and theoretical development of criminology and the implications it has for research and action. The fact that a uniform position can be found in a book written by authors from such a range of disciplines, interests, and theoretical perspectives indicates the most basic "healthy" sign in the field of prevention. We suggest that it reflects a certain maturity in this field that has been long developing and may make achievement in prevention more probable.

We find that after assessing the impact of a source of prevention (school, family, current programs, etc.) every author proceeds to indicate that "the _____ cannot do everything." This is followed by a statement concerning the complexity of the problem and therefore the necessarily complex preventive response. Thus, the entire thrust of the book is in the direction of prevention through the mobilization and organization of forces at the social-system level. This is also true of the chapters on prediction, programs, and the introductory statement by Lejins.

What is not explicit is how this varies, if it does, from the Chicago area projects and their modern descendant, community organization studies. The question raised is whether this book offers more than a summary of current efforts and thinking—does it advance our knowledge

243

or restate it? The answer is not entirely clear. However, we do think that, at a minimum, our authors have summarized and in most cases extended a recently developed way of thinking that can have profound practical implications and has obviously been influenced by recent theoretical statements.[1]

We suggest at least two fundamental differences between what is presented in this book and what has historically been the position of community-oriented preventive measures: first, the sincerity of the commitment to the need for the mobilization of the range of social institutions; and second, the recognition that the response must be motivated or implemented by the government. The remainder of this chapter will attempt to defend, in terms of their validity, and to develop, in terms of their consequences, these "differences."

In response to our contention that there is a difference in the quality of the concern for total community mobilization, one could ask: "But hasn't this been the case, at least since the beginning, of the multiple factor theories?" Our answer would be "yes." However, the recognition of this in the past has had little or no effect on the planning of major prevention programs. This situation is similar to that of sociologists who for years have recognized the role of personality factors in explaining human action in introductory or summary statements but have omitted it from their research and analysis.

Although it is most apparent in Mogulof's chapter, all the authors dealing directly with the formulation and implementation of preventive programs have attempted to indicate how the organization of efforts can be initiated and what impact it may have on the specific area with which they were concerned. Thus, Berg attempts to relate suggested changes in the economic system to necessary changes in the school and family; similarly, Powers attempts to bridge the gap between community action and religious action. The statements concerning the "mobilization for action" are not, we suggest, ways of avoiding problems, as they may have been in the past and as they are in much current action and writing, but a recognition of problems. This book treats the process of community organization or of institutional mobilization not as the solution but as the problem of delinquency prevention. We believe that this is a significant contribution to this field and one that should be pursued.

Consequently, the chapters are less conclusive than one may desire. We suggest that in this respect they reflect the confusion in the field and the difficulty of the problem. At this stage, the documentation of the issue and the statement of suggestions for resolution are all we can realistically anticipate.

[1] It should be clearly stated at this time that our discussion is not to be interpreted as an extension or product of the efforts of the contributing authors. We are attempting to perform the exegetical task we believe is required of us as editors.

The second "difference" identified previously concerns the role of government in prevention programs. Most of the current major innovative efforts at delinquency prevention are financed by the federal government. It is our contention, one that we believe is documented in this book, that active government intervention is necessary, not for economic reasons alone but for reasons related to basic characteristics of the problem. Some of these characteristics should be obvious. For example, some of the areas we have discussed from the perspective of prevention are elements of some level of government (courts, police, and school), and, therefore, change in them is directly dependent on action at the appropriate governmental level. In addition, there are those sources of prevention that are partially controlled and significantly influenced by government (e.g., economic and recreational). Therefore, many of the suggestions made by the authors in regard to change in content involve change in government.

There is, however, a more basic reason for the emphasis on action instigated, implemented, and stimulated by government. We are aware that those toward whom programs of this sort are most directly aimed are those who are least affected. The old model of the "client" as an active seeker of aid is no longer relevant for the field of delinquency prevention. The emphasis is on ways to "reach the unreachable." This is obvious in the war on poverty. Despite the desire for the involvement of the poor in the action program, it is perfectly clear that the impetus for initiation, direction, and intent comes from the Office of Economic Opportunity, and this is how it must be, given the target population—the "hard core" poor. A similar argument can be made, we suggest, and has been made for delinquency prevention.

This argument has been developed by Walter Lunden, although he uses it to reach a position we find unacceptable.[2] Lunden addresses the question, "Is there a community?" and replies that, at least for those sections of society toward which delinquency-prevention projects have been and are being aimed, the answer must be "no." Therefore, he concludes, we must return to a Civilian Conservation Corps type of recruitment in which the conservation would be of our youth and not of our physical resources. We agree with Lunden in his analysis of the present state of the community among large segments of our population, and therefore we move away from the conception of lower-class, urban life as presented by Whyte[3] and by those who have supported that approach. It may have been true in our recent past, when lower-class status was a position that was abandoned after two or three generations, but it does

[2] Walter Lunden, "The Theory of Crime Prevention," *British Journal of Criminology*, II (January, 1962), 213–228.
[3] William F. Whyte, *Street Corner Society* (Chicago: University of Chicago Press, 1943).

not seem to be an accurate position in the analysis of the current plight of lower-class (in particular, Negro lower-class) inhabitants existing in a mass society. The "Moynihan Report"[4] demonstrated this for the Negro lower-class community, and another report could document a similar condition for the white lower-class members who are the target population for prevention programs. There may still be organization, but there is no community.

It is the above that makes the role of government so vital to delinquency prevention. Various authors have discussed this problem from the concept of alienation of the poor and have developed its influence in the area of mental health.[5] We are suggesting that the same implications have been made throughout this book for the field of delinquency prevention. Lunden indicates that government involvement could occur only within the structure of a "police state." Whereas this is an understandable conclusion, we believe it is inaccurate.

It is inaccurate, first, because it makes certain assumptions about the level of government that would be involved, which we have not made. Once again, the poverty program is an example of efforts motivated and stimulated by federal planning and money but implemented at the local level. The concept of the "police state" is based obviously on the belief that control would reside at the funding, i.e., federal, level. Second, such a conclusion is unwarranted because it implies something about the target population that we would not want to state explicitly. It suggests that, if given opportunity and stimulation, the inhabitants would still not want or be able to change. The authors in this book have uniformly taken the position that changes in the forces that contribute to the destruction of the community will facilitate its "rebirth," and a consequence will be a reduction in delinquency (not its elimination). At this point the older emphasis on "natural leaders," community involvement, etc.—the area project approach—would again be applicable. We believe that it is not applicable, and hence more direction from external sources is necessary. We cannot operate on the assumption that there exists self-recuperative powers in something that does not exist (the community). As we indicated earlier, the concept "community" is the problem, not the solution. The authors here have been struggling with the problem of changing and of interrelating the forces at this level that could act in an ameliorative fashion on delinquency.

We are fully aware of a major consequence such a position has for

[4] *The Negro Family*, Office of Policy Planning and Research, Department of Labor (1965).

[5] See Maya Pines, "The Coming Upheaval in Psychiatry," *Harper's Magazine*, LIV (October, 1965), 54–60; and Arthur Pearl and Frank Riessman, *New Careers for the Poor: The Nonprofessional Revolution in Social Service* (New York: The Free Press of Glencoe, Inc., 1965).

theory and for practice. In regard to theory, it is obvious that we are ignoring to a great extent the contribution that personality factors can make to the explanation of action. This is not only a result of the orientation of the editors and authors but also a recognition, we believe, of where the greatest need is, given the validity of the above discussion, and of the fact that efforts in this area have consistently proven inadequate. In addition, as the chapters indicate, the division in practice is not as sharp as it appears in our summary. The interaction between the personality and the social system is not denied by the chapters or our summary: It is simply not developed. The most obvious consequence for research in the area of prevention has been discussed in Chapter 2 in regard to the need for different means of prediction and evaluation. Similarly, the concluding section of the Sullivan and Bash chapter documents the direct implications this has for the development of action programs.

Finally, we would like to offer some tentative suggestions concerning the relationship between the position in this final chapter and current criminological theory. Although historically wed to sociology (at least in the United States), criminological theory has been overwhelmingly concerned with the criminal and thus at best has been an effort in social psychology. It is not too harsh, we believe, to indicate that as a result: (1) attention has been drawn away from the analysis of the systemic sources of crime and delinquency at the level of the social system; and (2) theoretical efforts have been generally weak because sociology has not yet developed a way of incorporating the personality system into its method of explanation while maintaining the autonomy of each (Parsons notwithstanding).

In recent years we have seen the increasing awareness of the first of these "results" and the concomitant renaissance of sociological criminology. The obvious references are Cohen, Cloward and Ohlin, etc.—the subcultural theorists. It is within this framework that this book should be placed. This is not to indicate that there are not differences among and/or within these positions. Rather, it is the commitment to the influence, causal and ameliorative, of the social and cultural systems that unites these efforts. As we become more aware of these relationships we can expect our ability to engage in more effective preventive efforts to increase. At the present stage of our knowledge the efforts at eliminating external barriers to success and at modifying external sources of delinquency are directed more by intent than content. Our contributing authors have attempted to make this content more specific for limited aspects of the larger effort. We believe that these contributions are significant and should be evaluated on their theoretical, in addition to their more immediately pragmatic, relevance.

Although we have attempted to organize a book that would destroy, by its very nature, the provincialism of most texts, we have not accomplished this in one very important respect. We have not discussed prevention as it exists in countries other than the United States. Loveland, in tracing briefly the development of interests in criminology at the international level, has drawn our attention to the fact that since the United Nations has taken over the functions of the International Penal and Penitentiary Foundation an increasing amount of time at their meetings has been devoted to the discussion of prevention.[6] At the most recent meetings (Stockholm, 1965) three of the six items on the agenda were related directly to prevention ("Social Forces and the Prevention of Criminality"; "Community Preventive Action"; and "Special Preventive and Treatment Measures for Young Adults"). The summary of these sessions[7] indicates that the delegates were much concerned with the problems discussed in this book and with the implications we have indicated in this summary chapter. In addition, the report summarizes the content of some of the major preventive efforts in other countries. Thus, we can see that the problems of prevention concern criminologists throughout the world and that the content and intent of this book seems to reflect and to extend the concerns of the international delegates. We suggest that the reader consult these sources for a more detailed summary of prevention in other countries.

Theory, research, and action are "interminable" in a field such as prevention. We can only hope that the efforts represented in this book serve to organize the field, draw attention to the problem (for it has been too long neglected), and indicate the way(s) that seem(s) most appropriate to its solution in the current development of criminology.

[6] Frank Loveland, forthcoming in *Nebraska Law Review*.

[7] Rapporteurs' Summary, Third United Nations Congress on the Prevention of Crime and the Treatment of Offenders (Washington, D.C.: U.S. Bureau of Prisons, Department of Justice, 1965).

Index

A

Abrahamsen, David, 123
Alinsky, Saul, 56, 119
Allen, Francis A., 215
Allison, Junius, 214
Alstyne, Kenneth Van, 210
American Psychological Association, 29
Amos, W. E.; Manella, Raymond; Amos, William E., 133, 135
Southwell, Marilyn, 130
Anderson, Stanley, 166
Anderson, W. H. L., 178
Austin, David, 166

B

Barnes, Harry E., and Teeters, Negley K., 214, 216
Baroni, Geno, 119
Bazelon, David, 210, 217
Becaud, Joseph, 113
Beccaria, Cesare, 4
Bell, Daniel, 174, 177
Berg, I., and Freedman, M., 184
Berg, Ivar, 181
Best, Judah, and Birzon, Paul, 209
Bloch, Herbert A., 68
Bloch, Herbert A., and Geis, Gilbert, 214
Bok, Curtis, 211
Bonger, W. A., 102
Bonhoeffer, Dietrich, 121
Bovet, L., 69
Bowman, Leroy, 107
Brennan, James J., 193
Brown, Roscoe, 157
Burchill, George W., 132
Burgess, Ernest W., 22

C

Cambridge-Somerville Study, 76
Cardijn, Joseph, 113
Carlin, Jerome E., 214
Carlin, Jerome, and Carlin, Howard, J., 211
Carpenter, Kenneth, 117
Carr, Lowell J.; Barnes, Harry E.; and Teeters, Negley K., 100
Carr-Saunders, A. M.; Mannheim, Hermann; and Rhodes, E. C., 103
Cavan, Ruth Shonle, 53
Chapman, A. H., 199
Children's Bureau, Division of Juvenile Delinquency Service, 52
Church activities:
  chaplains, 110
  confession, 108
  evaluated, 120
  religion-centered, 108–112
  secularity-centered, 114–118
Church and delinquency problem, 100
Church and prevention, 107
Clemmer, Donald, 213
Cleveland Action for Youth, 237
Cloward, Richard A., and Ohlin, Lloyd E., 20, 175
Cohen, Albert K., 10, 20, 22
Collier, John, 151
Commonwealth v. *Green*, 209
Community demonstration programs:
  focus of, 232–235
  prototypes of, 235–240
Conant, James B., 20
Concentration areas of crime, high delinquency area, 17
Coogan, John Edward, 100
Cooley, Charles H., 38